FROM FARM TO OCEAN

A MEMOIR

by

D1710750

Captain Paul A. Jones

May Your Dreams
Come True

[signature]

Author's Bio

Paul A. Jones was born an only child on a small farm in north-central Kansas. He grew up bored, isolated, and as far from an ocean as one can be in the continental U.S. Paul dreamed of going to sea in a small sailboat. This is the story of how Paul achieved his dream. Paul went to first and second grade in a one-room country schoolhouse where one teacher taught grades one through eight. There were only seven other students, and no indoor plumbing, but the school did have a wood stove for heat. When Paul was eleven, his father died after a battle with cancer. He and his mother moved to a small town where he attended junior and senior high school and began learning how to interact with people. He delivered papers on a bicycle, milk from a panel truck, and sold shoes.

Paul attended college during the turbulent 1960s—there were protests, curfews, and the student union building burnt to the ground. He married and became a father to two daughters. He became an endodontist, but his passion was still sailing. So, at age fifty-one, Paul took a year off and sailed a forty-five-foot sailboat from Florida to Trinidad off the coast of South America and back, visiting most of the islands of the Caribbean with his first wife, older daughter, and her fiancée. He learned a lot about the world and himself during that year.

Paul struggled with alcohol; his first marriage fell apart. He overcame these struggles to become a better person and find love and contentment. He now spends his time with his beloved second wife, Judy, in Stuart, Florida. He is now healthier and happier than ever. He is blessed to have two wonderful daughters, two great sons-in-law, four grandchildren, and to have the acceptance and love of Judy's family. While far from perfect, Paul feels much closer to being the man his parents hoped he would be than he did in his teens and twenties. He is luckier and happier than most, having realized a childhood dream, loved, lost, and loved again.

Acknowledgements

I would like to thank my writing coach, Brad Wetzler (www.bradwetzler.com), for his advice and encouragement. Without it, I'd still be struggling to make progress.

I also want to thank my first wife, Linda, for doing the lion's share of raising our daughters—two amazing women who I love more that life itself. Linda also allowed me to live out my dream even though it probably was not hers.

Thanks also to my wife, Judy, who taught me what it is to love and be loved beyond belief. She has given me more that I can ever repay.

Lastly, I'd like to acknowledge my editor, Skye Kerr Levy (skyekerreditor.com), who made sense of my jumble of stories and gently guided me to make them clearer and more grammatically correct.

Dad, Mom, and Me on the Farm

Table of Contents

Prologue
Voyage

We were sailing south in the Gulf of Mexico, some thirty miles west of Naples, Florida. I was just coming off the midnight to 2:00 a.m. watch. We had been underway all day and half the night, pounding into a head sea. I felt my way into the cabin in the pitch black so as not to night-blind the crew member on deck or wake those sleeping below. As I lay there in the forward bunk, the boat's pitching raised my entire body about a foot off the bed and then slammed it back down. The mattress was soft, but I didn't think I would get much sleep, bouncing like I was on a trampoline. Eventually the sound of the water rushing by my head, just inches away through the inch-thick fiberglass hull, lulled me to sleep.

I had just drifted off when a loud crash by my head woke me. *What was that? Damn, we forgot to tie the anchors down!* One had come loose and was swinging back and forth on the bucking front of the boat, banging onto the hull and threatening to knock a hole, or even sink her.

I jumped out of bed and climbed into the cockpit, explaining the problem to Karl, who was steering the boat. He moved the throttle to dead slow to reduce the motion some. I clipped a harness to a jackline we had tied to cleats on the front and back of the boat. I inched my way toward the bow, keeping a firm grip on something solid—a slip could mean a fall, an injury, or even sliding off into the cold, dark water and being dragged beside the boat. I could drown before they could retrieve me. "One hand for you and one for the boat," was a mantra I preached to all who sailed with me, even on small lakes in the warm summer in Kansas. I repeated it to myself slowly as I worked my way to the bucking bow platform. I braced myself by gripping the slippery bow pulpit's stainless-steel tubing while pressing the windlass switch with my toe, but the clutch slipped, and the anchor still hung there below me—sixty-five pounds of cast iron with two sharp claws swinging through the night.

I knelt and tightened the clutch. When I pressed the switch this time, the chain caught, pulling the anchor up on the bow roller and into place. *Hooray!* I took a minute to catch my breath. Then I crawled onto the heaving bowsprit, which still threatened to buck me off the slippery deck. I looped a dock line through the cross brace on the anchor and tied a bowline. *The rabbit goes up out of the hole, around the tree, and back down the hole.* I'd tied this knot thousands of times, but never with this much at stake. If it came untied, I would have to crawl back up here again. I got it on the first try. I cinched it tight with all my strength, pulled the bitter end around a bow cleat, and tied it off. Once all the way around the base, then two figure eights, then a locking hitch, and once more around the cleat. That should hold it.

By now I was soaking wet and chilled, but I needed to repeat these knots on the second anchor. It hadn't come loose yet, making it easier to secure. After one more rest, I slowly and carefully crept back to the safety of the cockpit, unclipped, and went below. I took a brief, hot shower to rinse off the salt water. We had to take short showers: two hundred gallons of water needed to last four guys a dozen days in the tropics until we made landfall 1,500 miles away in Puerto Rico.

Warm and dry at last, I crawled back into bed for a bouncy thirty-minute rest before going back on deck for another two-hour watch. I struggled to stay awake while dodging fishing boats and tugs with barges. I hoped that the rest of the adventure would be a little less exciting.

For decades I'd dreamed of exploring the world by sailboat. Finally, I was taking a year off from my dental career to fulfill the dream. We would sail to most of the islands in the Caribbean. This sail was the beginning of that adventure. I had sailed to some of the islands before on our charter sailboat in the last decade, but only for a week or two at a time. I hoped that by having an entire year off, I could achieve my childhood dream of adventure travel and cultural discovery aboard a sailboat. My dream was coming true—I was on the high seas, beginning the year-long voyage. I told myself, *This upcoming trip won't be a disaster. I can do this.*

I had come so very far from my childhood as a small boy, isolated on a farm, to now sailing on the ocean blue. What follows is the story of how I got there and the adventures I had along the way through high seas, stormy nights, and lush tropical islands.

Chapter 1
Life on the Farm

I was born in August 1948, in a small hospital in a small Kansas town. I then spent the first dozen years of my life on a small farm in north-central Kansas about as far from an ocean as one could be: 750 miles from the Gulf of Mexico, over 1,000 miles from the Atlantic, and a little less than 1,500 from the Pacific.

My mother had been forced to quit teaching when she married my father in 1932, something unthinkable today. She was nearly forty-two and my dad had just turned forty-seven when I was born; they had been married for sixteen childless years. They used an early type of fertility treatment to help conceive me. I suspect it was Diethylstilbestrol, a drug that caused serious medical problems and early death in many of the female children but not males born through DES. On top of that, given that children conceived by women in their forties are often mentally challenged, I was lucky.

Our small, two-story house was off a dirt road a quarter mile down a gravel lane. It was surrounded by a large, treed lawn with a big vegetable garden. A gravel parking lot lay between our fenced yard and the barn and pasture. Across the lane was our alfalfa field. Our medium-size barn had room to hold some hay in the mow and had room for cows to be milked on the ground floor. We had a few other small out-buildings: a chicken coop, a grain storage building, and a garage.

My Dad farmed one hundred and sixty acres that he rented from his mother, and another eighty acres next to it that he owned. The farm was about one-third crop land and two-thirds pasture. We grew corn, wheat, and alfalfa, which we baled for hay for our cows, pigs, and sheep. I remember riding with my dad on the fender of his small Ford tractor while he plowed, mowed, and planted crops. I now realize how dangerous that was, but we didn't think about that back then. According to Politico, farming is one of the most dangerous occupations in America. Farmers are nearly twice as likely to die on the job as police officers and five times as likely as firefighters. The CDC reports that the number of farmers who were injured on the farm is ten percent greater than all the soldiers injured in the U.S. military since 9/11. Being a farmer meant hard work, discipline, and self-reliance. It also gave one the freedom to be one's own boss, be outside, and be one with nature and the land. Those were strengths I learned from my parents. I still love the outdoors, like to work outside, and enjoy fresh food.

The alfalfa we raised for cattle feed also replenished the land as alfalfa is a legume that adds nitrogen back into the soil. Dad would mow it a few times a summer, let it dry, and bale it. If they were wet, the square shaped bales would weigh as much, or more, than me. We would pick them up, load them on a flatbed trailer, and haul them into the barn. When the barn was full, we would create hay stacks of the bales outside. This was hard, physical work, but the baled hay could be fun too. One bitterly cold but sunny winter's day, Dad and I went to a farm sale. While the parents were bidding on farm implements and household goods, the kids played King of the Mountain on a pyramid of hay bales covered with snow. It was great fun to be pushed down the side of the haystack and slide to a soft landing in the deep snow.

The Wheat State

Kansas is the wheat state. I fondly recall looking out the window of our little house watching the wind wave the stalks of wheat. When Kansas University scores a touchdown (something unfortunately rare these days), fans wave their arms above their heads in a random order in what is called "waving the wheat." When life later took me to the ocean, the swell and crests of waves reminded me of those Kansas "amber waves of grain."

Dad used the Ford tractor to pull different implements to till the ground, plant, and harvest our crops. I would watch him circle the field, around and around, on the tractor. He mostly worked alone, but in order to harvest our wheat, we had to hire others. These workers were called "custom harvesters." They would begin in Texas and work their way up north to time the harvest for when the wheat was ripe. At our latitude, they usually arrived around the Fourth of July. They drove big, complex machines called combines. These labor-saving devices would reap (or cut) the stalks of grain, then thresh (or separate) the grain from the heads, blow the chaff away, deposit the grain into a bin in the combine, and then spit the wheat straw out the back in a neat row, which we would later bale. These were much lighter than alfalfa bales. I thought I was strong because I could easily lift them onto the trailer.

When the bin in the combine was full, the machine would auger it into a truck which, when full, Dad drove three miles to the Farmer's Coop in the small town of Beattie. We raised the bed to dump the grain from the truck through a grate in the ground into a temporary storage bin. The grain was then augured from the inground container up into a silo, or elevator, for storage. Eventually, it was transferred to rail cars to be shipped off for processing into flour, cereal, or animal feed. When there weren't enough rail cars available in bumper crop years, the silos became full and grain would have to be poured onto tarps on the ground—along with prayers that the rain wouldn't come and ruin it.

The farmer gets to store the grain for a certain amount of time for free, but eventually they are charged. The trick is predicting when to sell your grain, since the price fluctuates up and down depending on several factors. If you wait too long, storage costs could negate any gain and the price could always go down. Besides being physically dangerous and hard work, farming is also a risky financial proposition. When should you plant? Do you plant more wheat and less corn, or try beans or milo? How much fertilizer and herbicide do you apply? When do you harvest? Will you get enough rain in a timely manner, or too much? There are also hail storms, diseases, and weeds to contend with. The lessons I learned growing up on a farm have served me well throughout my life. I saw the benefits of hard work and taking calculated risks. Tilling the field, planting the crop, waiting for it to mature, and harvesting the grain taught me to be patient and accept delayed gratification.

The Menagerie

We raised cows for meat and milk, chickens for meat and eggs, sheep for wool (for some reason we didn't eat their meat), and hogs for meat.

I recall feeding the chickens cracked grain as well as crushed oyster shells to help them digest the grain. We bought the shells in fifty-pound bags from the feed store. I didn't realize at the time that these came from the ocean, a dream-length away from where we lived. I helped gather the eggs for us to eat and sell in town. When the chickens were big enough to eat, Dad would chop off their heads, Mom would dunk them by their feet in a bucket of boiling water, tie their legs to the fence at the end of our yard, as far from the house as possible, and pluck their feathers. Using an old butcher knife with a homemade replacement wood handle my father had made, she would pick the pin feathers, which are small budding feathers, off the chicken. She would then light rubbing alcohol in the lid of a coffee can and singe the remaining fuzz from the skin of the bird. Lastly, she would eviscerate them, cutting them up into pieces before putting them in freezer containers, saying, "Two legs, two thighs, two wings, one breast, one wishbone, one back," to be sure she had evenly distributed the parts.

We raised pigs, which I am sure we butchered, but I only remember them being castrated. We also raised sheep, which were treated somewhat more humanely. Dad rolled thick rubber washers up a hollow cone-shaped metal device. The sheep's balls were placed into the end of the cone and the rubber band slipped around the base. This deprived the organs of blood supply and they fell off a few days later. During shearing season, we'd hang a ten-foot-tall burlap bag from the rafters in the barn. A man came to shear the wool. Dad placed the bundles of wool in the bag and I would jump into the bag to pack the wool down so we could get as much in the bag as possible. I remember the lanolin making my skin soft, but I am sure I did not smell good.

We used to milk cows and I remember watching the large, metal cans being filled from the bucket we used to collect the milk. We would sit on a T-shaped stool made of two 2x4s nailed together.

I also recall Dad dehorning young cattle. They were driven, one at a time, into a metal shoot and immobilized. Dad would take large clippers and cut off their budding horns. The cows would bawl.

The Garden

My parents planted a huge garden where we raised potatoes, onions, tomatoes, sweet corn, green beans, spinach, lettuce, rhubarb, strawberries, and cucumbers. Mom would spend all summer harvesting the crop. When we'd had our fill of fresh fruits and vegetables, she would "put up" the excess—

preserving them in mason jars—for the long winter ahead. We stored the food in what we called "the cave," which was a root cellar dug into the ground behind our house about sixteen feet long and eight feet wide. We stored the jars of fruits and vegetables on shelves; the potatoes and onions were kept in bins on the floor.

The cave was a dark, scary place. When I was about eight, I remember being sent there to fetch another jar while we were entertaining relatives one afternoon. The cellar had no light, except from the door opening. When your eyes adjusted to the dark, you could find the jar of sweet pickles or beets that Mom needed. On my way back up the steps, I saw a snake lying across a step, halfway up. I didn't know what to do, so I just waited at the bottom of the stairs. Eventually my dad came to see why I hadn't returned, and I explained my dilemma. He calmly got a hoe and picked up the snake, removing it from my path and saving me.

I had an uncle who was an early organic and "no till" farmer. Instead of using pesticides (which later were found to be very toxic to birds) and chemical fertilizers, he learned how to use natural ways to grow crops. We accused him of being too cheap to buy the chemicals, but it now turns out he was right and ahead of his time. One of his daughters still farms his land and raises organic crops and beef.

The "Crick"

In the summers I was drawn to the spring that flowed from beneath a rock in a small draw in our pasture. I would drink the cool, clean water bubbling up from the ground. The water flowed from there into the small creek—which we pronounced "crick"—in the woods at the end of our pasture. The creek coursed through a wood of towering walnut and oak trees. It was my first experience with flowing water. I imagined that if I made a small boat, I could float down the stream to a river, then eventually to the ocean. It would take me to places far away and magical, surrounded by exotic lands and people, beautiful vistas, and adventures beyond my dreams.

But back then, just the creek itself was a kind of heaven. On warm summer Sundays after church, Mom would pack a picnic lunch: cold fried chicken, potato salad, homemade gooseberry pie (from wild berries we picked nearby), and a crockery jug of cold well water wrapped in wet burlap to keep it cool. Then we'd walk the half-mile to the creek to spend a leisurely afternoon on the wide, flat, grassy bank under the shade of the tall trees.

I had my first fishing experiences there. I'd take a long cane pole and line with a cork bobber and a hook baited with worms dug from our garden to fish for the small bullhead catfish that inhabited the stream. If you waited too long, the fish swallowed the hook, making retrieval harder. If you raised the pole too soon, the fish got the worm. It was great fun waiting in anticipation for the cork to slowly move up and down, indicating there was a fish on the end of the line. If we caught enough keepers, we would take them back to the house in a bucket of creek water; Dad would dress them, and Mom would bread them with cornmeal and fry them in lard for dinner, served with big helpings of mashed potatoes and green beans from our ample garden. I loved spending time by the creek with Mom and Dad.

My Uncle Leroy and Aunt Myrtle Jones lived on a farm on the other side of the creek. They loved to fish there on the opposite bank. Uncle Leroy used to say, "Days spent fishing don't count against your allotted lifetime." He may have been right as he lived a long, happy life. He was a jolly, short, slightly chubby, hard-working farmer who always seemed to have time to break away and go fishing.

Bootsie

I had a black-and-white collie mix named Bootsie who had only three legs. We loved to roam and explore the barnyard, pastures, and fields together.

Bootsie hadn't always had three legs; before I was old enough to remember, Dad accidentally cut off his hind leg with the tractor. My father's father had been a veterinarian, so I imagine Dad knew to bind the leg and bandage the wound to stem the bleeding and prevent infection. I'm sure he felt terrible about it.

In the summer, I would run with Bootsie barefoot on the soft prairie grass. I loved the feel of the blades between my toes. We would chase Killdeer birds, which would fake a broken wing and hobble away while we ran after them. Once we were far enough from their earthbound nests, they would take flight. They used this technique to protect the nest from predators.

Once I was running barefoot across the pasture to the stream, dodging cow patties and rocks when, for no apparent reason, I jumped for joy. Maybe just because it was a warm, sunny, summer day. Midair, I looked down and saw a long, non-poisonous bull snake stretched out on his quest for lunch. If I hadn't jumped, I would have stepped on him and gotten bit. What a lucky time to jump.

Beattie

On weekends we would drive into Beattie. It had about three hundred residents, a filling station where we bought gas, a grain elevator where we sold our crops and eggs, a post office, and a meat processing plant, or "locker," that would package and freeze the meat from our cows and pigs. The locker stored the meat in a walk-in freezer with individual locked compartments. Dad once took me to watch them shoot a cow of ours between the eyes before they butchered it. It didn't bother me; it was a fact of life that the cow would die so we could eat and live.

The hardware store was owned by an ex-WWII prisoner of war. He once talked matter-of-factly to our grade school classes about being taken prisoner by the Germans. There was also a small bank a cousin by marriage owned. There were a couple of clothing stores and a small food market. At the end of the one-block-long main street stood a pool hall. It had a couple of tables and a small bar. Dad loved to go there and hang out with his friends. I loved it when he took me with him. I don't think he drank or smoked, but he did surreptitiously chew Copenhagen snuff. He hid the cans in the barn because Mom objected. My maternal grandfather chewed it too, and Mom blamed her dad on getting my dad hooked on it. I was drawn to both smoking and drinking, as commercials glamorized them. Mom was a member of the Kansas United Dry Temperance League and always cautioned me not to imbibe. That just made me want to do it more. Mom's uncle and Dad's grandfather were alcoholics and it had ruined their lives, but I didn't know that back then.

On warm summer Saturday evenings in Beattie, we would watch black-and-white cowboy movies on a small, wooden, whitewashed screen while sitting on wood benches in a small park between two buildings.

First Adventures

As an only child growing up on a farm, miles from the nearest city or tourist attraction, travel was a big deal. It was a connection with the outside world that I could only imagine. In the winter, snow would drift and we couldn't drive to town. In the spring, rain would turn the dirt roads into mud with deep ruts that lasted until the road grader could smooth them out and make driving possible again.

There were no interstate highways, only hilly, dangerous, narrow, curvy, two-lane asphalt roads. Money was tight, and we had to stay on the farm to care for the animals, plant and harvest the crops. Occasionally we would take five-hour car trips to Kansas City to visit my aunt, uncle, cousins, and grandmother in their "big" stone house. I drove by it a few years ago and either I grew, or it shrunk; it wasn't nearly as big as I remembered.

Sometimes Dad would drive me to the old airport in downtown Kansas City to climb the observation deck and watch the airplanes taking off and landing. He was born before the Wright brothers first flew, and he was enthralled by the planes. I suspected he dreamed of traveling to faraway places too. Dad, always the good son, had stayed home to help his widowed mother run the family farm during the Depression while his siblings went away to Topeka, Kansas City, Chicago, and Oakland to earn livings and lead more exciting lives. I later learned that he had wanted to work on the railroad so he could travel and see the country. But he never let himself dream of flying in an airplane to a U.S. city, much less across the oceans to foreign lands with strange sounding names where the people looked and sounded different, ate exotic foods, and had customs and culture unknown to us. That was my dream.

It is the trend, promoted by Trump and his supporters, to fear the *other*. To keep those from *other* places—with non-white skin colors, other religions, and other customs—from contaminating our "pure, white Christian land." But monoculture doesn't work—in agriculture or in human societies. Keeping the blood line "pure" leads to genetic defects and prevents the growth of ideas and industry. It is not natural. Anyways, Dad and

I didn't talk about it, but I suspect he dreamed of flying off somewhere to escape the drudgery of farm work. Air travel was new and way beyond our budget—I didn't take my first flight until I was twenty-seven.

I was six years old by the time we took our first real vacation: driving to Colorado to see the mountains. I remember trying to be careful so I wouldn't hurt myself before the trip and miss the opportunity to travel. We had a brand new 1953 Ford. Perhaps we had had a good crop and Dad felt we could afford both a new car and a vacation. The neighbors said they would take care of our animals. My folks piled our clothes in the back seat and covered them with a blanket so I could lie down and look out the window. This was in the days before seat belts, car seats, or the interstate highway system, so we took the two-lane Highway 36 and spent the first night in a small motel somewhere in western Kansas. The room was tiny, but it was still a rare treat for me.

The anticipation of seeing the Rocky Mountains for the first time was thrilling. Clouds faked us out a few times, but eventually we were sure we could see the mountains. The most exciting part of the trip was the drive up Pikes Peak. It was a winding, gravel road with sheer drop-offs. My mom was scared. Dad got sick halfway up, so we didn't make it to the top. It may have been altitude sickness or an early sign of his undiagnosed leukemia. I don't recall much else, but it was still a marvelous time. I remember visiting Santa's North Pole in Colorado Springs with glee as I still believed in Santa.

Our next vacation, when I was about eight, was a train trip to California to visit my aunt in Oakland. We boarded the train in Kansas City in the middle of the night with my grandmother. I loved roaming the train and watching the scenery from the observation car. I watched the people on the train and wondered if they traveled like this often, where they were going, and what they did. I was jealous of their freedom.

Eventually we reached the coast. I remember seeing the ocean for the first time, amazed by the vastness of it, the endless horizon. I love the salty smell of seaweed, the sun setting on the water, and the waves rolling in from far away. Years later, when I became captivated by sailing, I heard a speaker claim that more people per capita from Nebraska are in the U.S. Navy than any other state. Our farm was ten miles from Nebraska. He claimed that being raised in the middle of the country, far from any ocean, made the sea seem like a wonderful, remote, and romantic place. Whatever you are far from becomes the dream.

We walked around Fisherman's Wharf, hearing the gulls squawking and seeing the ships that had traveled from afar. I had my first taste of shrimp. I loved the quaint beauty of San Francisco, the homes perched along the hilly, winding streets, and the cable cars.

We had a small Kodak box camera and my parents let me take a few pictures. The only one I recall taking was a photo of a giant green bean that my aunt grew. With all the amazing sites, why did I choose to record a large green bean?

I don't know if my mother loved the trip as much as I did, but she bought a tablecloth with drawings of the Golden Gate Bridge, Oakland, cable cars, and other local sites. She used that on our kitchen table for years afterward until it wore out. Clearly, California made an impression on both of us.

Childhood Impressions

In the evenings on the farm, if the wind was out of the south, we could hear a train whistle blow as it approached the crossing a couple miles away. I wondered where the train came from and where it was going. Looking back, I lived an isolated and lonely life, but it was idyllic in many ways—an almost Garden-of-Eden-like existence. We lived in a verdant plain. My parents loved each other and me. I was innocent, happy, and satisfied, except that I wanted to get away and explore, see new places, meet new people, and have an adventure.

I was perhaps spoiled, too. My first memory was pouting, "I want milk, I want it warm, and I want it in a bottle!" My mother read *Baby and Childcare* by Dr. Spock (not the one on *Star Trek*). One of my uncles, who believed in discipline, suggested that instead of reading it, she should have used the book to spank me. My mom only spanked me once in a fit of anger when I picked some vegetables before they were ripe—she said she regretted it to her dying day.

I would roam the fields barefoot in summer, play with imaginary friends, set up sticks and potatoes as toy soldiers, hang a burlap bag stuffed with other bags from a tree branch to use as a punching bag with an old steel bed frame as a ring. I tossed a baseball on the roof of our barn and played catch alone.

I used the books my mother read me and my imagination to transport myself to the wider world and seek adventures. Growing up on the farm gave me a love of the outdoors, and I also developed a longing for water and sailing. My experiences in nature, and reading about adventure, would plant seeds that would grow into pursuit of journeys I could never have fathomed as a small boy back on the farm.

As an adult, I have bought and memorized almost every song that Jimmy Buffett sings. Most of them encourage escape from everyday mundane life to enjoy paradise—often on a sailboat. The song "Life is Just a Tire Swing" speaks about his memories of growing up in isolation—just like I did:

And I've never been
West of New Orleans or East of Pensacola
My only contact with the outside world
Was an RCA Victrola

Chapter 2
The Family Tree

MR. AND MRS. PETER JONES.

My Paternal Great Grandparents,
Emma and Peter Jones, Sr.

Over a hundred million years ago, Kansas was covered by a vast, warm, shallow, inland sea. Over the millennia, the skeletons of various sea creatures were deposited on the bottom of the seabed and compressed into limestone. When the sea receded, these layers of limestone were near enough to the surface that they could be cut from the ground and shaped with simple tools.

Before it is exposed to air, limestone is soft enough to be cut with a hand saw. Once the limestone reacts with oxygen, it becomes hard and can be used for building blocks and stone fence posts. In the mid-19th century, there were few trees on the prairie. Settlers used this stone as building material. Simple sod huts made of blocks of prairie soil and grass were the first shelters, but they proved temporary, not nearly as satisfactory, strong, or permanent as building with the local limestone.

In 1855, my great grandfather, Peter Jones, Sr., came over from England on a sailing ship. It took about six weeks to cross the Atlantic. I wonder what motivated him to take on such a journey. What caused him to give up his homeland for a dangerous and arduous sea voyage to an unknown place so far away? Did I inherit some of his spirit—wanting to leave the farm for bigger adventures?

Peter and Emma lived in a small log cabin until 1864, when Peter quarried two-feet blocks of limestone to build a house a mile east across the creek from where I grew up. It still stands today. He hauled the blocks in a wooden cart drawn by a yoke of oxen. The stone was so heavy the axles and wheels wore out and he had to make new ones. He hauled sand from the nearby Vermilion River and burned lime in a homemade kiln on the farm to make the mortar to cement the limestone blocks together. He then drove the yoke of oxen to Atchison, Kansas, where he bought another wagon. He then used it to bring back native walnut trees that he cut and milled for floors and to panel the walls.

The Stone House my Great Grandfather Built

   Peter and Emma's only daughter, my great aunt May, lived alone in that house into her 90s. I remember visiting her there when I was a child. She was a beautiful, quiet soul who never married. She taught music and raised sheep. She told me about being afraid of Native Americans who traversed the farm when she was young. I still have a pair of stone tomahawks found on that farm.

May Jones, my Great Aunt

Family lore says that Aunt May had wanted to learn about our ancestors in England and had written some relatives there to research our family background. When she was told a reply had arrived, she was excited to read all about the family's history.

But once she read the letter, she never said another word about it—there must have been something or someone in our family tree she didn't want to brag about. Aunt May passed away when she was ninety-eight.

My father was born in 1901 and died at age fifty-eight. He was born two years before the Wright brothers' famous first flight; someday my grandsons may buy a commercial ticket for a space flight! My dad attended the same one-room country school that I did as a child; my grandkids can now take classes anywhere in the world via the internet on an iPad! They will see things in their lifetime that my father could never have fathomed.

My father was the oldest of the seven children of John Peter and Sylvia Jones. Dad's father, John, trained as a veterinarian in Kansas City. He treated their horses, cattle, pigs, and sheep as well as those of his neighbors. My father learned from him. I remember Dad performing surgery to save the life of a bloated sheep by plunging a knife into its belly to let out the air.

My Dad's Parents, Sylvia and John Peter Jones

I later learned that my grandfather was an awful person who used to beat his kids with a bullwhip. What could possibly have made him that way? Fortunately, the abuse didn't carry on to the next generation. My father was the kindest, gentlest person I've ever known. I was told that my dad finally stood up to his father when he was about to beat my dad's youngest sister for the first time. Until he had leukemia, my father was a hard-working and happy-go-lucky man.

My Father (back row, middle), His Siblings, and His Mother

Mom and Dad's Wedding Picture

My Mother's Side of the Family

My mother's parents and her two older siblings were born in Sweden. They immigrated through Ellis Island and settled on a farm near Beattie, Kansas, not far from where my father's grandparents had moved from England several decades before. My mother and four additional girls were born there in Beattie. The family lived together with an eighty-four-year-old aunt in a small, three-bedroom farm house. The only brother had one bedroom, their parents another bedroom, and the five sisters and the aunt *all* slept in the third bedroom.

My mother's youngest sister, my Aunt Caryl, was a remarkable woman. She taught for two years after high school in a one-room schoolhouse while saving up for college. Unfortunately, just as she was ready to withdraw the money, the bank failed. The FDIC was not there to bail her out—she lost it all. The banker didn't have any money either, but he did have a friend in Lawrence who let Aunt Caryl live with him and his family. She worked as a domestic for them for four years to pay her tuition. They gave her room and board. She graduated Phi Beta Kappa from Kansas University, the first in her family to attend college.

Aunt Caryl eventually married a handsome farmer and continued teaching. They never had children of their own, but she inspired, taught, mentored, and gave scholarships to an untold number of her students. She was my algebra teacher— one of the best teachers I have ever had. My daughter is a teacher too. I like the bumper sticker that says, "If you can read this, thank a teacher." While reading and writing are critical to success, so is mathematics. In her forty years as a math teacher, Aunt Caryl laid a solid foundation for many students to attain successful careers in science, healthcare, accounting, business, and technology, myself included.

When Aunt Caryl passed, I made sure to attend her funeral. It brought me back to similar sad occasions—watching my father, mother, grandparents, aunts, and uncles being laid to rest. "Amazing Grace" and "Jesus is All the World to Me" were sung. To illustrate how well Aunt Caryl dressed, the minister told us that one of her classes kept track for an entire school year and found she never wore the same outfit twice. Several years later the minister asked her if it was true; Aunt Caryl did not deny it. Three cousins and I gave brief eulogies about how much she had meant to us. I surprised myself by choking back tears while speaking. The cousin who was very close to her read two of her poems—Aunt Caryl had taken up writing poetry after her husband died. Another cousin told of the time Aunt Caryl had told her there were two things in this world that she really loved. The first was Jesus. She said she told Him everything and He had been a comfort to her in good times and bad. My cousin agreed. The second thing she really loved? Her microwave oven! I guess if you had spent the first seventy years of life using wood fire, gas, and electric stoves to heat food, a microwave oven would be nearly as miraculous as Jesus.

After the funeral, I drove around my old hometown to revisit some of my haunts. I couldn't help but wonder how my life would have been if I had stayed there after high school like some of my classmates did. I assume they were happy with their choice. Like the country song says, "Everyone dies famous in a small town." I had been so anxious to get out of town that I left immediately after graduation to attend summer school.

Chapter 3
School and Church

Orr School

I didn't go to preschool or kindergarten as neither was offered back then. I went to a one-room schoolhouse called Orr School for first and second grades. My first two years in the school coincided with the last two years the school was open—they closed since there were only seven students in the whole school. There were three others in my grade and four students in the upper grades. My great-grandmother had, at age sixteen, been the first teacher of that school, and my father and his siblings had gone there as well.

The school did not have indoor plumbing; we got our drinking water by hand-pumping a well out front. There were outhouses in the back and a wood-burning stove in the middle of the room helped keep us warm. I remember on frigid winter days the wind would blow through the cracks in the uninsulated wooden walls. We would sit around the stove trying to keep our feet warm by putting our shoes near the sides of the stove until the soles started smoking.

I recall listening intently when the teacher was talking to the older kids, hoping to learn something more interesting than my ABCs and 123s. One day I was talking to a classmate while the teacher was presenting something to the older kids, and she came up behind me and cuffed me behind the ear. Lesson learned.

At recess we would play games in the schoolyard. "Red Rover, Red Rover, Come Over" was a game in which kids would form two lines holding hands. A kid from one line would run over to the other, trying to break through between the kids. Whoever succeeded chose one kid from that line to go back to join his line, if he failed, he had to stay on that line. When all the kids were in one line, the game was over. When it snowed, we played a game called "Fox and Geese," a type of tag. First you tramped a large, spoked wheel shape in the snow. You had to stay on the track while playing tag. The hub was safe.

After Orr School closed, my folks would drive me into Beattie for school. There I attended third and fourth grades in an ancient school building built of the same native limestone quarried from the thick bed of sediment rock not far outside of town. By the time I was in fifth grade, they had built a new "modern" school made of concrete blocks and covered by bricks. It had a gym and linoleum floors.

During the first day of "town school" someone came by and asked if anyone played a musical instrument. I raised my hand because in country school I had played what we called the flutophone—a simple, inexpensive, plastic, flute-like instrument also called a recorder. In band class, I learned there was no flutophone section, so they assigned me the trumpet. Over the next decade, music became an increasingly important part of my life. I continued playing the trumpet, eventually becoming first chair in high school. I also loved to sing in church and school choirs and the boys' octet.

My dad had played the violin and my mother the soprano sax before I was born, but they had given them up by the time I came along. I still have those instruments. My earliest exposure to music was in the Methodist Church in Beattie. A few years ago, I wrote to my daughters:

Last evening I was listening to Pandora radio when the old gospel song "I'll Fly Away," sung by Randy Travis, came on. I downloaded his album "Worship and Faith" to my iPhone. I put on my headphones and took off on a walk. A particularly meaningful song came on and I was flooded with memories and emotions about my childhood.

Every Sunday we would drive into Beattie and attend the small Methodist church. My mother and father both sang in the choir and I vividly recall the joy the old-time gospel music brought us. I seldom allow myself to feel or display deep emotions, but religious music somehow brings them out. Here I was out in the dark, walking and singing at the top of my lungs to the tunes I remembered well from my youth, with tears of sadness and joy streaming down my cheeks. I was thinking of my parents and the love we shared. I only wish I could see them once more and tell them how much I love and miss them. How thankful and appreciative I am for all they gave me, how they guided me, and instilled ethics and strength into me that got me where I am today.

Chapter 4
Deaths in the Family

The first funeral I remember was for my uncle, Peter Jones, my father's cousin. I was six. He had run a stop sign after a night on the town and was killed when a truck on the highway crushed his car. The undertaker did a poor job patching his face up and I recall it was pocked, irregular, and caked with makeup. A couple of years later, my mother's father passed. I don't remember my mother being too upset, although I am sure she was. My father was already ill by then and I suspect Mom was more worried about losing him than she was her father.

When I was about nine, my dad became ill with leukemia. He was admitted to the University of Kansas Medical Center in Kansas City. In those days, long stays in hospitals were the norm. Mom and I would take trips on the train to visit him. Mom drove us an hour to Hiawatha where we would board the train. She would pack a lunch of cold roast beef sandwiches with mayonnaise on white bread. We would eat as I watched the scenery whiz by outside the train. Although I was sad to see my father ill, it was exciting to travel on the train. I loved looking out the window, seeing the rolling hills go by. Kansas City also meant more people, cousins to play with, and exploring the hospital. I remember I was not allowed to visit him in his room in those days. I amused myself by riding up and down the halls in a wheelchair.

Ironically, when I was in dental school a decade later, I worked in the bacteriology lab in that same hospital starting cultures of, among other microorganisms, the very same bacteria that led to my dad's demise. While in the hospital, Dad had contracted MERSA, a type of antibiotic-resistant staph infection. He had huge, ugly, painful boils all over his body. With his diminished immune system, he couldn't fight off the infection; it eventually killed him.

The original building where he stayed still stands, but the medical center has expanded exponentially. There wasn't much they could do back then to treat my dad's cancer. Now KU Med has become one of the best cancer treatment centers in the country. He might have survived if he were alive today.

Dad had been in and out of hospitals for three years. Mom and I were staying with my aunt, uncle, and cousin in Marysville when Dad passed away during the night. I was sleeping in the upper bunk in my cousin's room. I awoke during the night and just instinctively knew he was gone. Maybe the phone rang or there were voices outside, but I have no conscious memory of that. When I woke in the morning, my uncle came in and told me he was dead. He told my cousin to comfort me. I don't remember if I cried, but I must have.

Years later, I found the program from his funeral. The songs they sang were "The Old Rugged Cross" and "How Great Thou Art." The poem "Crossing of the Bar" by Tennyson was on it. If he had had a hand in the choice, was he telling us not to be sad? The ocean references seemed out of place for a Kansas farmer.

Chapter 4
Deaths in the Family

The first funeral I remember was for my uncle, Peter Jones, my father's cousin. I was six. He had run a stop sign after a night on the town and was killed when a truck on the highway crushed his car. The undertaker did a poor job patching his face up and I recall it was pocked, irregular, and caked with makeup. A couple of years later, my mother's father passed. I don't remember my mother being too upset, although I am sure she was. My father was already ill by then and I suspect Mom was more worried about losing him than she was her father.

When I was about nine, my dad became ill with leukemia. He was admitted to the University of Kansas Medical Center in Kansas City. In those days, long stays in hospitals were the norm. Mom and I would take trips on the train to visit him. Mom drove us an hour to Hiawatha where we would board the train. She would pack a lunch of cold roast beef sandwiches with mayonnaise on white bread. We would eat as I watched the scenery whiz by outside the train. Although I was sad to see my father ill, it was exciting to travel on the train. I loved looking out the window, seeing the rolling hills go by. Kansas City also meant more people, cousins to play with, and exploring the hospital. I remember I was not allowed to visit him in his room in those days. I amused myself by riding up and down the halls in a wheelchair.

Ironically, when I was in dental school a decade later, I worked in the bacteriology lab in that same hospital starting cultures of, among other microorganisms, the very same bacteria that led to my dad's demise. While in the hospital, Dad had contracted MERSA, a type of antibiotic-resistant staph infection. He had huge, ugly, painful boils all over his body. With his diminished immune system, he couldn't fight off the infection; it eventually killed him.

The original building where he stayed still stands, but the medical center has expanded exponentially. There wasn't much they could do back then to treat my dad's cancer. Now KU Med has become one of the best cancer treatment centers in the country. He might have survived if he were alive today.

Dad had been in and out of hospitals for three years. Mom and I were staying with my aunt, uncle, and cousin in Marysville when Dad passed away during the night. I was sleeping in the upper bunk in my cousin's room. I awoke during the night and just instinctively knew he was gone. Maybe the phone rang or there were voices outside, but I have no conscious memory of that. When I woke in the morning, my uncle came in and told me he was dead. He told my cousin to comfort me. I don't remember if I cried, but I must have.

Years later, I found the program from his funeral. The songs they sang were "The Old Rugged Cross" and "How Great Thou Art." The poem "Crossing of the Bar" by Tennyson was on it. If he had had a hand in the choice, was he telling us not to be sad? The ocean references seemed out of place for a Kansas farmer.

Did he long to travel, to go to sea? Was it prophetic that I would find solace on the sea? Bars at the mouths of rivers can be notoriously dangerous and difficult to cross to get to the open ocean. A pilot with local knowledge is often employed to guide ships in and out of them. Of course, "pilot" refers to God and "crossing the bar" to death.

Sunset and evening star,
And one clear call for me!
And may there be no moaning of the bar,
When I put out to sea,

But such a tide as moving seems asleep,
Too full for sound and foam,
When that which drew from out the boundless deep
Turns again home.

Twilight and evening bell,
And after that the dark!
And may there be no sadness of farewell,
When I embark;

For tho' from out our bourne of Time and Place
The flood may bear me far,
I hope to see my Pilot face to face
When I have crost the bar.

My father and I shared the same first name, so when he was alive, they called me Allan, my middle name. I remember riding home from my father's funeral and telling my mother that I wanted to be known as Paul from now on. I was thinking to myself that I had to take over the task of being the man of the house. I had no idea what that meant or how to be a man. My dad had been sick on and off for years. Many of my aunts and uncles had a hard time making the switch so they called me Paul Allan instead.

Without a Father Figure, in a New Town

Having Dad become chronically ill when I was about eight and losing him when I was eleven didn't give me a strong father figure growing up. I was much closer to my mother, who spent a lot more time with me alone on the farm while dad was out in the fields before I went to school. When I finally realized my dad was dying, I remember thinking that if I *had* to lose a parent, I was glad it was him and not her. I had nothing against him, I just knew her better. Or was it an Oedipal complex?

I had several uncles who tried, in one way or another, to help after dad died. I took bits and pieces from each of them, but none stood out as trying to take over teaching me how to be a man.

My cousin Dick probably had the greatest influence on me. He was only a couple of years older and had his own issues, but I looked up to him—especially when moving from the farm to town where he knew his way around. I also had many good, and a few great, teachers and coaches who I learned a lot from. Still, I don't recall guidance from anyone on how to plan a career, select good friends, what to look for in a wife, and how to live properly. Mom and the Church helped, but without Dad's guidance, I had to become self-reliant and figure it out myself. The side benefit of losing Dad was that we had to leave our lonely life on the farm and move to town where I suddenly had *many* more social interactions, friends, and activities. The summer after he died, we moved to the "big city" (to me) of Marysville, Kansas (population about 3,500).

At first, Mom worked as a switchboard operator in the local telephone office. Eventually she trained and became a nurse's aide at the hospital in Marysville. She made $2.35 an hour, working from 3 p.m. until 11 p.m. We also each got $63 a month Social Security. In the 1960s, two could live on that. We didn't think we were poor; mom had lived through the Depression and knew how to be frugal. My uncle helped us buy a small, two-bedroom house across the alley from his.

I can vividly recall the first night I had to stay home alone. It was a warm summer evening and we didn't have air conditioning, so the windows were open. After eating an early dinner, my mother left for work. I read awhile and then turned in soon after it got dark. I wasn't worried about being alone. My thoughts drifted to school, which would start in a couple of weeks. The house was still when suddenly I heard a faint sound in the next room. I wasn't sure what it was, so I listened carefully. Nearly a minute passed without a repeat. I was starting to relax when I heard it again. This time I was sure it was someone taking a step in the room next to mine. I was petrified. It was pitch black. I was too scared to get up and turn on the light. I heard it again. What could I do? If I lay perfectly still, maybe he wouldn't know I was there. At age eleven, I was too small and weak to fight back, and I didn't have a weapon of any kind. I heard it again. I was sure someone was walking around my mother's bedroom.

Finally, after what seemed like an hour but was probably only a few minutes, the sound stopped. I waited and waited but heard nothing else. Maybe he had left. I couldn't take it any longer—I jumped up, turned on the light, ran to the living room, and called my uncle to tell him I was alone and thought someone was in the house. He came right over, and we discovered that a gentle breeze was causing the shade in the open bathroom window next to my room to rub on the sill. We both had a good laugh. He told me that I would learn that many times the things you are afraid of turn out to be not nearly as bad as you imagined. The best way to tackle fear was to face it head on. I went back to bed but stayed awake until my mom got home from work at 11:30 p.m. She comforted me and said not to worry—my uncle was nearby if I had any more problems.

One night after a baseball game, a man named Don Morse asked me if I wanted a ride home and to go swimming in the dark in a creek several miles outside of town. He often hung around our games. Having grown up so isolated on the farm, I had never heard of pedophilia. Being the trusting sort, I went.

We drove out into the country in the dark. We stripped and swam in a small stream. He tried to show me how to float. I felt his penis on my backside but nothing else happened. We got out, dried off, and drove to the main road nude. I can still smell his sweat. Fortunately, he didn't take it any further than that and brought me back to town unhurt.

When my mom found out, she said, "Don't do that, they say he is queer." I had never heard the word before. I thought it just meant odd. He never asked me to go with him again.

Jobs I've Held

Before we moved to Beattie, I worked on the farm before and after my dad passed. I remember driving a tractor pulling a disk or rake when I was nine or ten. I remember getting tired and faking falling asleep on the fender. My dad came out and was mad. I would also help bale hay. Wheat straw bales were light enough that I could lift them, but if the alfalfa was wet, it was too heavy for me to lift. I had a college and dental friend who lost a leg trying to unjam hay from a baler. Farming is dangerous work. I remember gathering eggs and getting pecked by hens.

The first job I had in town was a paper route. The *Marysville Advocate* was a small weekly paper and I would deliver about fifty papers a day on my bicycle. It wasn't a particularly strenuous or dangerous job, although I was chased by a few dogs and had to watch for traffic.

In my next job, I delivered milk and other dairy products from a panel truck. The milk came in quart glass bottles and we delivered it to people's doors. I once dropped my 6-bottle carrier and the bottles shattered. Luckily they were empty of milk. Mr. Kraemer was a stern boss and wasn't very happy with me that day. During the school year I would work Saturday mornings and every day during the summer. I got paid a dollar for four hours of work. That's twenty-five cents per hour!

I learned to keep my milk carrier between me and any dog who tried to bite me. Only once did a small dog nip my heel; I thought he was not a risk, so I ignored him—at my peril. I also once had to jump from the truck door while it was still moving to get a running start. I guess child labor laws weren't a big deal back then.

I also sold shoes in town. I wasn't a very good salesman, but also did odd jobs for the owner, like polishing the floor with a large pad of steel wool under my foot and washing the store windows.

In college, I sold shoes and worked as a construction laborer in the summers. I sold shoes in dental school too. Next, I got a job at KU Med starting bacterial cultures on about everything you can think of: blood, spinal fluid, urine, feces—yuck! Back then we didn't wear gloves or masks. I recall accidentally sucking blood into my mouth while pipetting it for a culture. It is amazing I didn't catch some fatal disease.

One night another dental student and I snuck out of work and went to a nearby bar. We had a few pops before returning to work. I forgot to incubate some cultures before I left. I got fired for that. After that, I waited tables at a steak and ale. I was learning that I wanted to become a dentist so I didn't have to spend my life doing low-paying, menial jobs.

My Stepfather Henry

While Mom was working at the local hospital, my future stepfather's mother was a patient there for months. Back in the 1960s, a hospital stay was a few dollars a day. Henry's mother spent over two-hundred-and-fifty days in the hospital before she passed. Henry visited his mother there every day and reconnected with my mom. He had been a schoolmate of hers and farmed not far from us. His dad had also died in middle age and Henry, also an only child, stayed home and took care of his mother and the farm. Henry had pale skin, light blue eyes, and grey hair by the time I met him. He tried to be a father to me, but I didn't want to listen.

By the time I was a senior in high school, Mom and Henry were engaged. They married right after I graduated. He was wonderful and supportive to my mother at a time when I was away at college and didn't have the time or money to be there for her.

Henry loved red vehicles: he had a red Ford pickup and a red Ford sedan. I remember Henry using an old outhouse behind his new "modern" house; he said it was nasty to go to the bathroom inside. He had grown up with an outdoor bathroom and it was hard to make the change, I guess.

He also loved my daughters, Jennifer and Libby. He was so proud of them and loved to entertain them. He took them for a ride in his pickup to a pond on his farm so we could fish.

Henry was badly bow-legged and had his knees replaced. He was so proud of his new straight legs and could walk without pain. Unfortunately, soon after he came down with pulmonary fibrosis and had to be on oxygen. He did great for a while, but eventually they discovered he had an aortic aneurism. This was before modern stents had been developed so they did an open chest procedure. He never got off the ventilator and lived a month before passing away. My mother and I were with him when he died.

I have lived through the deaths of my father, grandparents, some uncles, aunts, and friends of my mom, but Henry's was the only death I've been physically present for. Just like on TV, the heart monitor finally stopped beeping and the EKG graph flatlined. I'd witnessed an autopsy in dental school, but being there for his passing was a surreal experience.

Chapter 5
Dating Girls

I was twelve when I had my first "real" girlfriend, Jan. She and I were in band together, so we had a musical connection. We began exchanging notes at school. We would go to the movies together and sit in the back row. It was there that I got my first kiss! Some other friends were sitting in the row in front of us. They saw us and gave us thumbs up. I don't remember how long the relationship lasted, but I felt I was *truly* in love. What a blissful feeling.

I vividly recall the day when Jan threw me over for Craig. I remember his smug look and how much it hurt. I wonder now why I didn't fight for her love or try to win her back. I remember my chest actually ached with the pain. Now I know that "broken heart syndrome" is a real thing, but at the time I didn't know why I was in so much emotional and physical pain. We had only kissed closed mouth and danced close. It may have been puppy love … but it was so real to me.

Jan eventually married another classmate who worked for years in a prison pharmacy. He came home early one day and caught her in bed with another woman. Craig, the guy who had taken her from me in middle school, eventually married my distant cousin, dropped out of college to go to Vietnam, returned to farm, and then retired to Arizona. He died of a heart attack one spring.

ATKISSON STUDIOS   CENTRAL   1961-62

My Junior High-School Class Photo

I am the kid in the goofy striped sweater on the right end of the front row. The other kids are wearing cool plaid shirts and sweaters. In this photo is also a girl who liked me then. She died too young from diabetes. I also see a guy I was in Boy Scouts with who died in a house fire recently. I see several others who are gone, two guys who went to prison, a good friend who had to get married at seventeen to a girl who was fifteen. He went on to have a very successful career in the grocery business. They are still happily married and are well-to-do. There is also a girl who is my cousin by marriage and lives the good life in L.A.

Another classmate was a professional musician until he lost his teeth. He went on to become a letter carrier.

I became guarded after the experience with Jan. I didn't want to get close enough to anyone to feel that pain again. It had come so soon after losing my dad, and I didn't have him to talk to about it. I was scared and never fully trusted friends—male or female. I am sure this has something to do with my failure to be fully engaged and in love—that's my excuse, at least. If you are not totally committed to anyone, rejection doesn't hurt as much.

I remember when, as a senior in high school, I went "parking" one night with a beautiful and well-endowed blonde who was a year younger than me. We had had a couple of dates and I took her to prom. She let me fondle and kiss her breasts.

"I love you!" I said.

"No, you don't!" she replied.

She must have known instinctively I was not in love with *her,* just her breasts.

Music and High School

In high school, I played taps on my trumpet at the cemetery every Memorial Day. I worried about being bored, so I decided to sneak my prized possession—a brick-sized transistor radio covered in a chocolate-colored leather case—in my horn case so I could listen to the Indianapolis 500.

I was afraid I would be caught and reprimanded, but I also really didn't care. The sun was shining, the soldiers were in their uniforms, their rifles at the ready. The speaker was droning on and on, but I was not listening—instead, I slowly eased the radio out of its case and raised it to my ear. I turned it up *just* enough, so I could hear but hopefully the attendees couldn't. I tuned in just in time to hear the exciting words, "Gentlemen, start your engines!" The motors roared to life.

Over the last forty years I have tried to listen to or watch this event each Memorial Day and the words never fail to bring tears to my eyes and a tightness in my chest. The announcers can really transport me to an event I have never seen with my own eyes. Their excitement was infectious as they described how the powerful cars careened round the track at breakneck speed, inches away from each other. I no doubt was using the race as a distraction from listening to Memorial Day speeches and recalling that I'd attended my dad's funeral just a few years before. I didn't want to reflect on missing a father to guide me in the world of girls, parties, jobs, and studies.

I once Googled the list of the top 100 songs for every year from 1963-1967 and picked the ones I remembered listening to. I decided to categorize them. The themes, I discovered, are universal: love, war, peace, change, dancing, and cars.

When I was in high school, Vietnam was heating up and war was on everyone's mind. The guys were subject to the draft and their girls were facing time away from them. The "Ballad of the Green Berets" was as patriotic as one could get. It was number one on the Billboard charts for several weeks and was the number one song for the entire year of our graduation, 1966.

Once I **went** away to college, the civil rights and peace movements were ramping up and protest songs were beginning to become the rage. Bob Dylan's "Blowin' in the Wind," later covered by Joan Baez and Peter, Paul & Mary, among others, seemed to sum up how those opposed to war, and for civil rights, felt.

How many roads must a man walk down before you call him a man?

Yes, how many times must the cannon balls fly before they're forever banned?

Yes, how many years can some people exist before they're allowed to be free?

Yes, how many times can a man turn his head pretending he just doesn't see?

Yes, how many ears must one man have before he can hear people cry?

Yes, how many deaths will it take 'til he knows that too many people have died?

The answer my friend is blowin' in the wind;

The answer is blowin' in the wind.

The end of high school is often the time in your life when you experience great change and half a dozen of the songs I researched were about change, leaving, decisions, or falling from grace. Bob Dylan correctly predicted that "The Times They Are a Changing." Things certainly were changing for us new graduates, for the rest of the country, even for the entire world. Dylan's "Like a Rolling Stone" was about a girl going from a comfortable life to being homeless; something we didn't think or talk much about back then, but becoming responsible adults on our own seemed daunting—not a sure thing.

Four songs were about dancing or parties. Attending school dances, parties with records playing to dance to, and dance concerts in National Guard armories with small time bands trying to make it big was a great way to listen to music and to get close to the opposite sex by dancing. I was just young enough, and our town so small and behind the times, that I missed learning to do the West Coast Swing (that's my excuse, at least). Fortunately, the simple and easy Twist came along just in time to rescue me. Of course, we loved slow dancing the most because of the closeness it brought.

Not unexpectedly, four songs were about cars and how much fun and independence they brought to our lives. Driving was freedom. Cars allowed us to listen to music while driving where we wanted, without our parents, and, more importantly, they let us go "parking" with dates. Living in a small town, we were just minutes away from isolated country roads where we could kiss, pet, and, for some, much more. A full two-thirds of my songs were about love, romance, marriage, and intimacy. Many of us were dating, having our first romantic experiences, even choosing life partners, so it is not surprising that we listened to love songs.

"Paradise by the Dashboard Light" by Meat Loaf vividly describes what many of us did and felt when we were young, in love, and parked in a car. That is how Linda and I gave each other our virginity and the promise I made to her then.

Will you love me forever
I couldn't take it any longer Lord I was crazed
And when the feeling came upon me like a tidal wave
I started swearing to my god and on my mother's grave
That I would love you to the end of time
I swore, that I would love you to the end of time
So now I'm praying for the end of time to hurry up and arrive

Chapter 6
My Mother's Scar

One warm, summer afternoon I was driving my mother somewhere. I had just obtained my license to drive and I was glad for the opportunity to show her what a good driver I was.

I noticed a wasp on the partly-open passenger-side window. I reached across my mom to swat it out the window when suddenly there was a loud *bang.* When I had reached for the wasp, I had pulled the wheel with me and steered the car into a light pole at the curb.

We were sitting on the seatbelts; back then, no one wore them. I looked at Mom and saw blood streaming down her face.

"Oh, Paul, you wrecked the car!" was Mom's first reaction.

I later realized that her glasses were broken when she'd hit the windshield. The glasses' temples were left inside. The part holding the lenses was ejected through the windshield and onto the street.

My mother's cut healed into a faint scar across her forehead that served as a reminder of my momentary inattention. My only injuries were on my forearms which were bruised by the wheel. I have no idea if we had adequate insurance, but two months later the car was repaired. I think she even had to pay for the telephone pole. I nearly orphaned myself, since my father had been dead for a few years by then. My mother eventually forgave me for wrecking the car, but every time I looked at her face, I saw the scar on her forehead, reminding me of the pain I had caused her. The two-inch-long white line across her forehead above her nose was angled enough so it was obvious it wasn't a worry line. It even showed up in photos.

* * *

This story could serve as a metaphor about my relationship with my mother. I was trying to avoid hurting her, but I ended up hurting her more than a wasp sting would have. We spent an inordinate amount of time together for the first decade of my life until my father died. We were close. I didn't want to disappoint her. I tried to please her yet wanted to be true to myself. When, as a teenager, I questioned the existence of God, she expressed extreme disappointment, but we didn't debate the issue. She was adamantly against smoking and drinking; of course, I was drawn to both. She encouraged me to study hard; I did just enough to get good grades, not really to learn as much as I could have.

I think now how hard it must have been for her to lose a husband after nearly thirty years, having to learn new skills, and go back to work to support us.

She did depend on me in later years. Once she couldn't handle her affairs, I paid her bills and made financial decisions for her. In a way, being an only child made it easier; I didn't have to get approval from siblings. I was with her when her second husband died, but I am sure I failed her in many ways. I was not there when she was dying, I was sailing around the Caribbean.

If my mother could see me now, would she be proud of the way I turned out? She would be disappointed that I don't go to church, that I got divorced, and that I don't visit the cemetery and put flowers on her grave on Decoration Day. She would be glad to know I have quit smoking and drinking. I think, all in all, she might approve. I regret I didn't visit or write her more while she was alive. I could have given more time to her.

I also wonder what my dad would think of me. I wasn't very close to him. He had so many burdens, getting mortally ill in his mid-50s. I do wish he would have lived long enough to see me succeed in life and have his grandchildren. I wish I could have taken him on an airplane trip, a train trip, a sailing trip. I am sure he had wanted to travel.

Chapter 7
The First Time

When I went away to college, I bought a small paperback book on how to sail. Since I had no boat, it didn't make much sense. Eventually, I rented a small sailboat at tiny Lone Star Lake, south of Lawrence, Kansas. The water was relatively calm and the trees a beautiful mix of reds, yellows, oranges, and greens. It was one of those warm autumn days.

The guy at the dock showed me how to handle the line and the tiller. Off I went. I didn't really know how to sail, but I sheeted in the sail and the boat took off, propelled only by the wind. Although I was thrilled, I didn't grasp the concept of tacking or the importance of knowing the direction of the wind. I was having a blast flying down the lake using only wind to propel me in the peaceful setting.

Before long I reached the end of the small body of water. Now what? I kept trying to turn the boat one way and then the other. And then, a puff of wind knocked the boat over. The water was warm, but I had no idea what to do. Pull the board down and stand on it? That didn't work. Before long, the boat turned upside down with the mast stuck in the muddy bottom of the lake and I was still treading water. Fortunately, the guy who had rented me the boat came to my rescue. He helped me right the boat and, since the wind had died, towed me back to the dock.

What an inglorious start to my sailing career. I had managed to do almost everything wrong and had even failed to return the boat to the dock. Still I was undeterred; I was hooked! I really *could* use the wind to propel me and a boat. I loved the peaceful feeling combined with the exhilarating sensations of the boat leaning, the wind on my face, the sun on my skin. The dream I had as a small child—on that isolated farm in landlocked Kansas—about traveling the world in a boat having great adventures, with just the wind to propel me, was now firmly planted in my brain.

Getting a Hooker for CJ

I wanted to escape my small town so badly I decided to go to college early—the summer before my freshman year—right after Mom and Henry got married. There were two KU basketball players in one of my classes: Jo Jo White, who was black and went on to become a star at KU and the NBA, and Carl Janis or "CJ," who was so white he was nearly albino. I nearly flunked out the fall semester while I was a pledge in the Pike fraternity. It could have served as a model for the movie *Animal House.* The spring semester I moved into a dorm where the scholarship athletes, including CJ, lived. Neither CJ nor I liked our assigned roommates, so we decided to switch and live together. We immediately bonded, despite him being the only white kid and star athlete on his high school team from the south side of Chicago and me being a non-athletic farm kid from Kansas.

CJ had a serious girlfriend back home who he really missed. "Their song," he said, was "Dedicated to The One I Love" by the Mamas and the Papas.

Each night before you go to bed my baby
Whisper a little prayer for me my baby
And tell all the stars above
This is dedicated to the one I love ...

When we would listen to it on the radio, he would pine for her, telling me how much he loved her and that he couldn't wait to marry her. We were both virgins, but she had given him a BJ. Years later Clinton would famously claim this was not sexual relations.

CJ decided he needed some experience so that he would know what to do when they got married. We heard there were ladies of the night in hotels in the 12th Street area in downtown Kansas City. We drove there and asked at the first place we found. The doorman told us to go to any hotel with a black doorman. We found one and I stayed in the lobby while CJ headed up to a room. The only thing he told me about the experience was the woman had asked him if anyone had ever told him he was rough.

CJ also had a couple of dates with a girl from Lawrence High School who worked in the basketball office. He had seen her friend, and he liked her better. We went on a double date with the idea that we would switch dates during the evening. It didn't work out that way; I liked her better too. When we got back to the dorm, I told CJ, "I'll probably end up marrying that girl." Sure enough, that girl was Linda, my first wife.

CJ realized that Jo Jo White was always going to get to play instead of him. He missed his girlfriend so much that he dropped out of school. He went home and married her, joined the Marines, did two tours of duty in Vietnam, and was killed in a car accident when he got back to the states. I will always regret that I didn't stay in touch with him while he was in Vietnam and afterwards. Ironically, Linda's friend from the double date died young too.

I often wonder what would have happened if I had stayed in the fraternity, flunked out of college, and gone to Vietnam myself, or not switched roommates, or had switched dates ...

I shall be telling this with a sigh
Somewhere ages and ages hence:
Two roads diverged in a wood, and I—
I took the one less traveled by,
And that has made all the difference.
–Robert Frost

Chapter 8
Becoming a Dentist

When I was in college at Kansas University, the Vietnam War was heating up. If I dropped out or flunked out, I was headed to the jungles of Southeast Asia with an M-16. This motivated me to study harder. My sophomore year I took organic chemistry taught by Dr. Clark Bricker, a perennial student favorite. There were over seven-hundred students in the class, but by the end of second semester he could call most of us by name. He inspired me to study harder. My grades became much improved.

Many years ago, I was sitting at a dinner with two friends, a dermatologist and a psychologist PhD, and a discussion came up about why we ended up in our respective professions. We all admitted that "it kept us out of Vietnam." Nothing defined our generation like that war. I didn't come from a military family and there was no tradition of service. My dad was too young for WWI and too old for WWII and he was a farmer, needed for the country. None of my ancestors served except my mom's oldest sister who was a nurse in WWII. She had died before I was born.

While I was at KU, demonstrations, anti-war protests, a curfew, and arson gradually came on the scene. One night I had been out studying and was driving back home. Cresting the hill and rounding the Chi Omega fountain, I could see across the valley the Student Union building engulfed in flames lighting up the night sky. I had worked construction the summer before and expanded the parking garage for that building. They never solved that crime. Those were not the carefree college days many experienced in a different era. The summer after my third year, there were race riots in Kansas City and so many problems in Lawrence that they instituted a curfew: you had to be off the streets by 6:00 p.m. National Guardsmen had recently killed protesters in Kent State.

My cousin Dick was once spending the night at the Law School. He was perennially late. It was just a few minutes before 6:00 as I drove him to the building. We passed a Jeep with Guardsmen armed with M-16 rifles ready to enforce the ban. I remember thinking, *Wow, this is real*. They canceled classes and we didn't have to take finals. And yet … I had a lot on my plate: I was getting married and had just been admitted to dental school.

* * *

I had worked in retail pharmacy one summer and decided it wasn't for me. I didn't want to spend the rest of my life counting pills to one hundred by fives and stocking shelves with Kotex. I also worked for a couple of graduate students one semester, helping them do research. But that, too, was boring, plus they complained they would never make much money.

On breaks I would get together with my cousin Dick and his good friend Charlie, who had dated the local dentist's daughter in high school, which may have motivated him to go to dental school. Charlie would talk about how great a career dentistry was. You make good money and have good hours, yet don't have the pressure of being a "real doctor."

I applied to dental school, took the DAT, and got in. Dr. Bricker, the organic chemistry teacher, remembered me two years later and wrote me a letter of recommendation. I will never know how much that influenced my acceptance, but I'm sure it didn't hurt. We were told that there were 1,500 applicants for 150 slots, and I got in.

In college, I was friends with a student with psychological issues named Paul Johnson who had a barber's license. We called him Paul the Barber. He applied to dental school and the admissions dean told him that if he would sleep with him, he would let him in. He declined. That didn't happen to me. Eventually Paul was drafted and when examined, he cried. They rejected him, which he was happy about. Paul later invited me to go to Woodstock with him. I didn't want to take off work and didn't really understand what it was all about. I loaned Paul some money to go and he never paid me back. He said the experiences and the drugs were amazing. Years later, one of my college roommates owed Paul money for a weed deal and knew Paul still owed me so he paid me instead. As much as I would have loved to experience Woodstock, it is probably just as well that I didn't go. Karma is a funny thing.

They didn't require an undergraduate degree for dental school, just some science classes, all of which I had taken already in my four years out of five of pharmacy school. In addition to the written test, I had to carve a big piece of chalk with a small knife into a certain geometric shape for the Dental Aptitude Test. I was always good at taking multiple choice tests. I could smell out the wrong answers. Since all the questions were multiple choice, if you could narrow it down to two to guess from, it improved your odds. And if you had no idea, you chose B. Those were the days before computers randomly assigned answers and that was the letter most often assigned by the test maker.

Ironically, the dean who offered my friend Paul admission-for-sex gave our introductory lecture the first day of class. He gave me the best piece of advice, "Keep your grades up, you never know if you might want to specialize someday." I didn't know anything about dentistry, much less what "specialties" were.

At the end of my first year, I was looking over the classes for the next year and saw "Endodontics" as one of the classes. I asked a classmate, "What's this endodontics?"

"That's a root canal," he replied.

I said, "Okay. What is a root canal?"

He explained that you drill a hole in the top of the tooth and remove the nerve. I'd had dental anatomy and knew how small and tortuous the nerve canals were.

"No, you can't do that!" I said.

I was about to enter my second year in dental school, and I had never heard of endodontics. Eventually I specialized in it.

Dental school was a blur. In college, I had had twelve to fifteen hours of lecture and maybe another five to ten hours of lab per week. In dental school, we had forty hours of lecture and lab every week. I usually worked another twenty hours on top of that, so I had to really learn to budget my study time. The semester that I had the least free time, I ended up making my best grades. We had a group of guys who would get together and study. Fortunately, one of my study friends was also one of my best friends—Archie Jones. Since we sat together alphabetically in class, he always sat next to me. He graduated first in our class. I was thirteenth.

Archie had attended KU and was about my size and height. He was a smart aleck and always joking. If the waitress fumbled, he'd say, "You must be new here." In an elevator once, a guy had a fashionable goose down jacket that was the new thing and expensive. Archie said, "Do you smell a duck in here?" Once he went with Linda and me to a place with go-go dancers near the same 12th Street hotel I took CJ to a few years before—that seedy collection of strip clubs, go-go bars, and cheap hotels. A scantily clad waitress bent over to serve the table next to us. I pointed to her rear end with my thumb and Archie pushed it into her. She turned around and saw me with my arm around Linda and Archie alone and grinning. She slapped him. "But it wasn't my thumb!" he said. No, but she got the right guy.

They had a program in dental school where some of the best students could graduate early. A group of ten got out after three years instead of four. I was in the group that got out after three-and-a-half years, but I went to school all three summer breaks, so I spent more time in school than those who went all four years.

When we found out that we were going to graduate early, Archie, Linda, and I went out to celebrate at a seafood restaurant called The Rusty Scupper near 12th Street. They ran a special of all the cheap white wine you could drink with dinner for free. Archie and I both got hammered. He looked at me as we left. We both said, "I can't drive!" Linda drove us home. I had a killer hangover the next day.

I also had to pass a clinical board exam before I could practice. It consisted of doing some fillings on patients and other things I can't recall. In addition to taking the dental part of the board, the state required a jurisprudence test of the dental laws of the state. We were told not to bother studying for it because it was not going to be offered there. As I started my board—drilling on my first patient—someone came up and told us they changed their mind and that we could take it at the end of the day. "We didn't study!" we said. They reassured us it was no problem—we could take it again if we failed. I missed passing by one question. I had to drive to Jefferson City, Missouri, a couple of weeks later to take the test at a board member's office. When I got there, he said:

"Do you know you are the only guy to ever fail this test?"

I wanted to punch him.

After graduating, I bought Bob Gillihan's practice in Lawrence and practiced general dentistry for two years. "Gilley" was a wild guy, nearly as wide as he was tall. He used to chew tobacco while working on patients and spit it in an old coffee can. One day he came in and saw I was with a lady he knew. She was well dressed, an elegant person. He popped his head in the treatment room and told her a dirty joke. I thought I was going to die and that she would be offended. She just laughed.

After a few months in the practice, it became clear to me that I would have to spend a lot of time getting better at many facets of dentistry. I liked doing root canals and thought I was good at them, so I decided to specialize. I applied to several programs and got into a few. Nebraska seemed to be the best fit and my mother and stepfather were living just seventy miles south of the program at the time.

* * *

In the medical field, one learns to hide one's feelings from the patient. Am I calm and cool, or just cold and unfeeling? There was a Bill Cosby skit in which the doctor says "oops" while working on a patient who is awake.

The patient says, "I know what *oops* means—what did you just do?"

When I first started practicing, I was tense. I was worried I would hurt the patient or make a mistake. The longer I practiced, the better I became at appearing calm and the less anxious I actually felt. When I did make a small mistake, I would wait until the procedure was over and then tell the patient in a calm voice what had happened. Often it wasn't a big deal. I recall doing a root canal on the wrong tooth on a referring dentist. He understood, I did the right tooth too, and he continued to send me patients. I also told my assistants to not initiate conversation with me while I was working. It distracted me from concentrating and comments can be misinterpreted by the patient. "Oh, Doctor, why did you do that?" "Is there still decay in the tooth?" "Do you want the big, long needle?" These are all the wrong thing to say over a patient.

But after years of hiding my feelings from patients, I was starting to become adept at hiding my feelings from my loved ones, too.

My Dental School Graduation

Chapter 9
New Father

As much as I hate to admit it, I was at first a reluctant father. I am basically a selfish person. At the time Linda became pregnant with Jennifer, our relationship was rocky, at best. But once Jennifer was born, I embraced her and loved being a dad. By then we had moved to Lincoln, Nebraska, where I did my graduate specialty training in endodontics. I was working part time on top of that so I had little time to enjoy our new baby.

Since my dad had passed before I was old enough to learn about being a father from him, as with other things, I was on my own trying to figure out how best to parent Jennifer. She was always tough, smart, and adventurous. She was my surrogate son; we went fishing, boating, camping, and hunting. She was a great student without even seeming to try. She led an active social life and had four close girlfriends who couldn't have been better people or friends. She was a couple of years ahead of her class in math and so went to high school to take math class when she was still in middle school. She graduated seventh in her class in a high school of several hundred. She got all A's at KU in Environmental Science, got her master's degree in urban planning at Portland State in Oregon, and had her first child at the same time.

When Jennifer was about twelve, we canoed into Quetico Provincial Park in southern Ontario. We packed in our freeze-dried food, drank water from the lake, cooked over an open wood fire, and paddled and portaged, carrying packs and canoes between lakes. We covered over fifty miles, with only a map and a compass to find our way. After the first day, I let her navigate.

She was a good gymnast and tough too. The first time she competed for her high school team, she came down hard while doing a tumbling pass. Instead of the spring floor she was used to, they had simply put wrestling mats on a wooden gym floor. She finished the floor routine with a broken bone in her foot!

Perhaps Jennifer's love of adventures developed before she'd left the womb. In college I had a fraternity brother named Larry. After college, he went into the Air Force and flew F-15s. We reconnected a few years later, after he got out of the service. He was driving an old VW bus he had converted into a camper. VW buses were the ultimate symbol of hippies and were often painted psychedelic colors—they expressed freedom and non-conformity. Between stories of flying jets, he told me how badly underpowered the bus was. It couldn't keep any speed into a head wind so he would sit at the top of a hill on the interstate and wait for a semi-truck. He would get enough speed downhill and then pull in behind the massive truck to tailgate its bumper. I think when you are used to flying wing tip to wing tip at Mach 2, tailgating a truck at sixty-five mph doesn't bother you.

Larry inspired me to get my own bus: a 1972 camper, the non-pop-top version. It had the slightly bigger engine, the back folded into a bed, and it had an icebox. We also bought a two-burner propane stove and I pop-riveted an awning on the side. When Linda was four months pregnant with Jennifer, we drove the bus from Lawrence to Houston and back, and then headed west. We stopped at the Ogallala Reservoir in western Nebraska, which is twenty-six miles long in the sand hills and is bound by sandy shores. The plains don't block the wind, so it is great for sailing. Next, we stopped in Cheyenne and Jackson Hole, Wyoming, where we pretended to be cowboys. Then we went on to the stunning beauty of the Tetons and Yellowstone National Park.

We stopped at the incredible Lake Tahoe where we ate avocados for the very first time and sailed on a gorgeous catamaran hand-built by a couple of teachers from California. They had cute girls as crew and a glass-bottomed boat. This, of course, fueled my desire to get a sailboat.

Linda and I made it to San Francisco, where we watched sailboats plying the Bay. Next, we drove down to Monterey, then headed up the coast to Oregon, Washington, and British Columbia. I took every opportunity to stare out at the Pacific, dreaming of sailing away to the magical, tropical islands beyond the horizon.

Somewhere just outside Olympic Peninsula National Park, we bought fresh crab legs and corn on the cob at a Safeway. We drove into the verdant woods and cooked and ate them with butter. We took the ferry from Anacortes to Victoria, British Columbia where we watched military jets take off and land. It reminded me of Larry. We then traversed the Canadian Rockies, looking at the beautiful robin egg blue, glacier-filled lakes, including Lake Louise, near Banff. We pulled into Calgary just in time for the Calgary Stampede with a rodeo, figure eight chuck wagon races, and all. Next it was the Columbia Icefield and then Glacier National Park. Then the Black Hills and back to Lincoln, Nebraska, where I was ready to start graduate school.

We had driven the bus eight thousand miles, over six weeks, and only stayed in a motel once and ate in a restaurant once. I grew a beard while on the trip. My love of travel was partially satisfied. For now.

Chapter 10
The Sailor Dog

The sea, once it casts its spell, holds one in its net of wonder forever.
—Jacques Yves Cousteau

My mom read to me before I knew how. I loved it when she would read the brightly-illustrated, simple Golden Books stories to me. The one I remember most vividly, because I begged her to it read over and over again, was *The Sailor Dog.* It was the story of a little dog named Scuppers who longed to go to sea for adventure. Scuppers too had grown up on a farm. After trying other modes of travel to find adventure, he eventually makes it to the sea, finds a small sailboat, and begins his voyage. Looking at the illustration on the page where he first reaches the ocean and spies his boat, I can see the utter delight and joy in his face. He has found his passion in life. I memorized every word of that little book.

This book planted a seed in my brain. Maybe I too could sail on the ocean, have great adventures, sail to and explore exotic lands, be self-sufficient, and discover the wide world far from the farm. I mentioned Scuppers often enough that one year my staff bought me a copy of *The Sailor Dog* for my birthday.

Mother, mother ocean, I have heard you call
Wanted to sail upon your waters since I was three feet tall
You've seen it all, you've seen it all
Watched the men who rode you switch from sails to steam
And in your belly you hold the treasures few have ever seen
Most of them dream, most of them dream
—Jimmy Buffett

Ten years of college, dental school, private practice, and specialty school had intervened and distracted me from pursuing sailing, but once I started my specialty practice, I had time to read about sailing adventures and learn to sail. I spent hours reading the works of Joshua Slocum, Sir Francis Chichester, Tristan Jones, and Bernard Moitessier. Most of them sailed on a tight budget. I also read books by William F. Buckley, Jr., who crossed oceans in large yachts in style with a full crew of friends, fine wine, and classic music. I was hooked. It was time to go for it.

In the spring of 1979, I took a Coast Guard Auxiliary "Learn to Sail" course and bought a fourteen-foot sloop rigged dinghy.

There was no turning back. I took every opportunity to sail on area lakes. Three years later, I bought a twenty-three-foot cutter rigged (three sails) boat with a small cabin just big enough to sleep in. Later, I moved up to a twenty-seven-footer.

Jennifer in Our First Sailboat

A friend who had sailed the British Virgin Islands often talked about how wonderful it was there. After spending eight years sailing midwestern lakes, I was ready to try salt water. Linda and I took a class—"Learn to Bareboat"—in the BVIs. The class was taught by Captain David Mayo, a grandson of one of the founders of the clinic by the same name. "Bareboating" is renting or chartering a boat without a captain or crew—you are on your own to dock, steer, navigate, and anchor the boat.

Captain Mayo showed us how to anchor, pick up a mooring (permanent anchor attached to a float), raise and lower sails, tack, gybe, recover a person lost overboard, cook aboard, dock, and maneuver the sailboat.

Captain Mayo taught us how to set the anchor properly. Picking a semi-protected anchorage makes for a good night's rest. Deciding exactly where to drop the hook so you won't swing into other boats or shallow water is important too. After letting out some chain, we would snorkel to check if the anchor was buried in the sand. Back on board, we would slowly back the engine to dig the anchor in. Then we watched two places with trees or hills in line on land to be sure we weren't dragging. Securely setting an anchor so it doesn't drag is an important skill.

Next, we learned how to pick up a mooring. Captain Mayo taught us to use hand signals to direct the boat from the bow or front of the boat approaching from downwind. Shouting is not good form and the person at the helm in the rear of the boat can't hear you or see the mooring ball, while the person on the bow can. It is best to have the stronger person on the foredeck, so Linda drove the boat while I pointed where she needed to steer. Then I raised the line and attached it to the boat.

It was amusing to watch the uninitiated try unsuccessfully to pick up moorings. They would shout and yell, get mad, miss the ball and line, drive around, and around, unsuccessfully until they finally got lucky. We watched a bareboat crew backing down too fast on an anchor in a spot with poor holding, dragging it all the way across the anchorage.

We also learned how to cook, clean up, and sleep aboard. Sleeping was wonderful—being gently rocked to sleep by the motion of the boat. Finally, after five days and nights aboard, we went ashore and learned the meaning of "getting your land legs." The floor still felt like it was moving back and forth and we nearly tripped or fell a time or two. It took two hours for the sensation to stop. It was even worse when we took showers ashore. I almost fell down the first time. After years of life aboard, I am no longer bothered by the transition from sea to land, and back again.

What a life-changing experience that bareboating class was. I loved snorkeling on the coral reefs filled with a kaleidoscope of tropical fish. All you had to do was step off the boat and you could swim as if in an aquarium. The water and the air were the ideal temperature. The culture in the Caribbean was a wonderful change of pace from life in America.

I had been hooked before, but now I was sunk. I couldn't get enough of sailing.

A year later we rented a thirty-seven-foot sloop for a week. After that we bought a forty-three-foot sloop in the Moorings charter fleet in the British Virgin Islands. At the time, they had bases all over the world and you could trade your time on your boat for a similar boat any place they had a fleet of boats. Their ads read, "The only fleet with more bases is the U.S. Navy!"

Our Charter Boat in the BVIs

For eight years we spent up to six weeks a year aboard *Lady Jayhawk* or traded our time on similar boats in the Moorings fleet. In the eight years we had the charter boat in the 1990s, I spent over two hundred days sailing to over forty-five islands or cities on thirty separate trips. I sailed the U.S. and British Virgin Islands of St. Thomas and St. John, Tortola, Virgin Gorda, Jost Van Dyke, Beef Island, Peter Island, Cooper Island, Norman Island, Anagada, Marina Cay, and Sandy Cay. Other Caribbean islands I visited included St. Martin/St. Maarten, Anguilla, St. Barts, St. Kitts, Nevis, Guadeloupe, Marie-Galante, Les Saintes, Grenada, Carriacou, St. Lucia, and Martinique. We also spent two weeks in Greece sailing from Athens to Kythnos, Syros, Tinos, Mykonos, Delos, Naxos, Santorini, Folegandros, Melos,

Hydra, and back. On other trips, I managed to charter or sail boats near Maui, Seattle, San Diego, Chicago, Charleston, Key West, St. Petersburg, and Sanibel Island. Not a bad sailing resume for a guy who grew up on a farm and was living and working in Kansas.

Every time I step foot on a sailboat, I feel the same way Scuppers did when he first climbed on his little sailboat, hoisted the sail, and felt the wind drawing the boat along the water. What do I love about sailing? I don't really know the full answer. Can anyone say why they love a particular fine wine, a sport, or any hobby? Sailing is part sport, part hobby, and part lifestyle.

To begin with, I love being outdoors. I love fresh air, the sky, and being away from buildings and crowds. I also love water. Without it, life would be impossible. Being on, in, or near water relaxes me. I forget my worries and enjoy life much more when I am close to water. I enjoy the physical aspect of sailing. Just standing and moving about on a sailboat is exercise. I find it exhilarating to become one with the boat. To feel its motion through my bare feet is pleasurable. I like the sights of land and water from a boat. Sunsets and sunrises are somehow more inspiring when viewed from the deck of a sailboat. I also enjoy the mental aspect of sailing: trimming the sails, keeping up with navigation, and maintaining the mechanical aspects of the boat are fun mental exercises for me.

I love nature. The birds and marine life fascinate me. Sailboats are a much more environmentally friendly way to observe the creatures of the world, as animals are less intimidated by a sailing vessel. I am thrilled to watch a pod of dolphins frolicking in the bow wave and staring up at me as I stare back, looking them in the eyes. Watching a whale broach, a stingray fly through the air, a school of flying fish skim just above the waves, or a sea turtle surface near the boat gives me a special connection with the animal kingdom. I marvel at the diversity and beauty of nature when I see a flock of ducks or geese take flight, watching frigate birds soar high above my mast, or spot bald eagles flying majestically. I love to watch pelicans dive for fish, schools of hundreds of silver-sided fish jump from the water in unison and reflect the sunlight, or jacks make gentle arcs as they jump.

I remember waking up one morning alone on our twenty-seven-foot O'Day sailboat on a lake near Lawrence, Kansas, and hearing a strange chirping sound on deck. I peeked out and saw a hundred barn swallows perched, nearly touching each other, lined up on the life lines on my boat. They sat undisturbed for several minutes before taking off for a day's bug catching. What a beautiful, peaceful experience that was! These events never fail to move me.

I also enjoy working *with* rather than *against* nature. You are getting an almost free ride when you sail. When you shut down the engine, you aren't burning fossil fuel and aren't polluting the environment, yet you can get where you want to go with the power of wind alone. Because it is a slow way to travel, it teaches patience, perseverance, and persistence.

I get a tremendous sense of freedom when sailing. With a sailing vessel, there are few limits as to where you can go. Humankind was born to roam. We have developed many ways to go from one place to another. To me, sailing is the most satisfying way to travel. I like being independent. When you are in command of a sailboat, you must be self-reliant. You use your wits, strength, and knowledge to accomplish something useful and meaningful.

So is it any wonder that a son of a son of a farmer came to love the song "Son of a Son of a Sailor?" Jimmy Buffett is the poet laureate of sailors everywhere. His songs and lyrics resonate in the hearts and minds of those who ply the seas for pleasure. His ideas and stories encourage one to live life to the fullest and enjoy all it has to offer—especially on a sailboat or at a waterfront bar. It is little wonder that my family and I came to love his songs, search out his concerts, and sail the waters he describes. I've come to know most of his songs by heart. My younger daughter, Libby, attended her first Jimmy concert while still in high school and when asked how it was, she replied, "It was great, but I've never seen so many drunk old people in my life!" Most were only in their 40s or 50s, but it's all relative when you're young. Libby chose "Son of a Sailor" for the father-daughter dance at her wedding.

In November of 1999, Jimmy gave a free concert at the quay in Gustavia, St. Barts. We were on our year-long sailing sabbatical and flew Libby down for the event. We hung out during the sound check in the afternoon before the concert and she was struck speechless being so near him. I didn't realize it until later, but I was offered a beer by Captain Fatty Goodlander, a sailing writer and radio talk show host I followed. Jimmy's daughter was also hanging out near us during the concert. We had a fabulous time and the next day we were anchored in a nearby harbor when Jimmy and his entourage came and anchored next to us.

There is a downside of sailing a small boat across a vast expanse of sea. It can often be tiring, boring, and entirely unromantic. Don't get me wrong, an offshore sail can be challenging, exciting, and fun … but it is also exhausting, dangerous, terrifying, and hyper- or hypothermic. Still, I personally love doing passages out of sight of land as a way to move a boat and my crew from one interesting place to another. As much as I love being rocked to sleep nestled in a cozy sea berth while the boat plows through waves or falls off them, dreaming of our next port of call, reality sets in when I am awakened after too little sleep to stand the 2–6:00 a.m. watch. Staying awake to watch for ships sneaking up on you or running you down, trying to dodge rain-drenched squalls filled with winds that will shred your sails, will push the boat and you to the limit and can scare the crap out of you.

Sailing safely along the coast from port to port gives one the fallback position of stopping short of the intended destination; something I have done more times than I care to admit due mostly to mechanical or physical failure. Depending on the weather and the route, I sometimes enjoy sailing within sight of land, watching the parade of buildings slowly recede past our stern. But even if our course parallels the shore, it is often safer and easier to head away from land. Shallow water, adverse current, boat traffic, shrimp and fishing boats, and confused waves bouncing off the shore often conspire to make staying near land not at all pleasant or relaxing.

Sailing at night is also difficult—although it is beautiful, too. The lyrics of the Little River Band's song "Cool Change" come to mind: "It's kind of a special feeling to be out on the sea alone, staring at the full moon like a lover." The rare, phosphorescent sparkle of phytoplankton stream from your stern as your wake excites them to glow in the dark. The stars are much brighter and more visible when not dimmed by city lights. Trying to pick out the constellations and wondering at the billions and billions of distant stars in the Milky Way, is indeed a special treat seen by few city-dwellers today.

Chapter 11
Off to Alaska

I practiced dentistry with Dr. Everson, a man who had flown around the world. He was also an avid golfer. He and his best golfing buddy bought around-the-world airline tickets, took three months off, and played golf along the way in as many countries as they could. Those tickets are not as expensive as one might think. His extended sabbatical from practice would later inspire me to take a year off and do what I loved doing.

After Dr. Everson retired, he and his wife drove his old Chevy pickup camper to Alaska and back. He said of all the places he had been, Alaska was the *most* amazing and impressive. High praise from a man who had seen it all.

Linda and I, her best friend Lyn, and Lyn's husband Spike took a two-week *Planes, Trains, and Automobiles*-type trip to Alaska. We flew to Fairbanks, played golf until midnight, took the train to Denali, rode a bus part-way up the mountain, rented a car and drove to Anchorage, took a whale watching cruise, rode a ferry to Juneau, flew in a small plane to Skagway, took a train built by gold miners, flew a helicopter up a mountain to hike on the tundra, and rode a river cruise to observe Native Americans fishing and their lifestyle. If you have not been to Alaska and it isn't on your bucket list, I highly recommend adding it.

* * *

When a dental school classmate invited me to go salmon fishing in Alaska, I jumped at the chance. Our flight out of Kansas City had been delayed four hours so we had missed the earlier flight to Anchorage. We spent the night at the Coast International Inn near the Anchorage airport beside a beautiful lake with hundreds of small seaplanes moored on the shore.

After an early morning scenic flight from Anchorage, over snow covered mountains to King Salmon in a turboprop commuter plane, we boarded an ancient de Havilland Otter seaplane for a twenty-five-minute hop to the Katmai Lodge on the Alagnak River, about three-hundred miles southwest of Anchorage, Alaska. There were no roads; the lodge was only accessible by air or boat. We stowed our gear in our room, met our guides, and had lunch. We donned our waders and took off down the river at thirty knots in large aluminum skiffs with 100-plus hp outboards (most motors had jet drives for heading to the shallower water up river). It was a chilly, breezy ride.

Within minutes of leaving the lodge, we saw bald eagles, brown bears, and beaver lodges. It took about forty-five minutes to get within a couple of miles of the mouth of the Alagnak River where it dumps into Bristol Bay on the Bering Sea. Although the low-lying scenery wasn't spectacular, zooming down the river was a thrill. As we snaked our way downriver, we saw salmon rolling, and occasionally jumping, and anticipated the fishing to come.

Our guide was Chris Swift, a thirty-year-old strapping rice farmer, an avid hunter and fisherman, from Katy, Texas. He was nearly as bald as me and sported a dirty blond goatee. He stopped the boat and we hopped out. I figured it was a good omen when, after he showed me how to cast, he hooked a fish on the very first toss.

We soon were catching 25–30 inch, 15–20-pound chum (dog) salmon with regularity. These fish fought hard and ran fast across the current. It sometimes took five minutes, or more, of fighting them on thirty-pound test line to reel them in. My arm quickly tired from casting the large, weighted, pink streamer on the heavy nine-weight fly rod. I landed so many fish that my arm started cramping. You know you are having a good fishing trip when you forget how many fish you caught. I know I caught and released at least a dozen chum and one nice coho (silver) salmon in the six or so hours we fished that first day. The first evening there, I sat on the deck outside our room on the second story of our cabin that overlooked the river. I could see for miles—the terrain was flat, and the river wound through it. At 9:30 p.m., the sun still shone brightly in my eyes. It still wouldn't set for over an hour. The river babbled; salmon jumped. It was absolutely gorgeous. The temperature was over 70 degrees.

Salmon that spawn in this river spend the next four years in the open ocean and then return to the same river and make their final run several miles upriver to spawn and die. The sooner you catch them after they leave the ocean, the better they are to eat. Chum have the highest percentage of protein, so the Native

Americans feed them to their sled dogs to give them the stamina needed to pull sleds and survive the brutal winters. Chinook (king) salmon had already run—the season ended the day before we had arrived. By far the largest of the five salmon species, kings weigh from 30 to 70 pounds. They have the highest content of cholesterol-lowering omega-3 fatty acids. The coho (silver) salmon were just beginning to run. They are a little tastier than chum and keep longer when frozen. The sockeye (pink) salmon run was over. That year they estimated the sockeye run was two to three million fish on this river alone. They were now further up river.

We were fishing in the river a few yards off a sandbar when Chris said, "Do you see the bear behind us?" The bear came down the bank behind us, looked around, climbed back on the bank, and disappeared in tall grass. A few minutes later he came back down to water fifty yards below us, crossed a sandbar, walked out in the river, and caught a fish. Then he took it back to a sandbar below us and ate it.

Chris told us it was an Alaskan brown bear, a type of grizzly that lives within two hundred miles of the water and eat salmon. They weigh up to 1,200 pounds and can stand ten feet tall. Chris assured us the bears are so full of fish this time of year they are much less likely to attack. The guides don't carry guns! We did *not* approach the bear, though more people are killed by moose than bear. The next day we saw moose swimming across the river a quarter mile above us. That fall, a self-described Grizzly Man and his girlfriend were killed and eaten by a brown bear not far from where we were. Evidently the fish were gone, and the bears were hungry.

The second day we got up early and again boated forty-five minutes down river. This time we caught lots of chum and a few silver salmon. The technique was to cast across current with heavy, large 9-weight flyrod, let the streamer drift downstream until the line ran out—being careful not to let the line impede the drift of the fly. Chum will hit with light taps, but we would wait for a good strike then hit it hard to set hook. You need to watch your knuckles on your reel hand!

For silver, we would cast to shore weeds and sight-fish, trying to cast to a fish you see. We used large, pink, weighted streamers, which were hard to cast.

We kept a few salmon to take home (the limit is five per person, including one coho). We also had a couple to eat for lunch. The guides applied their special seasoning and cooked them on small propane grills in the boats. Salmon never tasted so fresh. They had been swimming in the ocean a few hours ago and had been in the river a few minutes before we ate them. They were full of bright orange eggs the size of small pearls. Chris picked up a large hand-full of eggs he had just taken from the belly of a chum, tilted his head back, and ate a mouthful like he was eating a cluster of currants. Another guide named Glo Bug (after a fly of the same name) was nearly sickened by the display. He was a short, fireplug-shaped crabber from Eureka, California, with a full reddish-gold beard and full belly. He didn't look like too much would spoil his appetite.

I agreed with Dr. Everson: Alaska is an amazing place, the size is unmanageable, the climate so diverse, and the flora and fauna unique. As much as I loved visiting there in the warm summer months with endless sunshine and ice-free water, I doubt I could tolerate living there in the long, dark winters. No wonder some Alaskans suffer from depression and drug and alcohol abuse. I'm sure I'd be tempted as well. Of all the trips I've taken not on a sailboat, the ones on or near water are the most memorable. I have and always will be drawn to oceans, seas, rivers, and streams.

Although standing on a stream bank with a line and a pole made me feel like a kid again, I was still the happiest when I was sailing. I love the outdoors and exploring it on a liquid magic carpet that takes me away from the mundane world of work, worry, and obligation.

Chapter 12
Internet Sailing

Don't try to describe the ocean if you've never seen it
Don't ever forget that you just may wind up being wrong.
— Jimmy Buffett

I was an early adopter of CompuServe, the first major commercial online service and a sponsor of the BOC Around Alone single-handed sailing race. This was my first experience using the internet (before it was called that) to interact with ocean sailors via online discussions. The number of offshore sailors in Kansas was limited. I became excited about the Around Alone race so I booked flights to Charleston to watch the race start. I posted a question on the discussion group asking how to get on the water to watch it, thinking there might be a large ferry or small cruise ship. Instead, someone replied that I was welcome to go out with him on his brand new 65' aluminum Kanter sailboat. The boat was beautiful, with matching wood cabinet doors, a washer and dryer, and original art. The owner was retired military intelligence. Also onboard were his teenaged son, sailing journalist Herb McCormick, and an anesthesiologist from Ft. Lauderdale who had single-handed to Bermuda from Florida, and a few others. I don't remember much about the event, but I was hooked on ocean sailing and meeting people online to discuss, learn about, and to go sailing with.

Mark Schrader was the race director. I had already "met" him online through his postings. He had completed two single-handed circumnavigations, one as a previous entrant in the race. I heard him speak on another occasion, as I mentioned before. He was the one who claimed that growing up in the center of the country—like he and I both had—attracted you to the sea since it was a faraway, romantic, adventurous, almost mythical place.

This experience in Charleston planted the seed: I could find sailing companions online to help me fulfill my dream of offshore ocean sailing. I had enough sense to know I needed more experience before trying to sail alone across an ocean.

Captain Bob Cook

A few years later, I discovered Sailnet, another online sailing discussion group. You could post or answer questions about boats, passages, anchorages—whatever you were curious about. I was able to virtually meet hundreds of like-minded sailors on Sailnet with varying degrees of experience. As a resource, it really opened up the world of ocean sailing to me. It also allowed me to do the research needed to prepare for our planned year-long sailing trip … but that story comes later.

I met Captain Bob Cook on Sailnet. He had extensive single-handing sailing experience and did what he called "instructional deliveries." Owners who don't have the time or experience to move their boats long distances alone hire captains to do it for them. In addition to delivering the boats, Captain Bob Cook would find paying students—people who wanted to learn—to help him deliver boats.

When Jennifer was sixteen, we signed up for one of Captain Cook's classes to sail and learn aboard a beautiful Hinckley 49-foot ketch (a two-masted sailboat) from Key West, Florida, offshore straight across the Gulf of Mexico, 850 miles to Corpus Christi, Texas. Also onboard were the owner, a recently retired IBM executive, and a Marine Corps reserve general and his attorney wife. We began the trip anchored out off of Key West for a couple of days, getting informal lessons from Captain Cook. Finally, we raised anchor and we sailed past a few small uninhabited islands in the Keys called the Dry Tortugas, continuing seventy miles west to Fort Jefferson onto Garden Key.

Built in the 1820s, the fort is quite historic, and the waters around it have wonderful snorkeling. Lying seventy miles from the nearest road, and only accessible by seaplane or boat, it is more isolated than typical parks and mainland forts. Just the type of place I dreamed of sailing to on my own boat. The huge red brick fort became obsolete before it was even completed. Rifled cannon shells were developed that could penetrate its twenty-foot-thick brick walls. The fort served as a coaling station during WWI but is now a national park.

Dr. Mudd was incarcerated there for setting John Wilkes Booth's leg after he assassinated Lincoln. Dr. Mudd was freed several years later after treating victims of a yellow fever epidemic at the fort.

We hung out there for a couple of days, exploring the grounds, snorkeling, and learning about sailing. I was eager to get offshore, so I complained loudly when we didn't leave as soon as I wanted. I was tasked with navigating out of the tight anchorage and yelled at the owner's wife when she didn't follow my confusing direction. Finally, I upset the owner again by waking him when he was off watch. He was quitting smoking and was on edge. He yelled at me, but we eventually got along okay. I wasn't used to taking orders and he was used to giving them.

Soon after we left the island, I was out of sight of land for the first time ever. Some people are afraid of not being able to see the shore, but I was exhilarated by it. Boats are meant to be at sea and come to grief by running aground. The freedom to sail in any direction you want was exciting. GPS makes navigating much easier now, but back then we had only a compass and a sextant for celestial navigation.

There was very little wind for much of the first half of the trip, so we had to run the motor. We did a bit of fishing. We hooked a mahi-mahi, but I didn't land it. We had a couple of minor storms, but the boat and crew handled them without a problem.

This was our first ocean passage and I felt good about completing it. Jennifer and I learned a lot, didn't get sick, and had a great bonding experience. I also found I could spend a week aboard with strangers without going crazy. On a small boat, there is no escape. You can't cope by going into another room or just driving away like you can on land. I had read and dreamt about sailing on the ocean out of sight of land for years, but the experience was even better than I had hoped.

Chapter 13
Tom

I first met Tom in the mid 1970s shortly after moving to Lawrence, Kansas, and starting my dental practice. There were a group of people in Lawrence that Linda and I fell in with who liked to hang out and party. Tom was one. We hit it off almost right away. At the time, he was teaching auto mechanics at Lawrence High. Like me, he was an only child from a small town in Kansas. He also had a wife and two daughters. In addition to knowing almost everything mechanical about cars, boat, motors, and motorcycles, he had many other skills. He bought an abandoned foundation and build a three-bedroom house on it. He built an A-frame cabin at the lake. He loved to cook. We hung out at weekend pig roasts at the lake where we would stay up all night talking while he was cooking a whole pig. He taught me to duck hunt and fish. We would hang limb lines on the river and at night catch frogs (for their legs) by hand with a light on the river or the local golf course ponds. Tom had an old International Harvester Scout that he drove. It inspired me to buy one too. I paid six hundred dollars for mine and the floorboards were rusted out. Still, I took it duck hunting.

Our friend group formed a drinking, card-playing, and partying club. We couldn't think of a name, so we called it the No Name Club.

Tom eventually quit teaching and started a quick oil change service before Jiffy Lube was in existence. He lost it in the recession of 1984. Linda never liked Tom, probably because we always got in trouble together. When I was asked what Tom did, I told people he was an entrepreneur. Linda loved it when she saw this definition of an entrepreneur: "Someone who will do ANYTHING to avoid getting a job." Tom later got divorced and eventually remarried. They adopted a son and a daughter. Tom rehabbed an old farmhouse where he lived and started selling smoked meats. When Tom's second marriage fell apart, he moved to Topeka and began teaching again. He taught behavior and discipline problem kids in high school and finally found his niche. Tom was obviously smart, despite putting on a good old boy act. He had enough hours for a doctorate but never finished the dissertation.

Tom has owned a series of boats of all shapes and sizes, both sail and power for the last sixty-plus years, but when he had some health issues that made him doubt his ability to go out on the water, he sold his last boat. When I saw him last, he was bemoaning the fact that he was boat-less, depressed, and debilitated. He had survived a major heart attack but had a damaged heart. An uncaring doctor's offhanded comment suggested to Tom that he did not have more than a year to live. He was also suffering from PTSD because of a near fatal fall when his implanted defibrillator went off, knocking him to the ground where he lay for over an hour unable to get up from the freezing-cold ground until someone finally saw him and called 911.

Fortunately, Tom found a new doctor who was a sailor. He examined Tom and took the time to talk to him. Tom said his only regret was that he switched from powerboats to sailboats late in life and he hadn't had enough time to learn to sail better. The doctor encouraged him to buy a sailboat and get on with his life. He said, "Tom, you are no more likely to die of a heart attack on a sailboat than at home in bed. All tests look good, I just need to see you again in five years to change the batteries in your heart monitor."

This single comment rejuvenated Tom. Like any sailor worth his salt, he immediately bought a sailboat—a 1987 Hunter 28.5. He needed help rigging it and moving it from one marina to another on the Kansas lake where we both have had countless boating and other adventures for the last forty years. I jumped at the chance.

The boat had been lovingly cared for by the previous owners and, unlike us, was in great shape for her age. It was an unseasonably cool late July morning when we arrived at the dock. As luck would have it, the doctor who advised Tom to get a boat was there on his boat and we exchanged pleasantries. Tom told him he really appreciated his help, that he bought the boat, and was so excited to go sailing. The doctor replied, "That's great, Tom, you made my day!"

All sails were below. We figured out how to thread the Genoa into the roller furling foil and raise it. Next, we bent the main on the mast and boom. The main was a little undersized and not cut exactly right as I could never get the leach to shape properly, but the genoa was fine.

With some difficulty, we got the little Yanmar diesel to fire up. We slipped the lines and were soon motoring out of the marina onto the main body of the lake. Tom drove while I hoisted the sails and we were sailing in light and variable winds down the lake. We soon killed the motor. When the wind picked up enough the boat began to heel but then stiffed up and took off. Tom and I were both smiling from ear-to-ear to be sailing again on a beautiful, sunny, cool morning.

There is nothing so satisfying to me as spending time with one of my best and oldest friends, laughing, joking, and sailing on a well-found boat, plying familiar waters. I love renewing bonds of sailing and friendship, recounting good times and bad, telling stories, and learning how a new boat handles. Nothing is more healing to the heart, mind, and soul. Like Jimmy Buffett says in one of my favorite songs, "One Particular Harbor":

I know I don't get there often enough
But God knows I surely try
It's a magic kind of medicine
That no doctor could prescribe

Chapter 14
Libby, Libby, Libby

If you put Libby's, Libby's, Libby's,
On the label, label, label,
Then you will like it, like it, like it,
On the table, table, table.
—1974 commercial

Unlike our first child, I was fully onboard with having a second. Finally, after twenty-two years of school, I was established in a private practice. Linda and I were settled, for the moment, into a somewhat happy marriage.

Jen was early and little—five pounds, six ounces, if I remember correctly. Libby was almost a month late and weighed nine pounds. Linda was more than ready for birth; she was so depressed, I bought her a fur coat to try to cheer her up. When Libby was finally born, she was so beat up from the trip through the birth canal I remember thinking when I saw her face, "I hope it's a boy."

Jen had been a colicky baby. As she grew, she developed night terrors—a disconcerting condition to first-time parents. She would begin crying and screaming in the middle of the night but not be fully awake. Libby was a much happier baby. As she grew, she loved playing with Jen. I remember them dressing up and putting on "plays." But once she learned to read, that was all she wanted to do. I recall her going through a book a *day* when we were on vacation. She played soccer, tennis, and basketball but grew so fast she developed Osgood-Schlatter's disease, a painful knee condition that limited her ability to compete.

In middle school one of Libby's teachers, Audrey Wentz Chinnock, became a mentor to her. Audrey was just out of college and they bonded and related well. They stayed in touch over the years and when Libby was in high school, Audrey and her husband took Libby and a few classmates to Africa. They both had attended and inspired Libby to attend Miami of Ohio and become a middle school teacher.

Miami was a great school for Libby. McGuffey developed his famous reader while teaching there and many fraternities have their alpha, or first, chapter house there. Ironically, although they have sororities, there are no sorority houses. Instead, groups of female students rent large old houses and live together even though they may belong to different sororities. Libby lived in the dorm her first year and pledged, but in subsequent years moved in with twelve other girls in an old three-story house off campus called Endzone. One criticism Libby offered us when Linda and I were divorcing was that none of her roommates' parents had been divorced. Given the 50% divorce rates for baby boomers, that struck me as unusual.

Libby's roommate in the dorm, Susan, was from Chicago. They became fast friends and lived together in Endzone for three years. Libby became very close to most of the other girls in the house and has stayed in touch with them over the years. They have attended each other's weddings.

Libby and Susan did their student teaching in the Azores, a small group of islands about a thousand miles west off the coast of Africa. It was a good experience. I guess Libby is drawn to islands and foreign cultures too.

When Libby graduated, she decided to move to Chicago and live with Susan. Eventually, Susan got married and Libby moved into her own place on the fourth floor walkup of an old apartment building in Andersonville, a neighborhood noted for its Swedish founders. I loved visiting her in Chicago, my favorite city. True to form, Libby got her master's degree as a reading specialist from DePaul. She taught in the affluent neighborhood of Winnetka. The first year out of college, they hired her as a teaching assistant, but at half the salary of a teacher. I remember her saying, "Dad, some of my fifth graders have allowances greater than my salary!"

At her ten-year high school reunion, Libby reconnected with Matt Latham, a guy in her class. Jen and Mark had dated exclusively starting when they were in high school. In Libby's class, on the other hand, the kids ran more in groups. Matt was an accountant and had a job and a condo in Dallas. Libby had both too, but in Chicago. He didn't like Chicago and she didn't like Dallas. His parents still lived in Kansas City, so they agreed to move there.

The public schools in Kansas City had just instituted a hiring freeze. Libby got an offer at a suburban school but didn't really like the commute. She got hired at a private school called Barstow where they quoted her a salary. She asked for more, and they gave it to her. The demographics of the students were similar to those in Winnetka, so she felt comfortable with the parents. It took a year for Matt to move to Kansas City, so Libby lived with Judy and me the first year she was back.

Once Matt was in town, they rented a house and moved in together. Eventually they got married and bought a tiny house in old Leawood. They struggled to get pregnant at first, but with a little help from modern medicine and some financial help from Judy and me, they finally had Hattie, the cutest little granddaughter anyone could ask for.

Hattie Jane Latham

Chapter 15
A Seed is Planted: *Lady Jayhawk*'s Swan Song in the British Virgin Islands, May 1996

Lady Jayhawk's Sister Ship

Jen was nineteen. She and I planned to sail *Lady Jayhawk* (a 1988 Beneteau/Moorings 432) to Florida to try to sell her. Then, just two weeks before we were to leave, we got an offer on the boat. Although we wanted to have our first offshore sail, we also wanted to sell the boat. Jen and I decided to take one last trip to the British Virgin Islands. Linda wasn't keen on offshore sailing, so she didn't want to come. Libby was going to Africa with Audrey and her husband soon and wanted to stay home to get ready for her trip.

Since our airline reservations had us going by boat from Tortola to Tampa, we had to do some last-minute changes to get the roundtrip tickets back. We were unable to get to Tortola in one day, so we overnighted in the lovely San Juan PR Airport Hotel. We got all the way to the plane the next morning only to find it had a flat tire and we had to wait another hour. Deplaning at Beef Island is always a renewing experience—to be caressed by the gentle trade winds, smell the sea air, and feast your eyes on the beautiful pastel blue waters of the BVIs makes you feel like you have died and gone to heaven.

Jen and I took a taxi to Maya Cove and unloaded our bags. We soon got everything in place and motored out of the cut of Maya Cove. We raised the main, unfurled the genoa, and were sailing once again!

Since we hadn't provisioned yet, we decided to head to West End, the Ample Hamper. It took us a little over two hours to motorsail to Soper's Hole. There wasn't much wind and it was uncharacteristically from the SSE. We saw few boats in Drake's Channel. The water was calm as usual. Surprisingly, all but one mooring was taken when we pulled in. We were directly behind a motor yacht that we predicted would run their generator all night. They did. So much for peace and quiet in paradise.

Lymin' Times, the free TV and entertainment guide, said there was a band at the Jolly Roger, so we decided to go there. It also said Foxy would be performing the next day so we planned to sail to Jost Van Dyke for that. We dinghied to the Jolly Roger for dinner, where the band Focus was playing, consisting only of a guitar player and a keyboard player. Bomba (of Bomba Shack fame) was at the bar flirting with the tourists. It was a lovely but hazy night. We went back to the boat and turned in early after running the engine to charge the batteries.

I got up early and took a walk. There was a tugboat and a large catamaran wrecked on the bar between Tortola and Frenchman's Cay. They probably were casualties of one of the hurricanes—sad to see. After breakfast, we sailed for Sandy Cay. We snorkeled for nearly an hour and Jen saw an eel. We also saw quite a few parrotfish and some squid. Next, we motorsailed to Great Harbor.

At Great Harbor, we anchored and tidied things up a bit. We missed happy hour but went into Foxy's at about 6:30. Shortly after we got there, Foxy began to sing and tell jokes. Although I have a tape by him and a book about him, it was the first time I had seen him in person. He joked about how he used to date cooks from charter boats until a captain tired of that, kidnapped Foxy, and took him half-way round the world until he found a wife. Foxy said that he wore a pink hat with "PMS" written on the front. When someone asked him what that meant, he said Please More Sex. He said white people shouldn't call black people "colored" since white people are pink when we are born, red when we are in the sun, blue when we are in the cold, green when we get sick, and black when we die. He poked fun at St. Thomas and put in a plea for holding tanks on charter boats— without them the BVIs would become known as a turd world country.

When he finished performing, the buffet began, and we ate the best grilled mahi-mahi we'd ever had. Even the coffee was superb. During and after dinner, the same band that had played at the Jolly Roger performed. They sounded a little better even though they did the same songs from the night before. We were also entertained when a bride and groom came in, she in a full-length gown and he in a white shirt, tie, and black shorts.

It was hot and still again that night, but I had put up the windsocks, so it wasn't too unpleasant. As I went for a walk the next morning, I watched a large cruise ship arrive and the tourists being ferried ashore. I got ice, a brownie, and some wonderful French-style bread from the bakery behind the customs house. After a breakfast of cereal and brownies, we raised the anchors and the sails and set off for Monkey Point on Guana Island.

The only two moorings visible when we arrived were both taken. I found a large patch of sand and we anchored. Shortly after we anchored, another boat tied to the one mooring left. As they pulled beside our boat, they all gave the Rock Chalk Jayhawk chant. Our boat is named after the mascot of the University of Kansas, my alma mater. They were from Topeka, Kansas. Small world. On one trip with friends we met a couple on

Jost from McPherson, the same small town one of our friends had grown up in.

Jen and I snorkeled up to a small sea cave that had several schools of small yellowfish and one large grouper. After lunch, we motorsailed to Marina Cay. There we saw the boat *No Comment,* from Mission Hills, Kansas, an affluent suburb near our hometown of Prairie Village. The Noyes' boat, *Wildcat,* was moored next to us with an all-woman crew. We had met the Noyes the year before and had conversed via email and CompuServe since.

Anouk, a long-time resident of Trellis Bay, came by in her inflatable and sold us some earrings and a key chain. A guy also came by and sold me a t-shirt he had silk-screened. We went ashore and got more t-shirts—can you ever have too many?—and tried to call home but got the recording. Back at the boat, we cooked barbecued chicken, rice pilaf, and salad.

The next morning, we got up and had breakfast before motorsailing out between Great Camanoe and Scrub Island on our way to a group of small uninhabited islands called The Dogs. All three moorings were taken on the west side of Great Dog, so we took one on the south side. We motorsailed to Leverick Bay, got a few grocery items, and then on to Prickly Pear to pick up a mooring. We took the dinghy to Bitter End just in time to catch the final game of the Bulls-Magic semifinal series. Some avid Bulls fans were there to cheer "Da Bulls" on to victory. Michael Jordan had 45 points in a come-from-behind game to sweep 4-0.

There was only one other boat in the anchorage, so we relished having it almost to ourselves. Shortly after we finished the dishes, several drunk, obnoxiously loud people with New Jersey accents came roaring up in the dark to the beach and spent the next three hours talking and singing so loudly one couldn't even think.

I got up early the next morning and read. The wind finally had picked up a little and the forecast was okay, so we decided to go to Anagada; we had been coming to the BVIs since 1987 but had never been. I thought I had packed detailed directions downloaded from CompuServe, but I couldn't find them anywhere. All we had was a GPS, a 3-year-old cruising guide, and a chart.

We followed the directions in the cruising guide and fortunately a captained Moorings boat, with three couples from Kansas City, was heading in just behind us. We did a 360 and followed them in. The depth sounder read 5.6 a couple of times, which is what we draw. I knew their sailboat drew more than we did so I figured if he could make it, so could we. I think he cut the corner. We never saw the green buoy until we were tied to a mooring. Soon after we arrived, Jimmy, a Mooring's captain I had met before, pulled up. It was good to see him again.

We took a taxi (an old pickup truck) to Loblolly Beach to snorkel. I walked the long, pink-white sand beach. The entire area was protected by a barrier reef so shallow we did not find a way to get through it to the open ocean.

We came back, read, and showered on the boat. While hanging out, a couple of girls came by from the bakery. The sold us some wonderful five-grain bread, French bread, great chocolate brownies, and chocolate chip cookies—some of the tastiest baked goods I have ever had.

We went ashore for dinner and then slept in the next day. We were one of the last boats to leave in the morning. Fortunately, the wind was just east enough of south that we could make it to the Baths in one tack. It was the first time we could sail without running the motor. It was a delightfully relaxing trip with very little swell. There was a lot of swell at the Baths, so we headed for Virgin Gorda Yacht Harbor for lunch. It was hot so I tied a sheet to the bimini to block the sun. We snacked and played cards. After dinner we went up to the Bath and Turtle to listen to the band. We turned in early and slept late again.

It was an easy reach to Cooper Island, and we got there early enough that there were plenty of moorings. They have added a few more guesthouses so staying ashore there should be an option for some. After lunch we went snorkeling and saw a moderate-size ray and lots of fish. The sunset was wonderful and lasted nearly an hour. We fixed clam and mushroom pasta. We decided we needed some wine for the clam sauce, so I took the dinghy ashore and got a glass from the bar. I poured it into the mushroom jar and dinghy-ed back to the boat. Jen said she would have drank what was left but there was still a mushroom in the jar. I should have gotten a whole bottle or washed the jar out first, I guess. It was one of the best meals we fixed on our trip.

We got up early the next day and met Underwater Safari's dive boat. The dive master was from England. He was about six feet tall and weighed maybe one-hundred-and-twenty pounds. He looked about twelve years old, but was quite competent. We went to a wreck between Cooper and Salt. There was a tug and a small freighter that had been sunk by the local dive operators. They were on sand in about eighty feet. There were lots of garden eels. We saw a large angel fish and a trumpet fish. We stayed down twenty-five minutes and waited an hour before the second dive, which was just south of the wreck of the *Rhone*. It was only forty feet and we were down thirty minutes. We saw beautiful coral, lots of fish, and several lobsters. The dive master was able to coax two large ones out from under an overhang. The body of the larger of the two looked to be over two feet long—he was huge.

We decided we were tired of cooking, so we sailed to Trellis Bay for dinner at the de Loose Mongoose. We turned in early. It rained hard for the first time during the night. I got up early and went for a walk. I found the entrance road to Long Bay Beach. We had a long, leisurely sail to the caves on Norman Island.

More snorkeling again after lunch. There were large schools of sergeant major and yellowtail snappers that surrounded us. They evidently were used to getting a hand-out. Jennifer was very uncomfortable. She told me she had been traumatized at a young age by being nibbled on by small fish while snorkeling. We had been told to bring peas on our first scuba dive after the open water in the Cayman Islands. Well, she had a bag of them in her pocket and they started leaking out. The fish surrounded her while hunting for the peas. We now feel it is wrong to feed any wild life. Seagulls are in abundance and quite bothersome due to people feeding them. They swarm the boats looking for a hand out. On one trip a gull grabbed a piece of chicken off our unattended grill. Rats with wings!

After we had had enough, we motored around the corner and anchored in the Bight. There were only five other boats anchored when we arrived—solitude! Then it all changed; more than thirty-five boats arrived to spend the night. Fortunately, it was a large anchorage. It was fun to watch some of the misadventures of those trying to anchor.

I got up early and read while listening to the weather SSB net on my Sony SW radio. It sounded like it would be calm until we left. I hoisted the main and tried to raise the anchor. Not a good plan. The winds were gusty and shifty. I nearly crashed into another boat as we were sailing away. I hadn't told Jennifer that we were leaving in time for her to help. We finally maneuvered around and got the anchor up, viewing a large barracuda circling the boat as we left. We sailed to the Indians and picked up a park service mooring. I snorkeled around but Jennifer refused to join me due to a school of hungry yellowtail snappers. The sight was quite good. We raised the sails and set off for Soper's Hole for lunch at Pusser's.

I tried to look at some boats from Sunsail, but they didn't have any available. We tried to go to the Ample Hamper, but they closed at 1:00 p.m. on Sundays. Instead, we raised the sails, putting a reef in the main as it looked like there might be some gusty winds. We tacked up Sir Frances Drake's Channel for an hour, making five to six knots. The wind lessened so we shook out the reef. We still could barely make four knots, so I started the engine and we motorsailed to Maya Cove.

We dropped the sails for our final night and picked up a mooring. I got up early and took a walk, climbing up the hill behind the marina. The view was good, but the road was steep in places. I made it back in time to take a shower and pack. Our trip was over.

The taxi to the airport arrived at the arranged time. He must have been the only person we saw on the trip that was in a hurry. He sped so fast he even passed a police car! I guess it was good to get us in the mood for life in the fast lane back at home. We made it to the airport in plenty of time.

It had been a great trip. Jen and I are a couple of introverts; we don't spend much time chattering, generally. We enjoy our own company; being alone recharges our batteries. After lots of negotiating, we were due to close on our boat in a few days after returning home. It was a bittersweet moment. They say that the happiest two days in a boat owner's life are the day they buy and the day they sell. That may be true, but there have been many happy days in between.

Chapter 16
Halimeda

It became clear to me that *Lady Jayhawk* was not the right boat to sail offshore or to live aboard for a year. She had very little storage space and was not as tough as other true-blue water boats. Jennifer and I took an offshore passage class given by the Maryland School of Sailing on an Island Packet 40. We sailed 650 open ocean miles from Bermuda to Norfolk, Virginia, including crossing the Gulf Stream with Captain Tom Tursi, a first-mate psychologist from Melbourne, Florida, and two other students. It was excellent preparation for sailing offshore and living aboard.

I became convinced that an Island Packet was an ideal boat for my year-long sabbatical. Next was picking the size, I favored the forty foot, Linda liked the forty-five. We bought the forty-five. William F. Buckley, Jr. wrote that a friend of his father's had been married fifty-nine years. He explained that the secret to his long marriage was that he told his wife after they got married that he would make all the major decisions in the relationship and she could make all the minor ones. He admitted that after fifty-nine years, there had never been any major decisions to make.

We acquired *Halimeda* two years before the trip to properly outfit it and get to know the boat. I was pleased with the cutter rig, the strength of the hull, and the long keel. I liked its stability, sailing ability, suitability to living aboard, and its reputation for crossing oceans. But there is no perfect boat. It's like the man who never married because he would only marry if he found the perfect woman. When asked if he ever found her, he said, "Yes, I did. She was perfect in every way!" Why didn't they marry? "Unfortunately, she was looking for the perfect man." Still, this boat was good enough. As Voltaire said, "Perfect is the enemy of good."

Chapter 17
The Year-Long Voyage: Part I
1999

The Dream

When I tell someone that I took a year off from work at age fifty-one, it often doesn't seem to register. Perhaps they aren't expecting it and, in some way, can't hear it at first. I repeat the statement.

"You took a *month* off?" they ask.

"No, a *year*," I repeat.

Once they finally grasp what I did, they usually say, "Wow, I want to do that sometime and do ___." *But* always comes next: "But I don't have enough money." "But, I'd lose my job/career/spouse." Others say, "I always wanted to do something like that, but now I'm too old, too weak, too sick."

Reader, I want to tell you that you, too, can take a break, a sabbatical, an extended vacation—whatever you want to call it.

Some people operate on the spur of the moment with no plan. That doesn't work for me. I spent ten years dreaming about and five years planning my big getaway. It is said that we make time to do what is important to us. I dreamed and planned all while building a business and helping raise two daughters, who had been sailing with us since they were toddlers. By the time our older daughter was sixteen she had been sailing hundreds of times and had heard of my dream to sail around the world. Then, that day in the Caribbean, she said it. "Dad, when I graduate from high school, why don't you take a year off and let's sail around the world?"

Five years after Jen's stated wish to sail together for a year, she was engaged to Mark, who she had met in preschool and dated since they were seniors in high school. They both were graduating from Kansas University, so the timing was great. Portland State, in Oregon, had accepted her in their graduate school in urban planning, but would allow her to delay a year. Mark's degree in computer science was in such demand he could get a job anywhere when we returned. Mark was my height, dark, handsome, and athletic. Point guard on his high school basketball team, he played soccer and baseball too.

How many parents get to spend an entire year living with their twenty-one-year-old daughter *and* her fiancé—in such close quarters? There are no secrets in a forty-five-foot-long, thirteen-foot-wide, two-bedroom, two bath sailboat. Would we bond or come to hate each other? Would we learn too much about each other? I thought to myself that this trip would most likely make or break Jennifer and Mark's relationship. I didn't realize it might affect mine too.

The fourth member of the crew was Linda, my wife of nearly thirty years. She was a trooper for tolerating my love of sailing. As a child she had never learned to swim. Desegregation had closed the public pool in her hometown of Lawrence, Kansas, and her working-class parents couldn't afford, or didn't want to join, the Country Club for its whites-only pool. She was always nervous when the boat heeled or we went snorkeling. The trip would test our marriage too. We had had problems, but our relationship seemed solid at the time. We could also focus on planning Jennifer and Mark's wedding during the trip.

Two other family members were not with us: Libby and my mother, Ann. Libby was a sophomore in college studying middle school education and didn't want to take time away. During the trip we would end up flying her down to St. Barth's for a Jimmy Buffett concert and Christmas, and then again to Trinidad to celebrate her mother Linda's birthday. My mother was in a nursing home in Kansas and in poor health. She was a worrier, too. She always worried her only child might get injured. I hoped she would survive until we returned.

I had been looking forward to this break for so long. Running a busy dental practice is stressful and takes a lot of concentration. During nights and weekends, I always tensed up when the phone rang, or the pager buzzed. I might have to go into the office to relieve someone's pain. Sure, I had taken vacations, but they weren't long enough for me to unwind, relax, and enjoy myself. Instead, I wasted some of the time mulling over decisions I needed to make at work, treatments that could have gone better, or other job-related problems instead of being in the present. With a full year ahead of me to do what I loved— sail, see new vistas, meet new people, and commune with nature—I could also concentrate on the present, bond with Linda and Jen, get to know Mark better, and fulfill my dream.

I also saw the trip as a physical, mental, and educational challenge. I wanted to learn about the history of this part of the world firsthand. A U.S.-Civil-War-buff friend of mine once told me he had read a lot about the battle of Gettysburg but hadn't understand it fully until he walked the battlefield with his own two feet. I planned to sail through and walk the islands where Europeans had decimated the indigenous people, fought each other to the death for control of the islands, enslaved Africans, Indians, and deforested the landscape to plant sugarcane, which was once as valuable as oil is today. I wanted to swim in the ocean with the sea creatures, climb the hills and mountains, and feast my eyes on the lush flora, exotic birds and mammals there, and most importantly, sail the incredibly beautiful Caribbean Sea.

But could I pull this off? Could I complete a year-long voyage aboard a small boat, sail over 2,000 miles from Florida to Trinidad, visit the hundreds of islands in between, and make it back? I might face storms, pirates, sharks, injuries, illness. Would it improve my relationship with my family?

I couldn't wait to dance with the boat as it rode up and over the waves, leaning against the wind, balancing and bracing against the cockpit seat while gently steering through the ever-changing wind and waves. I loved the challenge of keeping an eye on the shape of the sails, while watching for oncoming waves; avoiding boat traffic and floating objects in our path; scanning the gauges for water depth, boat speed, wind speed and direction, and then compiling it into a course to steer the boat, at the best angle to the wind, and as close as possible to the direction we wanted to travel.

The Route

Next came the decision as to the route. I had dreamed about sailing around the world but that was too ambitious for a year and wouldn't allow time to visit foreign lands. Then I found that article in a sailing magazine about a good route to take if one intended to spend a year sailing the Caribbean islands. It called for leaving the east coast in May, sailing directly to the Virgin Islands, then head across the Caribbean to Trinidad for the summer months. This timing and route would keep us out of the hurricane zone for the peak of the season. It also gave us ample time to visit the diverse islands in between, some I knew and loved, some we hadn't sailed to. I wanted to enjoy the climate and learn more about the culture, the people, and the history of this part of the world.

I had done all the preparation I could and would find out if I was well-prepared soon enough. Many adventurers spend so much time preparing, they never leave the dock. Like the couple who owned a boat aptly named *Someday Isle,* they were always *almost* ready to go, but then something needed fixing, or they needed one more gadget or piece of equipment. I saw them, time and time again, when I visited my boat in St. Petersburg, Florida, over a two-year period. I never once saw them sail away to the islands they claimed to dream of visiting.

Others take off with too little preparation or experience. Sometimes they make it and learn along the way, others fail. They lose the boat, become injured, or soon become disillusioned and give up. I once met a couple who sold their cattle ranch in Montana and bought a boat to live aboard and sail to the islands. Two weeks into their first trip they became so frightened in their first storm that they sold the boat, abandoned their dream, and bought an RV.

I, on the other hand, would not be pulled off course. My dream was finally within reach.

All the Details

The full details for my fellow sailors include the following. The *Halimeda* was a 1996 Island Packet 45 built in Largo, Florida. She had the following dimensions: LOA 45' 3" displacement (approx.) 28,400 lbs; LWL 37' 7"; ballast 12,500 lbs; beam 13' 4"; sail area 1100 sq. ft. Draft; 4' 10" auxiliary power; 62 HP mast above DW; 58' 10" water capacity 240 US gal headroom 6' 5" fuel capacity; 140 US gal; cabins/berths 3/7; holding tank capacity 45 US gal; designer Bob Johnson, Nebraska.

She was a cutter rig, a full foil keel, and had rack and pinion steering which all contributed to her superior seakeeping ability and safety. She had a lot of room for her size, an incredible amount of storage space, and the ability to carry a great deal of weight. This made her a great boat for cruising and living aboard. The main had jiffy reefing with all control lines leading to the cockpit.

We made the following upgrades: house batteries were two 255 amp-hr Lifeline 8D batteries, and the starting battery was a 100 amp-hr group 27. The main engine had a Balmar 100 amp alternator. We had a Lugger/Northern Lights 5 kw diesel generator that had a 40 amp alternator and a 50 amp DC output to run a Freedom 100 amp 3 stage smart charger/inverter. We had a Link 2000 battery monitor/smart regulator. A FourWinds II wind generator and two BP 90 W solar panels provided additional charging capacity.

Instruments at the helm were all made by Brooks & Gatehouse and include Network Pilot, Network Wind, GPS Plus 12, Network Quad, and Network VHF. The autopilot had a Type II RAM drive and the ACP 2 computer. Some functions were repeated at the navigation station below on the B & G Network Nav. We also had a Raytheon RL 70 combination 4kw–48 mile radar and C-Map NT chart plotter with displays at the helm and navigation station.

We had a Raytheon VHF radio, a SEA 235 combination marine single-side band and amateur HAM radio, and a NEMA link to any one of our 3 Gateway laptops. This allowed us to plot our position on Maptech electronic charts using The Cap'n navigational software. The main navigation computer was a 333 mhz Pentium II with 128K of RAM and a 7 gb hard drive. It also had a DVD ROM drive. We also had a NAVTEX weather receiver.

We had a radar arch with dinghy davits made by Wells Marine. For communication in addition to the SSB we had an Iridium satellite telephone and a Motorola cellular telephone.

For entertainment we had a VHS tape player; a Lightware video projector for watching DVDs, TV, and a 60-inch screen; and a 12-disc CD changer/tape player/AM-FM stereo. We had two Motorola personal radios for communication between the helm and foredeck.

We had a 55 lb Delta anchor with 180' of high-tensile chain and a 60 lb Bruce anchor with 30' of chain and 200' of nylon rode. We also had a 45 lb Bruce and a 1 Fortress anchor with a spare rode. Our drinking water was run through a Seagull water filter, 30 gph portable manual bilge pump, Maxwell VWC2200 electric windlass. We had enough spare dock lines to tie up Gulliver seven times over (600 ft of 7/8" cut into 40 and 70 ft lengths).

We had two 16,000 BTU air conditioner/heater units, a combination Bimini and dodger, awnings for the foredeck and above the main boom, and two deck boxes. We had a spare main halyard and a spinnaker halyard. In addition to the standard, full-battened mainsail, stay sail, and 130% genoa, we added a cruising spinnaker with sock and a storm trysail. We also added a masthead tricolor navigation light for added visibility and a Davis radar reflector.

We had a Winslow offshore 6-person life raft mounted below, 406 Mhz EPIRB, abandon ship bag, parachute sea anchor, handheld Icom VHF radio and Garmin 45 GPS, emergency water and food, and offshore personal flotation devices. We had a very complete medical kit and a subscription to a Maritime medical consultation service. With DAN, we had medical evacuation insurance.

The forward cabin had a Handcraft Innerspring custom-made mattress with custom fitted sheets. The aft cabin mattress was divided in thirds for easy access to compartments underneath.

All this equipment allowed us to live aboard and cruise in comfort and safety. We had a full complement of paper charts and cruising guides onboard for all the areas we planned to visit.

In the galley we had a microwave oven, a 3-burner gimbaled propane stove with an oven, pressure cooker, blender, and toaster. We had a Magna party-sized propane grill. The huge icebox contained a 12-volt Alder Barber super cold machine.

Launch Day

The year-long sailing trip had finally begun. The diesel rumbled to life, the dock lines were untied, we waved goodbye to friends on the dock, and motored *Halimeda* out of Burnt Store Marina, through the channel, and onto Charlotte Harbor on Florida's west coast, south of Tampa.

Wind and current grabbed the boat near the fuel dock and turned me into the path of an incoming motor yacht, but I wrestled control and avoided collision. The rest of the docking maneuver went better. I hoped this inauspicious beginning was not a sign of trouble to come. We filled the fuel and water tanks and then headed out toward the Gulf of Mexico for our sail around the tip of Florida to Miami.

The Gulf of Mexico can sometimes be easy on the boat and crew. When Jennifer and I had "sailed" across it, east to west, a few years before there was not enough wind to fill the sails for much of it. We had to motor for more than half of the way. Some hazy days the ocean was so smooth and mirror flat, it was impossible to tell where the sea ended and the sky began.

Sailing offshore in open water, out of sight of land, has its joys and its challenges. It can be peaceful and tranquil, or raging and frightening. Unlike a car trip, one can't pull over to the side of the road to rest, ask for directions, get a bite to eat, or find a soft, unmoving motel bed for a full night's sleep. If something breaks, you fix it or do without—there are no repair shops mid-ocean. You need to have *more* than enough food and water for the trip because you never know for sure how long the voyage will take. Someone must always be on watch day and night.

The clear, blue sky and early morning sun painted our almond-colored hull with a warm light. The fresh breeze felt great on my skin. I had learned to sense the direction and speed of the wind by how it felt on my arms, legs, and face. My brain translated that information into the action of steering the boat at the proper angle to the wind's direction. Looking up, I checked if I had trimmed the sails correctly to best catch the wind. If not, I would trim them by easing or tightening the lines that attached them to the boat. The work of balancing sail shape or trim and course or direction to steer is the essence of sailing. I love the mental and physical challenge of keeping the boat going in the right direction at the best speed for the conditions. The briny smell of the shoreline—salt water, seagrass, and the muck of low tide—assailed my nose. Everything was perfect, the wind speed and direction were ideal. The weather, the temperature, and the gentle waves were relaxing. Perfect for the start of the trip. All the preparation was finally behind me and I could start to decompress and enjoy the ride.

The two-hour trip from the marina across the bay to the Gulf of Mexico was uneventful. But being a natural-born worrier, I couldn't help but go over details I might have forgotten and things that might go wrong. Was I as prepared as I could be? What if we got sick or injured, we got caught in a storm, or the boat broke down, or worse yet, sunk? Did I know enough about the many mechanical systems on the boat to keep them running? What if we got robbed or shot? I had to put all that out of my mind. There was sailing to be done.

We sailed the dozen miles across Charlotte Harbor to reach the Boca Grande cut. We sailed west past the cut for half an hour to clear the reef. The water in the gulf was much clearer than in the bay. Not the deep, beautiful blue of that offshore in the Atlantic and the Caribbean, but still a taste of things to come.

Once we turned the corner and headed south, the wind was blowing in our face. The waves were rocking us and pounding the boat. We set the autopilot to "steer" and only took the wheel to dodge the fleets of shrimp boats, a tug and barge, or fishermen in our path.

Sailboats can't sail directly into the wind. If we tacked back and forth at 45-degree angles off the wind and didn't use the motor, we would at least double the time and distance sailed. We were planning to pick up a fourth crew member in Miami in a few days so we motored instead.

I tell people, "It's the journey, not the destination," and that if I was in a hurry, I would have bought a power boat or an airplane. Most sailors will tell you the best time of any trip is when you turn off the smelly, noisy, hot, vibrating engine and the boat moves across the water propelled only by the wind and the sails. This time, though, we needed to hurry a little, so we motored directly into the wind. There was a 20 to 25 knot wind directly on our nose, creating four to six-foot waves that were steep and irregular. This caused the boat to pitch. She bucked like a bronco, raising her bow up and then slamming down as she fell off the waves. It made for a very uncomfortable ride. (See the Prologue for what happened along the way!)

We arrived at the cut near Marathon Key before noon the next day. As the sands shift, the Coast Guard moves the navigational marks to indicate the location of the deep-water channel. They were in a different location than shown on the paper chart, but the updated computerized charting system linked to the GPS showed them correctly. Thankfully so, as we were threading our way through areas of unmarked rocks and reefs that could severely damage our boat and are environmentally fragile. The fines for running aground and damaging seagrass can reach up to $100,000!

Once we turned the corner and headed east, the wind was finally on our beam and to our advantage again. We shut off the engine and sailed. The water was crystal clear and brilliant blue; the skies were almost as blue and clear. We had the ocean nearly to ourselves. All the hot, jarring, crashing ride down the Gulf was worth it.

We trailed a large, monofilament hand-fishing line about fifty yards behind the boat with a large squid-shaped lure. We attached a shock cord to the boat as a strike indicator. Once the cord sprang back and forth, we knew we had a fish on. We used heavy leather work gloves to roll the line onto a plastic donut-shaped hand reel. Once the twenty-pound fish was at the stern, we used a gaff to lift it into the cockpit and poured a few ounces of vodka in its gills to stop it from thrashing around. We filleted, breaded, and fried the fish for dinner. It was the tastiest, freshest fish I had ever had. It was incredible.

The rest of the twenty-hour trip up to Miami was a delight. We sailed about five miles off the low Florida Keys, seeing only a few other boats. The wind was 10–12 knots most of the time and we made 5–6 knots through the water. Our speed over the ground was up to 7.5 knots with a boost from the Gulf Stream current. The wind was blowing from the land, so the waves didn't have time to build. *Halimeda* kept rocking gently with her shoulder to the wind and a bone in her teeth (an old-fashioned term for the white bow wave generated by the motion of the boat through the water at speed).

Pulling into Miami's Government Cut, a busy commercial and cruise ship port, was a new experience for me. A huge container ship passed by us so close in the channel that I could read the labels on the shirts of the deck hands—but we didn't collide. I could have let the big boat enter first. Over the year I would learn to be respectful of their bulk and speed and not be frightened by them.

Chapter 18
The Year-Long Voyage, Part II: Ship Logs

May, 1999

May 15. I have just come off the 2:00–4:00 a.m. watch. It was unremarkable. We did see a strange ship or platform that wasn't moving. It was well-lit but had no discernable pattern or running lights. Must have been a research vessel, fishing trawler, or floating platform. They didn't respond to radio calls.

There has been very little wind. We finally quit sailing at 2:00 p.m. and have been motoring since. The ocean is like a smooth lake with only a slight roll. The wind does seem to be building up to 5 knots and has been finally coming from the east consistently. This afternoon the wind vane was spinning through 360 degrees and the true speed ranged from 0.0 to 2.4. I could see quite a lightning show 10 to 20 degrees off our starboard bow 50 miles ahead or so. That makes me hopeful we will finally get some wind again, which we will need because I estimate we have about 100 hours to go and only enough fuel to motor for about 75 hours. The fuel gauge quit working soon after we left the dock, so that is just an educated guess. We have been keeping a log of the hours we have been using the engine, but we don't know our actual fuel consumption.

Earlier this evening we saw several shooting stars and satellites overhead. During my watch, the Milky Way was most pronounced. Of course, we are making our own shooting stars in our wake; the tiny sparks of bioluminescent phytoplankton shoot along in our bow wake and trail behind the boat. It is as though we are plowing through a field filled with fireflies.

Time to turn in.

May 16. 4:11 a.m. I had the midnight to 2:00 a.m. watch. It was uneventful, but today was my worst day so far. I couldn't tell if I was seasick, had indigestion, or was suffering from an overdose of my cholesterol medicine. One day blends into another and I couldn't remember if I had taken my daily dose at bedtime or not, so I took one in the morning. My neck was acting up and producing a headache. Advil or Aleve usually fixes it, but I hesitated to take with the nausea. I had no appetite for the first time on the trip. Odors usually don't bother me but today they did. Finally, late this afternoon, I took the motion sickness medicine, non-drowsy Bonine. My stomach started to settle down and I was able to eat Karl's wonderful fish—creole style with beans and rice. Before turning in, I took Ibuprofen. I feel much better.

May 17. 12:25 p.m. What a difference a day makes: I feel great. We finally got wind. I took the helm during a squall. Winds were up to 30 knots. It was pouring rain. The sails were really straining. The log shows we were making 7.6 knots at one point. Karl made fresh mahi-mahi lightly breaded and sautéed with a mustard sauce and his now-famous hot German potato salad. We are eleven days out of Punta Gorda, 260 miles from San

Juan, and we have fish fresher than in the finest restaurants. We have been eating like kings.

May 19. 12:07 p.m. LAND HO!!!! After 10 days without seeing land, we finally sighted it. What an exciting moment! We still have 10 hours or more to go before we will reach the marina. Puerto Rico is still over 30 miles away, but we can see its beautiful green mountains.

Last night was the most exhilarating sailing of the trip. We had 18–20 knots 55 degrees off the port bow. We were screaming along under full genoa and full main on a close reach. The moon had set, but the stars provided enough light to see the water rushing by the boat. At night, you feel like you are going much faster than you really are. Still we were consistently going over 6.5 knots over the water and up to 7.9 over the ground. Fajardo, here we come.

This is what I had been dreaming about for all those years back in Kansas.

May 19. 4:57 p.m. In 14 days of sailing we just caught our fifth fish. The first day we caught a 2-pound mackerel. The first day out of Miami we caught a 5-pound mahi-mahi. Two days later we caught a 3-foot, 15-pound mahi-mahi. Since it was enough for several meals, we stopped fishing.

We are now about 15 miles from Puerto Rico. It has been a great trip. The weather has been benign, the boat has performed well. Having to stand watch 2 hours and having 6 hours off three times a day has not been strenuous at all.

* * *

After sailing along the north coast we rounded the northeastern tip of Puerto Rico and headed south down the east coast a couple of hours after sunset. With our primitive radar, we could see echoes of the unlit navigation marks to help guide us to Fajardo, halfway down the coast. I was puzzled when I noticed one of the echoes moving toward us! I realized it was an unlit boat. As it approached us in near total darkness, we could barely see it was an all-black, go-fast motor boat. As it pulled beside us we saw it held half a dozen men in black outfits with guns! One asked where we were going. Instead of pirates, we finally could tell they were customs and immigrations officers. I was glad I was wearing my brown pants!

They declined our request to guide us in but instead followed us into the marina, boarded the boat, and searched for drugs and stowaways. They were friendly and courteous, just young men doing their jobs. They left without a hassle, but it was an alarming experience to be boarded in the black of night by a group of armed men.

The next day I flew back to Kansas to attend Jen and Mark's graduation; a week later I will fly back to Puerto Rico to continue this adventure.

May 29. 4:50 a.m. Although we have been sailing for over 3 weeks, today I feel like we finally started cruising. Drs. Glen and Nancy Doyon are helping me with this leg. They are two Island Packet-owners from Philadelphia who I met on the Island Packet email list. They also both happen to be dentists. Until now we have been preparing to cruise and passage-making. It feels great to have arrived at a destination I can take time to enjoy.

We left Puerto del Rey Marina this morning at 9:00 and tacked back and forth along the east coast of Puerto Rico on reaches just for the joy of it. Isla Palominos was less than an hour from the marina and we had 12 to 15 knots of wind. By 11:30 we decided to anchor. We had lunch and I broke out my homemade dinghy. I rigged the sail and we set off to find a place to snorkel. We anchored in 10 feet of water over sand and grass. The fish were just okay, not great.

We decided to row ashore for drinks. I installed flotation tubes called Dinghy Dogs (invented by a dentist) just a little too high and they cause the oars to come out of the oarlocks when we rowed. I should get another set of attachment slots and place them a little lower.

Glen and Nancy had been to this island before. We walked the beach and settled into a little beach bar. Unfortunately, they only sold drinks to guests of El Conquistador resort that owns the island. We eventually found a guest that would buy drinks for us. We saw a beautiful green-winged macaw in a cage. I have a hard time watching these magnificent animals confined for our amusement. A tourist on Palomino told of a client of his that had three hundred tropical birds and lost all but nine in a fire. What a tragedy. When will humankind stop abusing other creatures?

We went back to the boat and Glen mentioned that our anchor chain was near a coral head. He checked the anchor when we first stopped and said it was okay. It was clear when we snorkeled that the moorings were the environmentally-friendly type with a U-bolt epoxied to a hole drilled into rock. I asked at the beach bar and was told they were free. We decided to pick up the anchor and take a mooring instead. They were marked DNRA, which I assume means Department of Natural Resources Administration. There were nearly a dozen at the anchorage.

May 31. On Saturday, we got up early and sailed to Isabel Segunda on Vieques. We picked up a mooring and rowed ashore. The "seafood restaurant" listed in Van Sant's *Guide to the Spanish Virgin Islands* was only a fish market. We set out in search of adventure and found a beautifully restored lighthouse containing a museum. The view was spectacular. From there we walked up town and found a beach bar that served sandwiches. We then sailed towards Culebra and anchored off the north coast of Cayo Luis Pena, an island just off the southwest coast of Culebra. When we arrived, we found over twenty powerboats anchored. I went snorkeling for an hour and the reef was in great shape. In the late afternoon all the power boats left and we had the anchorage to ourselves. It was rolly due to wakes of large ferries and small freighters passing between Luis Pena and Culebra but we had a peaceful night.

The next day we motorsailed to Bahia Almodovar on the southeast coast of Culebra. The marks shown on the chart were gone, but the range in Van Sant's book kept us on course. The water wasn't clear enough for us to see the reef, so we were grateful for the guidance. Several powerboats surrounded the anchorage inside the reef but there was an area in the center with plenty of room for us to anchor. The breeze was light but delightful. There were a few no-see-ems due to the mangroves, but not enough to be a problem.

After dinner, Glen and I stayed up to watch *Les Miserables* on the laptop. I finally figured a way to get good sound out of it. I simply take a compact disk adapter for the tape player and plug it into "line out" on the laptop. All I need is an extension cord for small headphone jacks.

We got up this morning and had to motor all the way to St. Thomas. We are now anchored in Christmas Cove, off St. James Island near the eastern end of St. Thomas. The snorkeling is quite good with lots of rays, puffer fish, parrotfish, angelfish, and many others.

June

June 1. Hurricane season starts today. I just heard the official forecast of fourteen tropical storms, with ten named and four major storms. It makes me want to get south as soon as possible. One boat insurance company forces you to get south of 12 north (on the south coast of Grenada) by July 15 for coverage. Barring major problems, we should have no trouble doing that.

We are near a choke point where many boats must go, making for a rolly anchorage. Yesterday evening there was just enough wind to allow me to use a line from the main winch to the anchor chain for a bridle that turned the bow into the waves. It won't work today unless the wind picks up.

Last night Glen asked me if I am constantly thinking about home, work, family, etc. I said that I occasionally do, but that I don't dwell on it. For the most part, I am relaxed and focused on enjoying the boat and my environment. It is wonderful to jump off the stern and spend an hour exploring a beautiful and diverse reef. I still love planning the route, attending to the details of running the boat, reading the cruising guide, looking over the charts, and setting my own schedule. I sleep when I'm tired, get up when I'm rested, eat when I'm hungry, read when I feel like it, and am enjoying myself immensely.

I met Jen, Mark, and Linda at the airport. Our family trip has finally begun ...

June 7. If one has to hangout in a marina, this is an excellent choice. Crown Bay Marina is new, modern, clean, safe, and friendly. Two different live-aboard couples recommended it. It is reasonably priced, close to many stores and services, has a great laundry, very good telecommunications/mail service, super restaurant/bar, dive shop, beauty salon, and a submarine! It is within walking distance to the airport. I understand that the nearby Yacht Haven Marina is scheduled to undergo extensive modernization and a new resort is to be built where the hurricane-damaged, boarded-up Yacht Haven Motel stands, but there is no evidence of any progress. One cruiser told us it is nicknamed Rat Haven. I'm glad we didn't choose it.

I have been slowly finishing up many small projects on the boat. I hung small gear hammocks in the cabins and one in the galley (that's the kitchen, for you landlubbers). They are good for storing clothing and fresh fruit. Note to first timers: hang it side-to-side, not front and back, near the wall. If you do, the motion of the boat will pulverize the food and spill it all over the cabin. I have spent days looking for a way to hang pictures on the bulkheads (walls). We finally found the solution: Plexiglas frames and double-sided tape. I hung the pictures and it makes the boat seem more like a home.

We spent yesterday taking out all the food we had stowed and inventorying it. We have quite a bit of canned goods, beans, rice, and pasta. We then repacked it so we knew where it was. We are going to the grocery store for meat, fresh fruits, vegetables, and other perishables.

Almost to a person, the locals have gone out of their way to help us. For example, I went into an office supply to ask for an extension cord for my headphones. They didn't have any but suggested I try Radio Shack. The owner took me outside and pointed the way to the store. I later went to another store asking directions again and the clerk took me outside and pointed out where I needed to go. This wasn't in the town's touristy section but the working part. Even the drivers are friendly and will honk to warn you before you step out in front of them when you have looked the wrong way for traffic, as they drive on the left here.

Tomorrow we plan to head out. We will probably spend one more night in the U.S. Virgin Islands before crossing over to the British Virgins. We may only spend a couple of nights there before taking off for St. Martin.

June 10. Great Harbour—Foxy's, Jost Van Dyke, British Virgin Islands. We still have no wind. We have yet to raise the sails or even take the sail cover off. Yesterday we left Christmas Cove St. James Island and motored to Cruz Bay. We anchored and prepared the dinghy to go ashore to clear out of customs. I called to see the procedure and was told we did not need to clear out. We raised the anchor and motored to JVD. We went through a heavy rain shower with winds of only 10 knots on the nose. It had slowed to a drizzle by the time we anchored. Mark and I went in to clear customs. The officer told us we could clear out at the same time if we only stayed three days. I was amused to see a notice that Jet Skis and weapons were banned and must be declared. The wording made it seem like Jet Skis were weapons.

It was hot, still, and humid. We walked up several steep hills to a vista near the western end of the island. It took us an hour and a half, and we were quite wrung out. We stopped at Foxy's afterwards and Foxy was there performing at his best. If you tease both men and women, is it sexist? If you chide all races, is it racist?

It is hard to imagine several hundred boats may be in this harbor for New Year's Eve, and even harder to envision several thousand people partying at Foxy's. It is supposed to be the best party in the world. I think we will give it a miss.

June 12. We spent a peaceful night anchored off Cooper Island, BVI. Jennifer fixed the most delicious pizza from scratch using flour, water, and yeast to make the crust. Toppings included fresh Roma tomatoes, canned mushrooms, Canadian bacon, Mozzarella and Parmesan cheese, and frozen spinach.

Thursday we sailed to Marina Cay and picked up a $20 mooring. We went ashore and did laundry, $3 per wash, $3 per dry. We got lazy and ate dinner at the Pusser's ashore. Since we didn't have reservations, we had to wait an hour. There were tables available, but not enough cooks. When we returned to the boat at least twenty fish over three feet long were swimming near the boat. I think they were tarpon.

June 15. We had planned to leave soon for St. Martin, but a tropical wave was forecast to intensify and pass through the area, so we decided to anchor in North Gorda Sound off Prickly Pear Island near Virgin Gorda, BVI. It turned out to be a wise move. We no sooner got our anchor down than the leading edge of the wave hit. Winds gusted to 38 knots and it poured. In the enclosed sound, waves only got about 2–3 ft. At least all the rain washed some of the salt off the boat. The rain only lasted about an hour, but the 20–30 knot winds kept up for most of the night.

The wind generator was very good and kept our batteries charged. I am glad we weren't sailing offshore that night.

We had taken non-drowsy Bonine in anticipation of the trip, so were all quite sleepy. We spent the next day resting, eating, and prepping the boat for the offshore leg. We rigged jack lines, ropes attached to strong points in the cockpit and the bow. They allow you to clip a tether from a harness to the boat to keep you from falling off, yet allow you to move about the boat. Falling off the boat offshore at night can be a fatal mistake, one to be avoided at all costs.

A couple on a Valiant 40 called *Whatever* from Chicago stopped by to chat. They had been living aboard for ten years. They gave us a few tips and complimented our boat. They were going to wait another day and sail south wherever the winds were most favorable. They had no plan and were sticking to it. I guess their boat was appropriately named.

We left at about 4:00 p.m. We decided to put a single reef in the mainsail in the protected waters of the sound. It was a good thing we didn't wait until we were offshore. We hadn't put the main up when we reattached the reefing lines and they had been installed improperly.

We sailed out the cut and around Necker Island on the way out. It has a villa that rents for $30,000 per week, including staff. Princess Di used to stay there. Once we were in the open ocean, the winds were 18–22 knots and the seas 6–8 feet. They were confused from the storm that had passed the night before. I'm just glad we hadn't left the day before when the winds were 35–

40 knots (gale force) and seas must have been 12–15 feet in this area.

This was Mark and Linda's first overnight offshore passage and they were tested. We couldn't sail to St. Martin directly since it was up wind. We could have sailed a zigzag course, but that would have doubled the distance. We could have motored into the wind, but that would have been most uncomfortable. We chose to motorsail for a compromise. It was still hard sailing. We were pinching, sailing as close to the wind as possible. I could see why the fellow on *Whatever* said he had not done that.

We decided on 3-hour watches. Linda and I had 3–6 p.m., 9–12 p.m., and 3–6 a.m. Jen and Mark had the alternating ones. Mark was a little queasy and laid down during our first watch. All but Jen had taken the non-drowsy Dramamine again and she was the only one to get sick.

We had a close encounter with a fast-moving ship I think must have been a Navy vessel. Mark stood his watch and did admirably. I was cat napping and on call when he saw ships. About 4:30 a.m. the engine alarm screamed. I shut the engine down and discovered we had a broken fan belt. We sailed until dawn and then I replaced it.

After a 20-hour passage, we arrived about noon on Monday. I showered before we got in. Everyone was tired, hot, and sweaty. Even sitting or lying down is tiring when the boat is constantly heeled and moving.

St. Martin is very nice, but customs at this port was a pain. The cruising guide said to go to the police station that was a 10-minute row and a 20-minute walk away. When we got there, we waited in line only to be told we must go elsewhere. We walked back to where we thought it was, but it wasn't there. We took a cab to an out-of-the-way place. The immigration lady made me fill out a long form. She couldn't read my writing, so she reprinted much of it. I was told to go next door to customs where I paid $14. The guy didn't read the form. I had written on it that we wanted to leave on the 18th. He asked me what time I wanted to leave and told him 9:00 am. He thought I was leaving the next day (the 15th). After filling out everything, he told me to go back to the first lady. She went crazy since I had the wrong date on the form. I had to talk to the guy's supervisor who said we had to leave on the 15th or promise to come back on the 18th. It was all very confusing, but part of the fun of island hopping, I suppose.

When we returned on the 17th, the immigration lady was gone from her post even though it was 45 minutes before the posted lunch break. We waited for half-an-hour to no avail. The custom's supervisor finally asked where we were going. When we told him St. Barts, he said, "Go ahead, you won't really need her stamp there."

We are cleaning the boat today and will be off on a tour of the island this afternoon.

June 20, Sunday. Happy Father's Day. The 3-hour sail to St. Barts was uneventful. We had anchored the first night at Anse de Columbier on St. Barts, one of my favorite anchorages. Mark and I swam to shore the first afternoon—it was further than it looked. I had heard that a hurricane had taken all the sand from this and other beaches on St. Barts, but fortunately there was plenty here. It may have been naturally replenished.

The next morning, we got up and rowed to shore. It is private beyond the beach, but one can make it to a hiking trail that leads to a small settlement in Anse des Flamandes. The beach is gorgeous and was deserted when we got there. The very scenic hike took about 45 minutes. It was a little challenging and warm in parts. Lilies and cactus lined the trail. A huge hollowed-out volcanic rock formed a mini echo chamber. We walked to the end of the half-mile long beach and checked out some great little villas and mini hotels. We then stopped by a small grocery and got fresh baguette and water.

Several small sea turtles occasionally swam by our boat. The water was clear enough for me to run the watermaker. A huge sailboat briefly anchored nearby. It was dark blue, called *Amadeus,* and was from Kingston, St. Vincent. I'd guess it was 100 feet long and worth several million dollars. With crew, maintenance, and dockage, it probably cost a million a year to keep up. Too bad we weren't born rich instead of so good looking. Too bad I didn't go work for Microsoft when it first started. But, as the Sheryl Crow lyric says, "It's better to want what you've got than to get what you want."

Actually, I am quite happy with our boat and wouldn't like a bigger one. This one is hard enough to handle in tight quarters, keep relatively clean, and maintain. I guess if you can afford a mega yacht, you can afford to pay someone to sail and maintain it. What fun would that be?

We spent our last night in St. Barth's at Anse du Corossol. It was a little rolly but not as bad as off the fort in Gustavia. I got up at 5:30 a.m. and prepped the boat for the sail today. We picked up the anchor at 7:00 and set a course of 187 degrees magnetic. Four hours later we were between St. Kitts and Statia. Winds were ESE at 22–25 all day. We had a double-reefed main, the staysail, and about half of the genoa out. We were on a close reach. Waves were 6–8 feet and the swells were out of the east at about 10 feet. It made for an exhilarating sail.

Once we made the turn between the islands, the waves settled down a little, but the wind kept up. It got as high as 28. It took us until 4:00 p.m. to reach the anchorage on Nevis.

June 21. Monday. Today I rowed ashore to clear into Nevis. I went to customs and port authority, both near the dock, and then immigration at the police station. It was relatively painless and inexpensive, though I was chastised for not checking in with the police right after we arrived on Sunday. I thought they would be closed, like customs, and since we hadn't gone ashore, we were probably okay.

I rowed back to the boat and we all went ashore for a taxi tour of the island. It is simply beautiful, very clean, lush, and has some great small hotels that used to be plantations. Montpelier was our favorite. Lord Nelson got married there. The views were great, the grounds filled with exotic plants, and it had an inviting pool. The sad part of these places is the slaves who toiled under the whip and worse to build and run them.

We had a mouth-watering lunch of lobster sandwiches at Golden Rock Plantation Inn. Tiny birds and lizards scurried about waiting for us to drop crumbs. This inn sits at the foot of the mountain and the edge of the rainforest. The sky was too hazy to see the adjacent islands, they are visible on clearer days. Still, the view was breathtaking.

We visited an abandoned bathhouse with creaky floors. The Nelson museum was less than we expected. The Hamilton museum was much better. Alexander Hamilton (the U.S. president on the $10 bill) was born on Nevis. He was quite a guy, according to the exhibits.

June 22. Tuesday. Thanks to Jennifer, we spent the day getting organized. She computerized the daily and weekly tasks and we printed them out. We got the outboard motor out for the first time and fired it up. I had been reluctant to use it for several reasons. It is a 2-cycle engine that is not very environmentally friendly. I thought it might be overpowering to my dinghy, it is one more piece of equipment to maintain, and I like getting exercise rowing. For the long trip from our boat to the dock, though, it worked quite well. The Dinghy Dogs generate some spray. Sailing is the wrong sport for you if you mind getting wet.

A squall line moved through and we got lots of nice rain. A beautiful sunset resulted.

June 26. Saturday. We are anchored below Fort Napoleon on Terre D'en Haut in Iles Des Saintes, a group of islands called The Saints. They are part of Guadeloupe, and thus French. We spent several days waiting for a weather window on Nevis that didn't appear. We finally decided to bite the bullet and do an overnight sail.

We left about 1:00 p.m. and had a pleasant motorsail until we cleared the lee of Nevis. The wind piped up to 25 knots and the waves were 6–8 feet. As the wind approached 30, we decided to roll up the big head sail. We later found that the line used to furl it was slightly fouled by a cleat, making the task very difficult. We had just dodged a freighter and the waves were very confused. We were rolling uncomfortably. This led to another bout of *mal de mer* for Jennifer.

We got back on course and spent the night in 20–25 knot winds and 4–6 feet seas with an occasional swell of 8 feet. We were on a close reach about 45 degrees off the apparent wind making 5–6 knots with a full main and staysail up. I found this to be very pleasant conditions. Linda disagreed.

We did have a couple of exciting moments. The boat has propane tanks in a locker on deck at the rail. A cap off the hose used to run the grill came off and blocked the drain. One tank was nearly empty and when the locker filled with water, it became quite buoyant and opened the locker. It then was floating and banging on the deck. I had to go forward and put it back. We were heeled over with the rail in the water. A wave gave me a dousing. At least the harness kept me onboard and the shower cooled me off. This happened twice. I couldn't get the cap out of the locker until we were anchored since it was trapped under the second tank.

I later found out that the rudder and tiller that I spent hours making for the sailing dinghy fell overboard sometime during the night. I must not have secured them well enough. Bummer.

Mark and I went ashore to get email. An art gallery with an internet café was closed for lunch. The boutique next door with internet access asked that we buy something before using their machine. Mark saved me from buying a turquoise blue batik shirt and advised me to stick to white. It was 365 Francs (about $60). I guess I really wanted to get online.

We are adapting to boat life. The winds are unusually high this year for some reason. This makes passages between islands more challenging, the anchorages more uncomfortable, and the dinghy rides to shore wetter. We went to shore at a makeshift dock beside the place huge ferryboats land. One ferry caused a 5-foot wave to come crashing ashore. My dinghy, mercifully, did not crash into the concrete.

There has been a haze for weeks now, making photography of the scenery fair at best. It is from dust blown from the Sahara Desert in Africa and makes sunrises and sunsets gray without any color. Hopefully it will stop when the winds die down, whenever that is.

Linda was stricken with a bout of dizziness last night. I tried calling the doctor, but all forms of communication failed. Sat phones, cell phone, SSB HF radio all don't seem to work here. It she gets worse again, I'll go ashore and try to figure out the French phones. Not an easy task since I think you need a phone card and to speak French. So much for staying connected with high tech gadgets.

We think we will go to Dominica tomorrow, then Martinique in a few days. We may make St. Lucia next week. From there it is only a few days to Trinidad and Tobago, our southernmost destination. Libby will join us there August 1th and Linda will make a trip home on August 10th.

June 28. Monday. I am a little numb. On Saturday I finally figured out how to use the French phones on Les Saints to call our daughter, Libby. She told me my mother had died. Mom was ninety-two and in poor health. Her health was a constant worry hanging over this trip. I knew she wasn't going to last much longer, but I hoped she would live until we finished the trip. With the satellite phone, I was able to call her often. Maddeningly, it wouldn't work in certain locations. I had spoken a while ago with her doctor. He felt she was stable enough to last until I could get the boat in a safe spot and fly home to visit her. I didn't quite make it.

I loved my mother very much and will miss her greatly. She taught me many things: honesty is the best policy, go to church, work hard, respect others, be on time, don't drink or smoke.

Obviously, I learned some lessons better than others. I could not have asked for a better mother. She had a good, but also hard, life. I knew she had loved my dad and they were a team. I'm sure it was difficult for her to lose him, but she did a wonderful job raising me alone. I could have been a better son, but I tried to balance my wants while attending to her needs. I tried to call and write regularly and visit as much as possible. She loved Linda, Jen, and Libby. I was lucky to have such a strong, loving, and wise mother.

Due to weather patterns, there are only two good windows to make the voyage from Florida to Trinidad and the spring window is rapidly closing. Hurricanes are notoriously difficult to forecast, but it is generally thought that being south of 12 degrees north is a safe place. Some insurance companies refuse to cover boats that aren't there by July 15th. I wanted to do that even though our policy only doubles the deductible for damage from a named storm and doesn't specify a location.

Les Saintes is not a place to leave the boat unattended during hurricane season. The closest spot is north to Pointe-a-Pitre on Guadeloupe. The wind has persistently been out of the east-southeast, making most of our sails close-hauled. The wind speed has also been uncharacteristically high, which causes difficult passages. Linda is usually incapacitated, and Jennifer gets sea sick. It takes us a couple of days to recover from the longer passages.

I figured that since we were heading north, we would finally have an easy reach. This was not to be the case since the wind shifted to the east-northeast making this four-hour sail nearly as hard as the others. Mark unexpectedly had a bout with seasickness when I asked him to go below and navigate. He successfully fought it off and avoided feeding the fish. But we made it to a marina and successfully docked stern to. The marina and the surrounding complex seemed to have fallen on hard times. Several of the restaurants and businesses were closed and most condos unoccupied. The Moorings, a major sailboat charter company, no longer has its base here. Sunsail, another charter company, still has boats here. On the plus side, there were many slips available and the remaining restaurants weren't crowded. We had a wonderful seafood lunch and an outstanding wood-fired pizza dinner at very reasonable prices.

I got up very early this morning and went for a walk. Guadeloupe is as much a part of France as Hawaii is the United States. I like the French islands because the food is outstanding, bathing suits skimpy, the culture so unlike the U.S., and I don't speak the language. I take perverse pleasure trying to get by without being able to communicate verbally.

It is my understanding that strikes are as much a part of French culture as baseball is of ours. We were told the fuel dock at the marina was closed because of a strike. American Airlines wasn't flying from Guadeloupe because of this strike. I walked through some very old and rundown sections of town, but I didn't feel threatened. My theory is anyone wishing to cause me harm would not get up at 7:00 a.m. I don't think I would have ventured there after dark. I did find a small shop and bought a delicious baguette.

We took a taxi to the airport and boarded a flight to St. Martin. The monitor said St. Martin, but I was asleep when they called a flight in French. Linda woke me and we started to the gate. The lady sitting next to me asked if we were going to St. Martin. We said yes. She said the flight they called was to Martinique. I have come to rely on the kindness of strangers.

I then met a second angel at the American Airlines ticket counter in St. Martin. I had very mixed up tickets and she took time she didn't have to fix my problem. Once we had boarding passes, I started to go to the restroom when I heard her page me to another gate. The room was absolutely filled with people, but I did finally make it to where she was.

She told me our flight had just been cancelled, but she could get us on the only other flight out to the states. The connections would be tight, and we would probably miss the last flight out of Dallas. I was nearly moved to tears by her kindness and compassion amidst the chaos. She seemed to be the only one who knew what was going on as other employees constantly interrupted her with questions and requests. She was never bothered by it and answered them while continuing to work on our reservations. Once again, the reputation of slow, discourteous service in the Caribbean was proven wrong.

We decided to have Mark stay with the boat just in case the batteries ran down or a storm came up. We are so lucky to have him as a future son-in-law. He is a hard worker, a quick study, and a lot of fun to be around—such a trooper. I feel much better leaving the boat with him aboard.

July

We made it back to Guadeloupe with only minor delays and problems. We plan to sail to Dominica today. I figure if the ticket agent at the American Airlines counter in Dallas didn't know where Guadeloupe was, you might not either, so feel free to look at a map.

Wish us well and keep us in your thoughts and prayers.

July 8. Thursday. Happy Birthday, Mark! We made it back to Dominica yesterday afternoon, after returning from the States and Mom's funeral.

We finally had a wonderful reach. Sailboats are said to be on a reach with the wind blowing across the beam (side). This point of sail is the easiest and fastest, especially on our boat. We had winds 15–20 on the beam. We had the genoa and a single reefed main up and averaged over 7 knots.

We picked up a mooring in Prince Rupert Bay, off Coconut Beach Hotel, near Portsmouth. "Honest Boy" Alexis met us as we sailed in. He said the mooring was free and procured a freshly caught tuna for us for dinner.

I got up early, intending to sail to Martinique. We have several sources of weather information but none of them worked this morning. There is a HAM net at 7:00 a.m., but there was too much static to tell where the waves were. The weather fax didn't come in on the regular frequency and the auxiliary one had too much static to read. David Jones, the Caribbean weather guru, was garbled on his broadcast. Finally, as we were nearing the south end of the island about to go into open water, I heard him clearly say that the tropical wave would reach us today with 25 knot winds, lots of rain, and gust to 45 knots. He advised two boats near us to spend the night here and leave tomorrow. We decided to follow his advice and motored up to a mooring off the Anchorage Hotel, near Roseua, the capital of Dominica. Oscar met us on the way in. He took me to shore to clear customs. He runs a taxi/tour guide/laundry/etc. business.

Dominica is a lush, beautiful island. Oscar assured me that crime wasn't a problem here. Since it was Mark's birthday, I took everyone out for the evening. We ate at the Anchorage Hotel. The food was delicious, and the restaurant was right on the water. The dining area was open air. It started to pour as we were ordering our food. No problem, we just moved to a table away from the windows.

July 10. Saturday. It is 4:30 a.m. as I write this, and the party on shore is just hitting its stride. What a TGIF kind of day it has been. We are moored off a lovely, small waterfront hotel that is filled with revelers and "one of the two best Calypso bands in the islands," according to Oscar. The band didn't start playing until 11:30 p.m. and it is showing no signs of letting up. I suspect it will go until dawn, only an hour and a half away. Oscar told us we were in for a treat and I guess he was right. I slept through much of it, but the music was very loud.

The water was a lot calmer tonight. Last night there was a large swell, thanks to the tropical wave that passed through. The waves were 2–3 feet but on the beam or side of the boat. That causes the boat to roll 15–20 degrees back and forth several times a minute. That makes getting in and out of the dinghy a bit of a challenge since the rail of the boat is raising and lowering 2–3 feet. Surprisingly we slept well—rocked to sleep by the waves.

Oscar came by about 8:00 a.m. yesterday to see if we wanted an island tour. We gave him our laundry and agreed to meet him at the hotel in an hour. Since we are so close to the hotel, we rowed instead of taking the motor down. It started sprinkling as we got to the dock. We stopped by the bank where I cashed some traveler's checks. Next, we headed to the middle of the island. There had been a landslide during the night blocking one lane of the main road. This caused us a 10-minute delay, but the cars coming the other way to town were backed up for miles.

We saw a small container ship approaching the commercial dock as we drove by. Oscar explained that bananas are a major export for the island. Many small farmers will bring pickup truck loads of bananas every week to the dock. Prices are miserably low, partially due to some trade war the U.S. started. However, the government subsidizes the price somewhat by paying the farmers to pack and transport them.

Our first stop was Emerald Falls. The falls get their name from the beautiful, green hue of the pool they feed. The water is crystal clear, but the lush vegetation filters the light producing the color. Some parts of the island dry up during winter when the rains stop, but not here. Dominica has four mountains over 4,000 feet. The highest is over 4,700, almost as high as Denver, Colorado. As a result, they get plenty of rain. Islands make their own weather. The higher the island, the more rain they get.

With all the rain Dominica gets, she has plenty of rivers. As we approached the island, a large brown area extended out into the sea due to the runoff from the heavy rain as a result of the tropical wave. They utilize this resource by piping some of the water from natural mountain lakes and rivers to four hydroelectric plants, producing 75% of their electricity cleanly and cheaply. This is an example of utilizing nature rather than fighting her, just like sailing.

We drove back into town and then up a verdant valley formed by the Roseau River to Trafalgar Falls. They are a set of three lovely cascades over one hundred feet high. Our guide said they are called Mama (largest and widest), Papa (tallest), and Baby (smallest). We took a moderately difficult twenty-minute hike to the base of Mama Falls where Mark and I went for a swim in the refreshingly cold water. Plunging into the water was quite an exhilarating experience.

We stopped at a roadside stand and bought sodas, soap, and vanilla. Then we drove to a lovely tiny restaurant overlooking the valley and river. We had a common local lunch that was delicious: a plate full of rice, slaw, plantains (looks like banana but starchier), yams, dasheen (blueish-purple colored and tastes like potatoes), and river shrimp Creole style. Wonderful.

Back in town, we saw a beautiful botanical garden, filled with a large variety of flowers, shrubs, and trees. We saw a living tree trunk nearly eight feet in diameter lying horizontally on top of an old school bus it had crushed when a hurricane blew it down in 1979. The tree was still alive, but the bus didn't look too good.

After a little rest and email writing, we rowed back to shore for the twenty-minute walk to the internet café. The owner was a young man from Saskatchewan. The Bank of Canada had transferred him to Dominica a couple of years ago. They wanted to send him home after a year, but he chose to stay. A year ago, he renovated a second-floor loft above a small hardware store. He serves drinks and snacks, has two terminals with 48K access, and a great open-air view on two sides of the busy intersection below and the ocean a block away. He said he loves the pace and people of this island and doesn't miss the winters back home.

We walked back to the dock, rowed to the boat, and cooked a dinner of tuna, tomatoes, potatoes, onions baked with mustard-yogurt. It was quite good.

July 11. Sunday. We just pulled into Rodney Bay Marina, northwest of St. Lucia. It is quiet and calm here. We got up early yesterday and had a superb sail to Martinique. We had 15–18 knots of wind on the beam for most of the trip. I had all three sails up and they drove the boat at hull speed much of the way there. For *Halimeda* that is 8.2 knots or the theoretical maximum speed a monohulled boat our length can attain. The waves were minimal, the sea and sky delightful shades of blue, and the temperature ideal. This was the type of voyage in my dreams.

As we approached Martinique, a squall hit. Winds gusted to 38 knots, rain limited visibility to a few feet and stung the skin, and our over-canvassed boat heeled perilously. We quickly reefed the main sail and headed on a reach.

Halimeda handled the situation with her usual aplomb, giving us a secure feeling about her forgiving strength. Fortunately, we were close enough to land that the waves were minimal. We couldn't see the land ahead or the ship anchored somewhere off our port beam. Radar didn't help due to the heavy rain. Luckily it was short lived. We soon saw the lush coast ahead.

We were the only boat in the quiet anchorage with a black sand beach, palm trees, and cliffs on either side. A few locals were hanging out on the dock, strolling the beach, and swimming. Several daring youths were cliff-diving not 200 yards off our stern.

After setting the hook, I swam to shore. I saw some wonderful coral, several species of small tropical fish, and literally millions of silver sides, 2–4-inch silver fish that swim in unison. This school was about twenty feet in diameter and nearly a quarter mile long. The sun was low enough to cause their scales to sparkle. It was quite a sight.

I went back to the boat for lunch and was then joined by the rest of the crew for snorkeling. We just arrived at shore when Linda began crying. A small jellyfish found its way into the top of her swimming suit, stinging her in a very tender area. Shortly afterwards, Jennifer got stung in the mouth, Mark on the arm, and me on the neck. That put an end to the snorkeling.

Anse Noire had looked like a perfect anchorage, but then came the jellyfish, and after that someone was burning trash on shore. When a shower passed through, it started to smoke and stink. There was just enough wind to blow the acrid odor into our boat. Without much wind and with the recent rain, a few pesky mosquitoes found their way onboard. When a large ferry would pass by, its wake would cause quite a roll. The clear, moonless night would have been perfect for stargazing, had it not been for two bright streetlights high on the hill above the cove. I guess there is no perfect spot, but we enjoy looking for it.

This morning we slept in. We only had 26 miles to go and I planned on a fast reach. The wind didn't cooperate—it was lighter and more on the bow. Instead of making 8 knots, we averaged a little over 3. It was *just* enough wind sail. We had plenty of time, but Linda complained that my promised 4-hour sail turned into an 8-hour one.

Jennifer made tasty lentil burgers and homemade French fries. That was quite a treat after a long day. We will probably play cards and then turn in. Tomorrow I hope to get some work done on the boat.

July 16. Friday. We just cleared into Bequia after a 9-hour motorsail from St. Lucia. The winds were about 10 to 15, usually enough to sail. Our main halyard was chafed so I didn't want to fully raise the main. Our Yanmar diesel engine objected by overheating so we sailed into the anchorage. Of course, we were racing a squall line with lightning, wind, and blinding rain. Who said sailing is boring?

We spent three nights in Rodney Bay on the north end of St. Lucia. It is quite scenic and has a modern marina. We could walk to the email place, so Mark and I were happy there. We then sailed south to the Pitons. This portion of St. Lucia is the most physically beautiful island I've ever seen. The Pitons are twin peaks rising 2,500 and 2,600 feet nearly vertically from the sea. From one side, the shorter forms a nearly perfect isosceles triangle. The seabed drops nearly vertically at their base. Trees and other plants somehow cling to portions of them, other parts are bare, sheer rock faces. The tops are so pointed they look like they could puncture a balloon.

We went for a hike on the grounds of the upscale $1,000/night Hilton Jalousie Resort. It has a perfect beach and a pool near the water. There are about eighty villas scattered on the lush treed hillside above the beach. Most had ocean views and small pools. Brilliant tropical flowers and fruit trees lined the roads. Ripe mangoes, coconuts, breadfruit, and cocoa pods lay in the gutter. We climbed nearly halfway up the valley then rested at a sports facility with a great view of the beach. *Halimeda* looked like a tiny toy boat far below. We ran out of steam before reaching the main hotel on the ridge several hundred feet higher and nearly half a mile away.

We then walked back to the waterfront and had a drink at Bang, a charming place. Owner English Lord Glenconner (Colin Tenant) came strolling up in a flowery cotton robe, sandals, and an ancient straw hat flanked by twin Jack Russell terriers. He told of coming to the Caribbean in his twenties, probably fifty years ago, to inspect a Trinidadian plantation that he had just inherited. He found conditions impossible—the phone company had been on strike for eighteen months with no resolution in sight. He sold the plantation and bought the largely deserted island of Mustique with the proceeds. Over the next thirty years, he developed it into a haven for the extremely rich and very famous, including Mick Jagger, Princes Margaret, David Bowie, Rachel Welch, etc. When that finally got too much for him— "They kept wanting me to go to dinner with them!"—he sold out and bought the Pitons. After taking twenty years to develop the plush Jalousie resort and then selling it out, he is left with Bang and a large adjacent tract to develop. What a fascinating character. He had an elephant on the beach for years until she died tragically from an overdose of unraised bread dough.

Bang is very unassuming and reasonably priced. Lord Glenconner is proud that locals and yachties feel at home there. He encouraged us to stop at St. Vincent, as well as Mustique, and gave us the names of contacts there. He said that St. Vincent is not touristy at all. It has a reputation of being filled with boat boys who hassle sailors, but Lord G. said that is no longer true. The problem was cultural since the locals aren't used to tourists. He said that the falls and the rain forests there are spectacular.

July 19. Monday. I fought the surf and the surf won.

Yesterday was Sunday. Most places were closed so we decided to take a hike to Hope Beach. It was about a forty-five-minute hike up a steep winding street and then a fifteen-minute trek down a rocky steep path to a lovely palm filled plain with a half-mile long beach.

I decided to try body surfing, although I had never done it. I was able to swim out beyond where the waves were breaking by diving under them. I never got the hang of riding them back. I kept trying it further in. Finally, one wave broke over me as I tried to ride it. Unfortunately, it slammed me face first into the sand with a great deal of force. I could feel my entire spine twisting, my face shoved in the sand, and my left eye scraping along the bottom. Fortunately, all I got was a large bruise under my eye and a very sore back. Linda reminded me that I am too old for such foolishness.

Bequia is a charming island with much to offer the cruising sailor. We found a great sailmaker to quickly and cheaply sew us canvas awnings for the boat. A pleasant and quite competent diesel mechanic fixed our overheating problem and serviced our engine. Despite the lateness of the season, there were nearly a hundred boats in the harbor. It could easily hold twice that number.

Bequia has a century-old tradition of whaling from small, hand-made, twenty-six-foot boats that are sailed and rowed out after the giant creatures. The harpoons are launched by hand. I can imagine they get quite an exciting ride. If one really must kill whales, this would be the only sporting way. I really wanted to buy one of these exquisite boats.

July 26. Monday. If there is a heaven on earth, the Tobago Cays must surely be it. As Chris Doyle's *Sailors Guide to the Windward Islands* (8th ed.) states:

"[They are] a group of small deserted islands protected from the sea by Horseshoe Reef. The water and reef colors are a kaleidoscope of gold, brown, blue, turquoise, and green. There are small sand beaches and clear water. On cloudless nights the stars are case across the sky like wedding confetti thrown in an excessive gesture of bonhomie. Even squalls can be dramatically beautiful as they approach from afar."

In fact, the Grenadines are littered with magnificent islands, anchorages, people, and cruising boats. Bequia, Mustique, Canouan, Mayreu, Tobago Cays, Union Island, Palm Island, Petit St. Vincent, and Petite Martinique are some of the islands in the archipelago. It is a shame we can't visit them all and spend several weeks here. Maybe next time.

We reluctantly bypassed St. Vincent on the way down, against the advice of Lord Glenconner and several cruisers. It looked lush and fascinating. It is the largest island in this group that includes the Grenadines. The Tobago Cays have no relation to the large island of Tobago, which is part of Trinidad.

July 28. Wednesday. We are on an overnight passage from Union Island in the Grenadines to Trinidad. So far, it has been the easiest and most pleasant offshore trip I've ever been on. The moon is full, and it is nearly as bright as day out. The winds are 12–15 knots, just enough to drive us at 5–6 knots. We left about 12:30 p.m. and want to arrive sometime after 8:00 a.m. tomorrow. So far, we are right on schedule.

We them became lost in island time and passed around a bit of gastroenteritis. My guess is either a virus or food poisoning due to some feta cheese. We all had it, but it was mild and very short-lived. (I spoke too soon. Mine returned in a couple of days.)

July 31. Saturday. I am amazed at how many places there are to send and receive email. I think the laptops are the best pieces of equipment we have. I can't imagine cruising without them. Except for the cruising guides, we have barely looked at paper charts the entire trip. I know we should probably have them out too, but so far, the electronic versions have served us well.

On the trip down from Union to Trinidad, the Autopilot quit working. I had it looked at after we arrived, and it worked fine. The only thing I did was pull the solenoid and spray some lube on the contacts. Fortunately, we had a most benign passage.

Everyone was able to stand watch and take turns on the helm without getting seasick.

We are settling into Trinidad, staying at Crew's Inn Marina. It is a very modern, new complex. It is delightful; it has a pool, great laundry facilities, clean showers, and is in a very protected location. The docks are brand new. We have the correct power to run all appliances (many countries have different types of electricity that are incompatible with our system). Water and cable TV are free, and we even have a landline telephone onboard that works great. One could get used to this. We keep meeting people who tell of coming here intending to stay for a week or two and haven't left months or years later. The first people we met were from Shawnee, Kansas, not far from where we live. They have been here for three years.

We had the greatest pizza and pasta for lunch yesterday just across the inlet. We had huge portions of delicious food, freshly prepared in an immaculate setting. Including drinks, it was 20 USD for four people. Every repair and restocking facility imaginable is here and is of top-quality with rock-bottom prices.

We rented a car for 15 USD per day. There is an active cruising sailor social network here. Already we have met some interesting and talented people. It is fun to see how others live this life. Some are on a much more restricted budget. However, at this marina, ours is one of the smaller boats. There are some huge sailing and power yachts here.

This weekend is a national holiday: Emancipation Day. We could go to a steel drum concert, the opera, or a costume party. There are too many choices.

Mark is very nearly done updating our web page so we will try to upload to it this week. He had done a great job and is very talented. I am so blessed to have a wonderful wife, two incredible daughters, and now the best son-in-law-to-be one could hope for.

August

August 2. Monday. Libby made it here just fine. She had a close connection in Dallas, making it to the gate just as they were closing the door. We had an exciting drive to the airport. Since it is a holiday, many locals were parked, walking, or standing on the side of the road celebrating in the smaller towns we passed though. Visibility was poor and we had a right-hand drive clunker as a rental car—what did we expect for 15 USD per day? I thought her flight arrived at 8:00 p.m. and we didn't get to the airport until 8:40. The flight got in early, but she didn't get through customs and immigration until 8:50. We missed the turn to the airport. We didn't see a sign, so we went several kilometers past the turn before we realized it. We later learned that the sign blew down but wasn't replaced since everyone knew where the airport was.

Today we are loafing around. We hope to do some tours tomorrow and maybe go to the beach. I have several minor boat projects and a couple of major ones I need to get done while we are here. I'll get started in earnest tomorrow when all the chandleries and repair facilities reopen.

August 5. Thursday. Today we took a daylong tour from Trump Tours to a nature preserve in the rainforest. We went birding at the Asa Wright Nature Center, a 200-acre conservation estate 1,200 feet up in the lush rainforest in northern Trinidad. The trip was spectacular. The views along the way were delightful. We saw a myriad of birds and an incredible number of plants. Of course, it rained on us, but that's what you would expect in a rain forest. We had a delicious lunch of fried eggplant, flying fish, rice, slaw, and fruit for desert. On the way we saw a large dasheen plantation. Dasheen is a vegetable whose roots are like potatoes and whose leaves are like giant spinach.

Of all the groups of plants in the rainforest, epiphytes are one of the most interesting. They do not need their roots in soil and are attached to tree trunks and branches. Epiphytes are not parasitic; they live on airborne moisture and dust particles. I think they are a good metaphor for sailing. A sailor strives to be free of land-based attachments. Rather than forming dependent, parasitic relationships with the earth, sailors try to live without robbing the earth of its resources and instead work in harmony.

Tonight, we will be attending a potluck for marina tenants. It is nice meeting fellow cruisers and hearing their stories. There is a great social network of people who are out there doing what we are doing.

August 11. We have become too comfortable here in Trinidad. The running joke on the way down was if there was a project we didn't have the time or energy to do, we'd say, "We'll do it when we get to Trinidad." Well, we are here and we still say the same thing.

I finally got around to signing up for an internet service provider, so we have direct, fast internet access from the boat here in the marina. It is like a drug. Mark and I are spending hours online. Tomorrow, we must go sailing. I'm trying to line up people to do the many odd jobs on the boat that I'm not qualified or don't have the time and energy to do.

This morning I went for a walk with six fellow cruisers. We walked nearly to the top of the mountain range on the north coast. The views were breathtaking. It was so clear I could see all the way to the south end of the island, forty miles away. The road was paved, and the switchbacks made it not too steep. Still, after an hour and a half of trudging steadily upwards, one gets a little tired. I quit early and headed back.

The wildlife here is amazing. You hear green parrots squawking while they fly over the marina mornings and evenings. Vultures, bats, songbirds, and hummingbirds all fly within sight of the boat. At the Caroni Swamp, a national wildlife sanctuary, we saw the scarlet ibis, the national bird of Trinidad. They are large brilliantly-red birds with 3-foot wingspans, 6–7 inch beaks, and long legs. They fly in flocks of up to a hundred. We must have seen over a thousand. They are very rare and incredibly beautiful. We also saw egrets, herons, boa constrictors, an alligator, and a four-eyed fish. This strange animal has a pair of eyes under the water and a pair above.

Linda and Libby flew home last night. Jennifer's college roommate, Anne, joined us. It is hard to believe we've been here almost two weeks. We are continually amazed at the reasonably-priced food and services, the vast quantity of marine parts and services, and the friendliness of the cruisers and locals alike.

It is truly a small world. George, a charter captain who took friends sailing in the BVIs over thirty years ago, is probably indirectly responsible for my interest in sailing in the Caribbean. He skippered a boat owned by a group of doctors from Kansas City. One of my good friends from twenty years ago had gone sailing with him. That friend told me how great the BVIs were. I met George when he had a boat store in Kansas City several years ago. Now he and his wife, who grew up not far from where my wife grew up, are cruising full time. Today he saw "Prairie Village, Kansas" on the transom of our boat and stopped by to chat and reminisce.

We had a wonderful French cook named Anne on several sailing trips to the Caribbean. I hadn't seen her in three years but ran into her here at the marina. She is cooking full time on a gorgeous 72-foot cutter named *Blues.* Jennifer had been teasing me when I would look for her on boats along the way thinking we would never find her. Anne is living in St. Barts when she is not on charter.

We have learned that Jimmy Buffett may be performing in St. Barts in November. We are "Parrot Heads," as all dedicated fans of his are called. Libby went to a concert of his in July and is totally hooked. We booked a flight for her to come down and meet us there. We also plan to spend Christmas and New Year's there. Anne said she would probably be there both times.

August 13. Friday. One should never start a voyage on a Friday the 13th. We are tempting fate by departing today from Chaguaramas and sailing to Chacachacare, but, so far, we have done fine.

Chacachacare was a leper colony, run by priests and nuns, until thirty years ago. It was finally abandoned when a cure was found. It was then used as a base for Venezuelan revolutionaries. It has been visited by Columbus and Donald Trump.

It is lush and mountainous with several deserted and deteriorating buildings to explore. As we walked through them, I couldn't help but think of all the suffering that must have happened there. We saw abandoned beds, desks, and chairs. During the night we heard screams that sounded like a leopard or other cat. Columbus also mistook the cry for that of a cat. It was just howler monkeys, but it still was frightening. It is amazing how rapidly nature is reclaiming this island. Manchoneel trees, which are said to be as toxic as poison ivy, and thorn bushes have overgrown much of it. It is a beautiful place, with many abandoned homes and roads. We dinghied ashore to an old road that was once paved. Much of it is now washed out. We worked our way to an abandoned village and entered a couple of buildings. It was spooky. Large holes occupied by land crabs dotted the paths between dwellings.

We then took the dinghy to an old dock near another village which was populated by vultures. We walked on a paved road towards a lighthouse. We stopped by a beach on the other side of a narrow isthmus and were swarmed by mosquitoes. We opted to abandon our hike and explore the island by dinghy. It is amazingly beautiful from the water but quite inhospitable ashore.

The anchorage is peaceful and pleasantly cool. There are perhaps a dozen boats anchored in this mile-long bay. A family with several children is camping ashore with a large campfire. I just hope that for their sakes they didn't use Manchoneel wood for the fire. Vultures are soaring above the tall, forested peaks. The roofs of a few vacant, ramshackle buildings peek through the dense foliage.

The failing light reveals a faint pink cloud above the cliff behind us. A sliver crescent moon hangs lazily above the forest. A cool breeze caresses my skin as I type this while sitting in the cockpit. Despite the camaraderie, the internet connection, and long, hot showers at the marina, I am much happier here.

August 15. Sunday. Happy Birthday to me. I don't feel fifty-one, whatever that means. If one is healthy and has a good state of mind, age is relatively meaningless. I know people who looked, felt, and acted old in their 20s. I have met people who looked, felt, and acted young in their 90s.

Today we decided to motorsail to Maracas. There wasn't enough wind for much of the trip, but it was delightful just the same. Jennifer's friend, Anne, enjoyed the sail. We passed through a couple of islands on the northwest tip of Trinidad and then traveled along the north coast. The islands and the mainland are mountainous. One island, Monos, is less than a mile wide and nearly a thousand feet tall. The twenty-five mile sail took us past a steep mountain ridge that ranges from fourteen-hundred to over twenty-one-hundred feet. That peek is barely two-thirds of a mile from the ocean. Since it is the rainy season, the entire range is covered with brilliant green trees. We watched a spectacular squall line meet us with winds over 25 knots and rain that obscured the land. Fortunately, it passed before we reached the anchorage.

We dropped the hook in twenty-five-foot water in a beautiful cove with only one other boat. We ate lunch and dinghied to the mile-long beach. We walked the entire length and enjoyed the thousands of locals playing in the shallow sandy surf. Jennifer, Mark, and Anne went for a swim while I sat in a lovely open-air beach bar. I drank in the wonderful scenery and a Coke.

Later we walked to one of the many small beach stands and had a hot shark bake, a local favorite consisting of a baked dough shell filled with a couple of pieces of freshly fried shark served piping hot. Several condiments are available, including garlic sauce, hot sauce, and tamarind. It was quite tasty.

We returned to the boat, cleaned up, read until dark, had a light supper, and watched the movie *Animal House*. I had forgotten how funny it was. It reminded me of the fraternity I was in for a semester in college.

I have been away from work for four months now. One-third of my year off has passed. I am finally settling down and enjoying myself. It is wonderful to have time to sit, enjoy the scenery, and not be in a hurry to go somewhere or do something. It is great to get up in the middle of the night, lay in the cockpit for half an hour watching the stars without having to worry about getting up early to go to work. Last night I could hear a band warming up and the waves crashing on the beach in the distance, the crickets ashore, and the occasional squeak of a bat as it flew by. I even saw one buzz the cockpit just after I saw a shooting star. Life is good.

August 20. Friday. We took another sail today, this time to Monos Island, just 5 miles away. John and Shirley Gokool, Shirley's sister June, and several of their relatives joined us. Caryl, John and Shirley's daughter, is a dentist from Trinidad who worked with me in the States. She gave us their number. They have been entertaining us royally since we arrived. We have sampled the local foods: doubles, roti, potato pies, avocados, mangos, and a spicy fruit salad John called *chow*. Rain appeared eminent as we motored away from the dock, but somehow it avoided us, and we had a wonderful day. We anchored the boat and took the new dinghy to the Gokools' friend's beach house. We had a picnic and, for dessert, John cut up cucumbers, tomatoes, onions, garlic, Scotch Bonnet peppers, and fresh mangoes he picked from nearby trees. Wow was it hot, but it sure was tasty.

After dinner we took the dinghy across to a small open-air restaurant where a steel drum band was playing. The sounds they made were magical. The band contained nearly an equal number of men and women. Many of their songs were recognizable, some weren't. A few people danced. We sat at a table outside under a palm tree by the water. A half-moon shone brightly, and a few puffy clouds drifted lazily by. Despite the bright lights, we could see a few stars twinkling above. The temperature was perfect.

The crowd was as entertaining as the band; the place was packed with crusty yachties like us. There also was a large table of Trinidadians having the time of their life. One of their party was a middle-aged fellow with Down syndrome, dressed to the nines with neatly coiffed hair and a short, graying beard. After a while, one of the ladies went with him to the dance floor. Suddenly, he was transformed into John Travolta. He was amazingly graceful and energetic. Several ladies took turns trying to keep up with him. When they gave up, he continued his show alone. He was obviously having the time of his life, as was the transfixed crowd. He danced through two sets before finally taking a series of bows. He received a standing ovation from the crowd. Reveling in the spotlight, he shook hands with many diners as he left the floor.

My father's brother had Down syndrome but died of appendicitis as a young man, years before I was born. I saw a picture of him for the first time shortly before I left on this trip. I only hope that at least once in his life he had as much fun and recognition as this gentleman obviously was having. I admire a culture that welcomes such an individual into its merrymaking.

August 24. Tuesday. We finally went to the market on Saturday. The area is at least two city blocks long and half a block wide, filled with booth after booth of the most wonderfully fresh vegetables, spices, fruits, and many other things. We stocked up on lots of goodies. We also entered the meat and seafood market. Somehow, I don't think it is up to USDA standards, but everything seemed clean. There was no evidence of refrigeration. Being open air, there were numerous flies around. We saw live chickens in cages, to be slaughtered and plucked while you waited. Many kinds of fish including nurse and hammerhead shark, snapper, tuna, and shrimp. Carcasses of beef, pork, lamb, and goats hanging from the rafters and butchered to order.

Some vendors were selling live goldfish, others songbirds. The place was packed with people buying up the produce. Prices were incredibly reasonable. We got dasheen, tomatoes, a local green called callaloo, oregano, potatoes, onions, pumpkin, tuna, snapper, doubles (a local favorite: curried chickpea flatbread sandwiches), sweet peppers, Scotch Bonnet hot peppers, breadfruit, garlic, limes, okra, and cilantro all for about 13 USD. We still had plenty of fresh mangoes and avocados from the Gokools.

I baked the tuna with limes, onion, and garlic and fried some potatoes with onions and garlic for dinner. Sunday, I fixed shrimp Creole. Yesterday was cleaning day. If you keep up with it, it doesn't take too long. As a reward, we ate lunch at Joe's and then took a nap. Jennifer made wonderful minestrone for dinner. In addition to beans, rice, and tomatoes, she added yellow squash, christophene (a local squash), callaloo, hot and sweet peppers, cilantro, and okra.

The tropical weather is finally getting a bit more active. There are several systems heading generally in our direction that have the potential to cause trouble. We are in about the safest spot here at the marina. We have been lulled into complacency due to the relatively quiet season so far. We had hoped to go to Tobago this week but may wait and see what develops. One would hate to come all the way here to hide from hurricanes only to meet one face-to-face.

August 29. Sunday. We finally went to sea again. We left the dock Saturday afternoon and motored to Maracas. We had an early dinner and slept late. We then took off for Tobago. It was directly up wind and against a 2–3 knot current. We motored the entire eleven-hour trip. The sea got rough since we were, in effect, in the open Atlantic. Jennifer and Mark both got sick and I very nearly did. We had been on land too long and had lost our sea legs, I suppose.

We had to take the boat to Scarborough, the main town, to clear customs. Since it was Sunday, no one was at immigration. The customs man told me to come back tomorrow. Even though Trinidad and Tobago are one country, one must clear customs and immigration when going from one to the other.

The small anchorage was very rolly and there wasn't much on shore, so we motored to Store Bay near Crown Point. There is a nice beach with several small hotels ashore. Since Tuesday is a holiday, Independence Day, and Sunday is a traditional Tobago party night, they call it "Sunday School," there was a large crowd on the beach. Could be a long night, but the marina is wonderful: cable TV, phone and internet connection aboard, AC, newspaper delivered to the boat, a pool, and an exercise room.

September
As a surprise Linda's best friend, Lyn Lynch, flew down for Linda's birthday this month. We had a great time and stayed in a resort where we played a round of golf on a rugged course. A couple of cows were grazing on one hole. We had a great dinner and everyone but me smoked cigars. A full month, without much time for writing logs.

October
October 1. Friday. It seems like we are spinning our wheels this week. We did get quite a bit done on the boat. Only a couple

more projects and we will be ready to go to sea again. On Thursday we met the Gokools again and went to a local pottery site. They showed us how the locals make everything from tiny clay lamps to huge urns by hand. They find the perfect clay, knead the clay with sand to give it the proper consistency, then the potter shapes it. We saw the handmade kiln being used to fire the pottery. John explained that some of the jugs were used to cool water before refrigeration. He told us of the Festival of Lights in November. Small bowls are used as lamps to decorate the streets and buildings.

We then went to John and Shirley's home where we had a delicious lunch of curried duck, crab, rice, roti, pea soup, callaloo, and strawberry ice cream. After lunch we drove to the central mountain range where Shirley grew up. We saw where her brother had turned the mountain-top home into a wonderful bar and restaurant. The view was spectacular, overlooking a verdant valley. John picked softball-sized avocados, peppers, and oranges for us and served them with Caribs and Cokes. What a spot to "lime"—a Caribbean word meaning to relax and party.

We got our fifteen minutes of fame this week; we were featured in the Wednesday Shawnee Mission section of the *Kansas City Star.* Libby sent them the story and some photos.

October 8. Friday. We have escaped the clutches of Trinidad and are in the other spice island, Grenada. It was hard to leave, but it was time to go. Tuesday, Linda and I got up early and took a walk up the paved road toward the radio station at the top of a mountain. A flock of nearly fifty green parrots squawked loudly as it flew overhead. Howler monkey screams echoed eerily up the mountain valley. As we climbed, we could see for miles to the southern end of the island. Trinidad is truly a wonderful place with its scarlet ibis, beautiful tropical flowers, rainforests, mountain, friendly people, and great boating supplies and services.

Trinidad wasn't problem-free, though. That afternoon, without warning, a huge thunderstorm boiled up west of Chaguaramas. It produced 25-knot wind out of the west that built four-foot waves crashing into the harbor. Mark and I took the dinghy into the anchorage in hopes of helping our friends on their boat. We saw several boats getting slammed into each other. Lightning was crashing nearby. We decided we couldn't do anything and were in danger. The waves and blinding rain made it difficult to work our way back to our boat. Once there, we watched in horror as boats across the way had their masts swinging wildly in 90-degree arcs threatening to crash and entangle each other.

The boat in the slip next to us was too far in the slip and the anchor on its bow crashed into the dock until someone mercifully tightened the dock lines. Huge waves broke over the floating dock at the end of the marina, threatening to slam a great catamaran up, which would destroy both in the process.

Courageous, or crazy, dockhands and boaters fended it off by hand until the captain returned and set an anchor out.

Halimeda was well tied up. We put out two extra-large fenders on the dock and sat smugly in one of the less bouncy slips. Still, she rolled 30 degrees each way. Her long, full keel and our heavy stores dampened the motion. We decided it was too rough to stay aboard and cook. We instead walked across the dock and had dinner in the restaurant overlooking our slip. The rolling slowly abated through the night.

In the morning we heard tales of woe on the radio net. The cruising guide and the information booklet both warned of the poor holding and danger from west winds. We had been lulled into a false sense of security. In retrospect, I am thankful we decided to stay in a slip rather than anchor.

The overnight passage to Grenada was quite benign. A nearly 2-knot current assisted us, and the boat's clean bottom made us seem to fly. Island Packets aren't supposed to be good light air boats. We were making over 5 knots through the water in less than 10 knots of wind. With the current boost, we were doing 7 knots over the ground. We left two hours earlier than planned as I had counted on making 5.5 knots. We had to sail higher and slower than we could have to prevent arriving before dawn. Even in 10 knots of wind, the water was amazingly calm.

Grenada so far has been less than hospitable. The customs agent was surly and the immigration officer was in another office twenty minutes away. A squall blew through the anchorage causing us to nearly hit an adjacent boat. We had to re-anchor in a rainstorm. Linda and I walked for forty minutes in a narrow, muddy, pothole-infested road to the bank. Rush hour traffic zoomed buy, splashing us. There was no sidewalk, of course.

Now there is no wind. We had to put the screens in the windows for the first time because of flies and mosquitoes. It is hot enough that we are tempted to run the air conditioner. Having shore power spoiled us. I find myself wanting to check my email onboard instead of finding an internet cafe. The closest good restaurant is a dinghy ride and then long walk, or taxi ride, away.

At least the water is clean enough to go for a swim off the stern of the boat. We are looking forward to going to a beach, scuba diving, and taking windsurfing lessons.

October 19. Tuesday. Our stay in Grenada has turned more pleasant. We did quite a bit of hiking and went to the market twice. We did a dive on a wreck of a sailboat, which makes you realize that boats are mortal. We passed on the dive on a 600-

foot cruise ship because it was too deep. Yes, they are mortal too. We tried our hand at windsurfing. It was harder than it looks, though I think with some practice we could get the hang of it. As usual, Jennifer picked it up quickly.

There are some great homes here. There seems to be quite a bit of building going on. I heard the economy is expected to grow at over 6% this year and unemployment is down from 25% to the low teens. They have a new administration that is dedicated to improving things. They cut taxes. Maybe the Republicans were right.

We were getting ready to leave when we heard that a wave southwest of us had the potential for tropical development. We decided to head to a hurricane hole close by just in case. We were the first boat there. The next day nearly thirty boats poured into the large, well-protected spot. The forecast is calling for the storm to become a hurricane and hit near us in forty-eight hours.

Yesterday we did what we could to prepare *Halimeda* for a hurricane. We set three of our four anchors. We took the genoa and staysail off their furlers, and stowed them below. We ran their halyards up with messenger lines. We filled the forward head with the sails, fenders, cushions, and sundry things that might be damaged or give more surface area to high winds.

We spent a lot of time listening to the weather on the radio. Fortunately, during the day, the storm began to slowly turn to the north away from us. All the preparation may not have been in vain. Feeder bands can still give us quite a bit of wind and high swells can make things rough.

October 20. The storm was a non-event; we are safe and sound. There was no wind and hardly any rain. We will give it a day or two to settle down and then head north. Our hope is that it will stay far enough east to not affect the island up north. We are especially worried about St. Martin since we are flying in and out of there for a few upcoming trips. We are still in Grenada looking for a place to send email. Today is sunny and breezy with the wind out of the south.

October 25. Monday. We finally got underway again yesterday. We had been waiting for a weather window for what seemed like a month. One tropical storm threatened and passed. Then another was mentioned as a possibility, but never developed. Since we were heading to the unprotected Tobago Cays, we decided to wait.

We finally found a great little internet place on Grenada called "Sailor's Headquarters." It is run by a tiny French couple. She bakes wonderful bread and rolls. He builds, repairs, and sails small boats. They sell a few hand-painted t-shirts, some jewelry and a couple of pictures. They have fast internet, but a maddeningly slow computer. It took us two hours to get a couple dozen email messages, but what else did we have to do? Besides, the view was great, there was a nice breeze, and it was fun to hear them speak French.

I had lost the rudder and tiller from the dinghy I built, so I had Tony has built me a new one. He wanted us to stay and crew on the local boat race he was sponsoring. We wanted to but really needed to start heading back north.

When I started the outboard for the new dinghy, it backfired and crushed the end of the third finger on my right hand between the cover and the starter handle. It may be broken, but I can move it. I doubt any treatment is necessary. It is swollen and the color of a red grape. It makes pulling ropes slightly uncomfortable. I put a little splint on it to keep from banging it on parts of the boat.

What a joy to be sailing again. The wind was on the beam and 15 to 18 knots for much of the trip. *Halimeda* loves that point of sail. She is very easy to control and tracks like she is on rails. We were trailing fishing lines but didn't get a strike. Very disappointing. I had promised sushi for lunch and tuna steaks for dinner. Instead, we had macaroni and cheese for lunch and tomato, okra, and zucchini over rice for dinner.

Today we will get to deal with customs twice. We plan to clear out of Grenada and into St. Vincent and the Grenadines. I have gotten used to dealing with officials, but I still don't like it. We are eagerly awaiting the Tobago Cays. They aren't related to the Trinidad's Tobago but are part of St. Vincent and the Grenadines. They are behind a double reef, making them well protected from waves, but they are fully exposed to the wind. That gives us a delightful cooling breeze and charges our batteries with the wind generator. Snorkeling and scuba are great there too. There are no shore side facilities, but locals bring bread and ice and dive boats will pick you up and take you to the dive sights nearby.

October 25. We are anchored inside the reef on the south of Union Island. We found great internet access, so we decided to spend the night. There is a stiff breeze blowing off the Atlantic but not much wave action. We just watched the full moon rise. It began with an orange glow through holes in the clouds that looked almost like a jack-o'-lantern. We can see the twinkling lights of Carriacou, Petit St. Vincent, Petite Martinique, Palm Island, Mayreau, and Union Island. We can barely make out the anchor lights of a couple of boats at the Togabo Cays. The water is so clear we could see the bottom, thirty feet below, as we pulled in this morning. Jimmy Buffett is crooning on the CD player. Life is good.

I've been doing quite a bit of reading lately. I finished *Little Green Men* by Christopher Buckley. It is about a super-secret branch of government whose agents kidnap people while dressed as aliens to perpetuate the myth of UFOs. *Red Hunter*, by William F. Buckley, Jr. who is Chris' father and a great sailor, was better than I thought it might be. It is based on Senator McCarthy's life. *The Hungry Ocean*, by Linda Greenlaw, was a great memoir, describing her life as the captain of a one-hundred-foot sword fishing boat in the north Atlantic. *The Perfect Storm*'s author, Sebastian Junger, says Linda Greenlaw was the best captain on the East Coast. They go out 600 or more miles and fish for 30 days or more. The weather is sometimes unbelievably bad, and they survive on hardly any sleep. She was in that storm and describes it in her book. I thought Greenlaw's book was better than Junger's.

October 28. Thursday. Houston, we have a problem. We decided to leave for the Tobago Cays on Tuesday. We did a final batch of email, stopped for a delicious pizza, and readied the boat for the trip. Then I turned the key … and nothing happened. My troubleshooting pointed to the starter motor. We lowered the dinghy and I went to shore in search of a mechanic. He didn't answer the radio call since he was at lunch. He had another boat with a problem ahead of us but promised to be at the boat by 4:00. He finally showed up at 4:30 and agreed with my diagnosis. He removed the starter motor and took it to shore in hopes he could fix it. He soon called to say it wasn't repairable. I was to come to his shop the next day and he would try to locate a replacement since we have no spare aboard.

He spent most of the next day trying to locate a starter—in vain. I finally called the U.S. and got one FedExed. It just might get here tomorrow, or Saturday. If so, we will head directly to St. Martin and miss the Tobago Cays. Oh well, we spent a few days there on the way down, at least.

October 30. Saturday. The starter arrived on the ferry late this afternoon and the mechanic put it on. What a sweet sound: the main engine running again.

Two ferryboats arrived at about the same time. A downpour hit just before the larger one pulled in. The scene can only be described as organized chaos. The concrete pier was only a dozen feet wide and less than 100 feet long. It was covered with people, kids, dogs, cars, trucks, handcarts, boxes, bags, food, and crates. People were pouring on and off the boats. Others were loading and unloading cargo. Little old ladies were organizing their tubs and sacks of produce. Young men unloaded a huge sound system consisting of a half-dozen refrigerator-sized speakers and several smaller boxes of gear. At one time, four boats were loading and unloading at once. Somehow, all the packages seemed to get to the right place. The only problem I saw was a poorly-wrapped piece of glass break. It was promptly thrown overboard between the boat and the pier along with the cardboard packaging.

The skipper wouldn't let me have my FedEx package directly; an agent had to come and take delivery. The small storefront boutique that doubled as the FedEx office was closed for a two-month vacation (!), but there were numbers to call for help. The day before I had spoken to a lady who would get the starter, so I assumed she was coming. After an hour and a half, the boat was nearly unloaded, and most people had left the quay. I called again and was told that she had just left to meet the boat. She finally ambled down the dock and eventually picked up the package. She said that she had left earlier but it had started to rain so she turned around. I was just glad she came at all. One man waiting for a package commented that you need patience in the islands. I couldn't agree more. Still, it is amazing that only four days after our starter motor died, it has been replaced and we are ready to go.

October 31. Sunday. We hope to clear out this morning and head directly to St. Martin. With any luck, we will arrive sometime Wednesday.

November
November 1. Monday. Yesterday started great. We had 15-plus knots just forward of the beam and a 1-knot-plus boosting current that had us blasting along at well over 8 knots for much of the afternoon and into the evening. We had a few lulls, but it all came to an end early this morning. We have had less than 5 knots of wind all day. I finally gave up and lowered the mainsail. The whining growl of the motor and the clackity-clack of the watermaker have become almost unnoticed background noise.

We've read, slept, lounged, and stared at the horizon for hours on end. Linda has a touch of the *mal-de-mer* and is sleeping with the aid of Meclizine. I thought I would never tire of staring at the ocean, but I am getting close. The water is an incredible color of blue. The islands on the horizon remind us that we have a destination somewhere. We still have almost two-hundred miles to go. At 6 knots, that translates into over 30 hours. I suspect we will have wind before we get there. I just hope it isn't too much.

Late yesterday afternoon, a dozen miles off the coast of Bequia, Jennifer spotted a huge splash on the horizon. We watched in awe as a whale or two spouted giant plumes of mist. It somehow seemed appropriate that we spotted the first whale of the trip off Bequia, an island noted for its whaling tradition. The natives controversially still hunt these magnificent creatures.

November 3. Wednesday. We are anchored in the incredibly beautiful aquamarine waters of Simpson Bay, St. Martin. Monday we finally caught a fish. It was a gorgeous yellow, blue, and green mahi-mahi. Just as I was about to gaff it, it spit the hook out and swam away. It was a bittersweet moment. I was almost glad it got away—it was so pretty, I wasn't sure I could kill it.

Tuesday, we sailed much closer to Montserrat's volcano than before. In the dark we saw what looked like a huge ash plume rising from the peak. Lightning flashed inside it and illuminated it. Later, after the sun came up, we clearly saw a large ash cloud rising out of the top. We were about five miles upwind, so unless there had been a major event, we should have been okay. An impressive sight.

A couple of hours later, the shock cord we had attached to the hand fishing line exploded with a loud crack. Mark grabbed the spool as it was unreeling. I donned my sailing gloves and pulled in the front two thirds of a 5-foot king fish. Evidently a large shark had chomped the tail off the fish after it was hooked.

I estimated it once weighed fifteen pounds. It was still alive but without its tail, it couldn't fight much.

We poured vodka in its gills to kill it and I filleted it. We got at least five pounds of meat. Too bad we don't have much freezer space.

We sailed on to Nevis where we intended to rest for a few hours. We had been underway a little over forty-eight hours when we arrived. If we had continued to sail, we would have made landfall at St. Martin after dark. At the anchorage, we saw friends we met in Trinidad—Pat and Julie Murphy on *Antares*. We offered them a couple of large fillets. They invited us to join them on their impressive sailboat, a Gulfstar 60, for a potluck dinner with three others, a friend of theirs from Chicago and a couple on another boat from the U.K. they had recently met. Julie made a delicious bouillabaisse from part of the fish. It was most tasty. Jennifer sautéed another large piece in a bit of olive oil with curry, garlic, and onion and made rice. The other couple brought a yummy curried chicken. What a feast.

After an enjoyable evening of eating and talking, we raised anchor about 10:30 p.m. and motored overnight to St. Martin. We dropped anchor at 7:30 a.m. We are excited about meeting Libby and going to St. Barts for the weekend to party with Jimmy Buffett and the rich and famous.

November 8. Monday. What a weekend! We cleared out of St. Martin shortly after 8:00 a.m. and set sail for St. Barts an hour and a half later. The trip was difficult. We had 20-knot winds on the nose with 6–9-foot seas. We had several rain squalls and we were bouncing around. After four hours, I finally turned on the engine and motorsailed with only slight improvement in motion and velocity. It took us over six hours to make the eighteen mile trip. We were all a little tired afterwards.

The harbor at Gustavia was packed already, but we managed to squeeze in. I finally had to set a second anchor to keep from drifting into an adjacent boat. I dinghied to shore and cleared customs. It is one of the most friendly, efficient places to enter.

We noticed a lot of people snorkeling around our boat in an area that usually has little of interest. Finally, we figured out they were swimming with a dolphin. Mark joined them and got as close as three feet to the amazing mammal. He said it was an incredible experience to see how graceful, powerful, and fast this lovely creature was.

We went to shore and did a little shopping. Libby got a bracelet and Linda looked at one at Cartier. It was gorgeous. The price was 6,000 USD. To say that Barts is upscale is an understatement.

We had had a part we needed for our grill shipped to Libby, so we finally got it fixed. For dinner I grilled some more of the kingfish. We had more than enough for the five of us and that was only a quarter of the meat.

After dinner we went back ashore to check out Le Select. This weekend is the celebration of the 50th anniversary of this scruffy bar immortalized by Jimmy Buffett in his "Cheeseburger in Paradise" song. Jimmy sailed to St. Barts for some time off after his first and only mainstream hit twenty-five years ago. Here, he became fast friends with the owner and has spent a lot of time on the island since.

I got up early Saturday morning and went to shore. I stopped at one of several French bakeries and got *pain au chocolate* and baguette, so fresh it nearly burned my hand. I brought it back to the boat for everyone.

On shore for more shopping, we got t-shirts, prints, and some replacement fishing lures (we lost one on the way down when it snagged a fish trap). We found out when and where the concert was. It was to be on the small waterfront stage on the quay called "Quai General de Gaulle" at 8:30 p.m. The concrete parking lot in front of the stage is only about 50 feet by 200 feet so it was clear there couldn't be a very big crowd.

I found a concrete water and electric box with a good view of the stage and decided to claim it for our seat. I spent the next eight hours sitting and lying on it to save it for the concert. I did take a couple of bathroom breaks and went back to the boat to shower while other family members kept vigil. Mark and Libby fed me the obligatory "Cheeseburger in Paradise" from the nearby Le Select. It was a great spot for people watching. I saw everything from an old salt with a foot-long gray beard, a straw hat on his bald pate, wearing a sarong and riding a bicycle, to a bikini-clad young lady with an elaborate tattoo of a naked woman on her left shoulder and breast.

In the middle of the afternoon they began a sound check. Eventually, one-by-one, members of the band began to warm up. Suddenly Jimmy Buffett appeared and did three numbers. Fortunately, Mark, Jen, and Linda heard him from the boat and dinghied in to catch the last two songs. There were only about a hundred people around, so my family was able to go to the stage and watch. Libby was right next to Jimmy as he signed autographs and joked with the crowd on his way back to wherever he was staying. She said she was so excited she was speechless and her legs were shaking.

After dark fell, the crowd slowly built. A local steel band played to warm up the fans. Le Select was doing a booming business. They set up two portable bars right next to the stage. It was quite a carnival atmosphere with Parrotheads—diehard Jimmy Buffett fans—in their crazy costumes and hats, rich and famous locals decked out in their finest duds and jewels, rough and tumble waterfront types, kids, dogs, and assorted lookers-on.

The fact that there weren't more than a couple of thousand souls attending this free concert was due to the nature of St. Barts. It has no major resort hotels, just a few upscale small hotels ($1,500/night plus), and several pricey villas scattered around the island. The airport can only accommodate small "STL" (short takeoff and landing) planes. They must stall in a near vertical descent over a ridge to land on a tiny downhill strip that ends abruptly on a strip of beach and a bay. Only a few sailing catamarans and power ferries take visitors the fifteen miles from

St. Martin each day. Charter or personal yachts bring a few visitors and small cruise ships do stop there. The one there this day left at 11:00 p.m. so most passengers wouldn't be able to make the concert either. I spent time talking with a cute retired couple off the ship from the U.K. who had never heard of Jimmy Buffett before.

The family joined me at my stake-out. As we were waiting, a 20s-ish, dark-haired beauty in a white dress with flowers in her hair and a radiant smile began chatting with a crewmember from the large schooner just a few feet away from us. Mark began talking with another crewmember who told him the girl was Jimmy Buffett's oldest daughter.

Mark and Jennifer were on their way back from the nearby public toilet and shower when they were stopped by the guy who was providing security for Jimmy. He was about 6' 10" and 280 pounds and looked like he had spent time playing in the NFL or NBA. He was stopping them so the band could file off the large motor vessel three boats down from us. Jimmy gave Mark a high five as he ambled by on his way through the crowd to the stage.

The concert was fantastic. Jimmy and his Coral Reefer Band played many old favorites and a couple of new songs. The crowd was enthralled. We were only fifty feet away. By standing on the small, four-foot-high bench we had an unobstructed view of the stage. People were dancing, singing along, and generally having the time of their lives. Despite the smallness of the area, the pier wasn't completely full of people so one could still mill around, get a drink, dance, and party. They played for nearly two hours and did a couple of encores. Jimmy's daughter joined him for the next to the last number and his three younger children joined in for the last one. It was like Jimmy gave us a private concert.

When he finally left the stage for the last time, they played "The Night I Painted the Sky," a song about the night he helped set off a firework display on St. Martin. As the lyrics described his delight in shooting fireworks, they had a huge multicolored display illuminating the harbor. It was the perfect end to the perfect night. On the way back to the boat, Libby said it was one of the best nights of her short life.

Sunday, we packed up the boat and headed for a wonderful anchorage a few miles away. Mark and I went for a snorkel and saw a sea turtle and octopus. When we got back to the boat, Jennifer calmly told us to check out the large motor vessel that pulled in and anchored right next to us not forty feet away. It was *Our Delight* from Juneau, Alaska, the boat that Jimmy and the band were on before the concert. Sure enough, Jimmy and his family and friends were aboard. They went swimming, took family photos, had lunch, and went kayaking. Having them as neighbors was the perfect end to the perfect weekend.

As we raised anchor and sailed back to St. Martin, Libby commented that it felt like we didn't just see Jimmy Buffett, we hung out with him and his family! We had planned this weekend for three months, sailed nearly four hundred miles out of our way to get here, and flew Libby down for the weekend. It was quite a feat but well worth the effort; it was the weekend we will never forget.

November 15. Monday. We are safely anchored in Les Saintes just south of Guadeloupe. We are recovering from one of the hardest passages of the trip. On Friday we sailed twelve hours from St. Martin to Nevis and arrived at 11:00 p.m. We tried to sleep but it was terribly rolly. The next day we sailed for twenty-four hours in rough conditions, fighting wind and current. The waves were irregular, and we passed closer to the volcano at Monsterrat than I cared to. We dodged some squalls, oil tankers, and islands on the way. I was fighting a cold, chills, and body aches.

This afternoon we will hopefully leave for a much easier eighteen-hour overnight passage to Martinique. In addition to picking up Christie, Mark's sister, we will send Linda home to be with Libby for Thanksgiving. We are dodging what we hope will be the last hurricane of the season that is forecast to hit the Virgin Islands and pass near St. Martin. The worst we should get there is unusually high seas. We hope to find an anchorage sheltered from them. We worry about the friends we have in the Virgins, but are glad to be two-hundred-and-fifty miles south of the track of Hurricane Lenny.

November 23. Tuesday. We are back in Les Saintes after riding out the storm in Martinique. Lenny's waves caused major damage, all up and down the island chain. We still don't have good reports of the damage to St. Martin and St. Barts, both of which apparently took a direct hit. Radio reports seem to indicate that dozens of boats were drug ashore or sunk, including *Yahoo,* whose crew we met. I heard about a large freighter deposited on the runway at the St. Martin airport. Today I heard of winds gusts up to 180 knots and of at least one person who died after abandoning a sailboat.

We were tucked in behind a point near Anse Mitan and weren't affected by the waves to speak of. We did have quite a bit of rain, 25–30 knot winds, and some rolling. We did see three unattended boats drag anchor and drift away. I gave one fellow a ride in our inflatable dinghy to his drifting boat at the peak of the storm. It was a challenging ride with waves hitting six feet high. We were a couple of miles from shore.

Martinique was quite nice. The food was good, the scenery spectacular. It was unfortunately too rough to scuba. We rented a car and used it to pick up Christie at the airport on Friday and drop Linda off on Saturday. We also took the ferry across to Fort de France, the major city of Martinique. It is an old but fascinating city. The waves had deposited mountains of debris on the waterfront, but crews were already cleaning it up.

The only internet café in Anse Mitan had ceased operation. The phones didn't take credit cards, and most people didn't speak English. We felt isolated.

The day after tomorrow is Thanksgiving, one of the few holidays they don't celebrate here. We will probably have lobster instead of turkey. Christie leaves Friday from Pointe-a-

Pitre on Guadeloupe. We have nine days after that before we fly home for two weeks. I hope the airport on St. Martin is back in operation by then. It will be a busy time but great to see everyone again.

November 26. Friday. We are back in Marina de Bas-du-Fort, where Mark stayed on the boat while we went home for my mother's funeral. Things are busier here now. While we were away at dinner, four identical Farr Millennium sixty-five-foot sailboats pulled in. They are participating in an around-the-world-race for the year 2000.

We finally got to scuba in Les Saintes. It was amazingly clear for it being such a short time after the hurricane. The anchorages and towns on the Saints are protected from waves by their location. Like their sister island, St. Barts, they are low enough to receive little rainfall. The taller islands make their own weather by reaching into the clouds and producing rain. Since they didn't get enough rain to grow sugar cane, African slaves weren't imported. Most locals are Caucasian and speak French, though many speak Creole, a dialect mostly spoken by the African descendants on the larger French islands of Haiti, Guadeloupe, and Martinique.

The wind was light and still uncharacteristically from the west southwest, so we motorsailed the twenty miles. As we pulled into the marina, we saw a beautiful, dark blue, ultra-modern, three-masted schooner that was well over a hundred feet in length. Christie asked what it cost. I estimated it was deeply into eight figures and probably costs a phone number—over $1,000,000—a year to operate. Maybe when Mark's company goes public, he will buy one and take us for a cruise.

Last night we went to Cote Jardine, a wonderful French restaurant near the marina. The owner waited on us. For *entrées,* what we would call appetizers, we had fresh water prawns, duck salad, cheese in a pastry, and goose liver pate. For *plat* (main course) we had giant shrimp, whole stuffed boned fish from the south of France, beef filet, and grilled mahi-mahi. For dessert we had crème brûlée, profiteroles, and a scrumptious chocolate cake/mousse combination. The sauces where incomparable, the presentation delightfully beautiful, and the décor unique. French red wine with dinner, Guadeloupe Rhum after the meal, and small French rolls rounded out the meal. Everyone agreed it was the best meal they had ever had. Jennifer said she would never have to eat again. Granted, it wasn't turkey, dressing, and the trimmings and we missed our families, but it was a pretty good Thanksgiving dinner, just the same.

November 30. Tuesday. We got Christie off on the plane and finished a few things on the boat. An aluminum radar reflector came loose from the backstays near the top of our fifty-nine-foot mast, so I got to go up and cut it down. As I have said, heights aren't my thing, but I was amazingly calm. The view was great from up there, when I took the time to look.

The sail from Guadeloupe to St. Martin was one of the best of the trip. We had enough wind to sail for most of the trip, but not so much that it was bumpy. The one-hundred-and-eighty-mile trip took us just twenty-eight hours. We had no rain, lightning, or close encounters with ships. We caught a small mahi-mahi the second afternoon. Since it was so small, maybe we should just call it a mahi. We grilled it cut in half—it was mighty good.

The first thing I noticed as we approached St. Martin was that the beautiful green mountains are now totally brown. Evidently the few leaves that weren't blown off were battered so much they turned brown. They had had winds up to 150 knots for quite a few hours. Scary.

The lady at Budget Marine said she heard there were over a hundred boats lost. The French side reported fourteen confirmed dead and twelve missing. The Dutch side doesn't release casualties. We visited the place on Simpson Bay where some people we know were supposed to stay. The roof was blown off and the sea wall washed away. The owner said they were booked through the New Year and had to cancel everyone out. Some had been planning to spend New Year's there for up to ten years. I took a picture of a two-by-four board driven through the trunk of a palm tree by the wind just outside their office.

Overall, though, things are amazingly normal. The internet place was open, along with the marina, grocery stores, and ATM. Sambucca, the restaurant where we had eaten lobster before, was closed with some damage. There is a hundred-foot-long steel freighter on the beach by the runway of the airport. I suspect that what I had heard on the radio was that *from the sea* it looked like the freighter was on the runway. Several masts were sticking out of the water in the lagoon and several boats were on the beach inside.

We tried to get the boat into the lagoon tonight, but the bridge never opened. It opened this morning. I want to get the speakers in the cockpit and the VHF fixed, neither has sound. The electrician wanted me to bring the boat inside since it is calmer there, but the holding isn't good, it is crowded, and we will have to use the holding tanks. I'm not excited about it. I'll try again tomorrow.

December

December 6. Monday. We are somewhere over the Florida Keys on our way home. What a strange feeling it is to fly again. We did the Anagada Passage in less than twenty minutes by air. It took us twenty hours by sea. It is also strange to be wearing long pants and shoes for the first time in months. I am eagerly awaiting our visit to Kansas. It will be great to see Linda, Libby, the rest of our family, friends, and staff again. I really miss them. We picked the right time to head for St. Martin; just days after our arrival, the trade winds returned with a vengeance. They blew 20–30 knots from the northeast day and night. Waves offshore were reported to be 13–20 feet! The passage from

Guadeloupe would have been difficult if not impossible in those conditions.

To add insult to injury, it started raining Saturday afternoon and didn't stop until early Monday morning. Over seven inches fell during that time. Since we had a twenty-minute dinghy ride to the airport, we were praying they would end in time. Fortunately, the sky was only partly cloudy this morning and our canvas duffel bags kept fairly dry.

I thought I heard of a major snowstorm in the Midwest last night so it should be interesting. The temperature here in the islands dropped to the low to mid 70s as a cold front passed north of us. I slept with a fleece blanket the last few nights. It was the first time I had felt cold in months. You know you are spoiled when the 70s make you cold.

December 21. Tuesday. Libby flew back with us so she could be with us for Christmas and New Year's. The movie on the flight home was *I'll Be Home for Christmas*, a coming of age comedy. At the end, I suddenly found tears streaming down my cheeks as I realized I wouldn't be home with my mother for Christmas for the first time in fifty years.

It was great to have been home and to see everyone again. I found that I really missed my family, office staff, and friends. I also I missed long, hot showers, a bed that didn't roll, a ceiling without a hatch that needed closing several times during the night as rain squalls pass, and sleeping late without having to get up to listen to weather.

And now that I'm back aboard *Halimeda,* I find that I missed warm weather, a bed that rocks me to sleep, seeing the stars, swimming whenever I like, and the ocean. The grass is always greener and the ocean always bluer.

December 24. Merry Christmas! Swedes celebrate Christmas on Christmas Eve. I recall as a young child going to my grandfather's home in Beattie on Christmas Eve to celebrate with all my aunts, uncles, and cousins. As an only child, isolated on a farm, I looked forward to playing with my cousins. My dad dressed as Santa and delivered gifts; I didn't realize it was him.

My earliest memories of the day include *Dopp i grytan* or "dip in the kettle," the traditional noon meal. Legend has it that the cooks were so busy preparing the smorgasbord for the evening that they didn't have time to prepare an elaborate lunch. Instead, they put a pot of broth and meat to simmer on the stove. Bread was laid out to dip in the kettle of broth. Nearby were some cheeses, cookies, and the obligatory coffee. This was a simple, easy meal that was used to sustain guests while the hostess was busy preparing the more complex dishes for the big evening meal. Guests would drop by at their leisure and dip bread in the kettle of broth, grab a bit of meat, and snack away while visiting about the past year's events.

In the evening, everyone would gather for the giant potluck dinner. *Lutefisk* (we substituted creamed codfish) was my favorite. Ham, sausage meatballs, herring salad, potato balls, beans, rolls, and rice cooked with milk and sugar. The latter had an almond hidden inside. The one who got it was supposed to be the next to get married. For dessert we had *Fruktsoppa,* an old-fashioned Swedish fruit soup that is a thick mixture of sweetened, cooked dried fruit topped with whipped cream.

After the meal we would sit down and read the Christmas story from the Bible, sing carols, and exchange gifts. For many years the men brought a gift suitable for a man and the women one for a woman. The gifts were supposed to be limited to a dollar. After the inflation of the 70s, this became more and more difficult. My Aunt Caryl played Santa and always asked if you had been good before handing you your gift.

The only Christmas present I remember longing for was a BB gun. Mom clumsily wrapped a toy car track to sort of look like a gun, but I was pretty sure it wasn't. Eventually the oblong box showed up wrapped the day before Christmas and I was ecstatic. It was one toy I loved and played with for several years, terrorizing the local sparrow and pigeon population and mowing down toy soldiers made of sticks or old potatoes.

This year we had Christmas in the Caribbean—a far cry from snowy Sweden, or snowy Kansas, for that matter. We had dinner Christmas Eve at L'Escale, an amazing little waterfront restaurant. They serve wood-fired pizza, grilled fish and meat, and pasta. One waiter played loud pop music and mixed songs together, which the patrons really got into and sang along with their favorite tunes. Many people got up from their tables and danced wildly. Others lip-synced while pretending the large pepper grinders were microphones.

The waiters literally ran from table to table, only stopping long enough to dance animatedly to some numbers. Whenever someone ordered bananas flambé, they dimmed the lights, blasted out the theme from Hawaii Five-0, and poured the burning rum from a large ladle onto the plate while the waiter lowered it to the floor. This created a flaming stream of liquid four feet long. During one episode, the guy seated next to me started doing pushups while his date stood on his back pretending to surf.

The enthusiasm was infectious. It wasn't a traditional Christmas dinner, but it was most memorable.

December 30. It is hard to believe that tomorrow is New Year's Eve. The weather is so delightful here, the water and sky so blue, and the natives so friendly. Yesterday, Linda and I drove all over the island while I took pictures. As a reward for her patience, I took her to Eden Rock for lunch. It is a picturesque small hotel with four restaurants on a tiny peninsula on a lovely long beach. Jimmy Buffett has a song entitled "I Wish Lunch Could Last Forever," and he must have been here when he wrote it. We had a table by the beach.

Mark is really mastering the windsurfing. He goes nearly every day. I went the day before yesterday. To keep from slipping, the board is covered with a non-skid surface, not unlike sandpaper. I fell off and crawled back on so many times I sanded the skin off my knees and elbows. Today I went snorkeling instead around a couple of large rocks. It took me forty minutes to swim around them. Incredibly, a one-inch rust colored fish swam just inches in front of my mask for the entire time. I saw thousands of small fish and a couple of mid-sized barracuda.

It's about to be a new year and we are over half-way through our year-long journey. Time flies.

Chapter 19
The Year-Long Voyage, Part III: Ship Logs

January, 2000

January 5. We successfully made it through Y2K, celebrating on the quay at St. Barts. There was a band and a good-sized crowd. It was anticlimactic compared to the Jimmy Buffet concert. The boats were much larger. *Ticonderoga* was the only boat still there. It had seemed quite large in November, but was now dwarfed by the huge motor yachts tied to the quay.

The people watching was good. There were fireworks everywhere, including large ones not legal in the States. Kids were setting off strings of large firecrackers in the crowd. It was scary. We ate dinner aboard *Halimeda*. Afterwards the official fireworks display took place within good view of the cockpit.

New Year's Day we set off for St. Martin in windy rough conditions. We got Libby to the airport early Sunday morning for her flight home. We readied the boat for the trip to St. Thomas during the day and at a local casino watched the Chiefs lose a heartbreaker.

At about 7:00 p.m., we raised anchor and set sail for the Virgin Islands. Winds gradually built to 20–25 knots and waves to 6–9 feet. We only had a single reefed main and the staysail up. Sailing downwind is generally easier but it can be a challenge. One must continually watch for a gybe. If you let the stern pass through the eye of the wind the main sail can uncontrollably slam from one side of the boat to the other. In strong winds it could conceivably break the stays holding up the mast. To avoid this, we rigged a preventer, or line tied to the boom, from a cleat amidships.

Squalls occasionally passed with rain and winds up to 35 knots. Since we were going off the wind and down current, we were making 8 knots over the ground much of the time. Occasionally, while surfing down a wave, we hit 10 knots. The waves would sometimes roll the boat extremely from side to side. Still we were only heeled 10 degrees for most of the trip. Sailing back upwind will be much rougher unless conditions ease. We plan to make that trip mid-January.

We arrived in the British Virgins about 7:00 a.m. the next morning and sailed up Sir Frances Drake's channel to the USVI. By eleven we picked up a National Park Service mooring near Cruz Bay and dinghied to clear in to U.S. Customs. We had a nice lunch at Mongoose Junction and then motored to Crown Bay Marina on St. Thomas. This is the spot where Linda, Jennifer, and Mark joined me in June. We have come full circle.

January 10. Monday. We met Mark's parents, brother, and sisters last Tuesday evening at the St. Thomas airport. They stayed ashore on St. John while we spent the week moored nearby. Both St. Thomas and St. John are U.S. Virgin Islands.

St. John pleasantly surprised us. The new National Park Service moorings are plentiful and free. The water was quite clear, so the snorkeling and scuba was some of the best of the trip. The beaches and reefs were in great shape and still beautiful. Even the weather was wonderful with highs in the 80s, lows in the 70s, sunny, and almost no rain.

Lawrence Rockefeller owned much of St. John. In the late 50s he donated it for a huge national park. As a result, it is sparsely populated and quite scenic. Hurricanes did almost no damage to it this year.

The waters display a full spectrum of blues, outlining the lush green mountainous islands. It is all picture postcard perfect. Reminds me of a story a charter boat captain told of a return client who brought along several small bottles. When he asked her why, she said she wanted to bring back samples of the different colored waters to show her friends back home. Unfortunately, the water is clear, the color is due to the different bottom colors—her plan didn't work.

Despite being mostly national park, St. John has great restaurants, shops, and services, which we have taken advantage of to get our civilization fix. It has also been a great opportunity to get to know Jennifer's future in-laws better. We have had a splendid time and enjoyed ourselves immensely. It is amazing how much fun we have had together.

In late December, a large high-pressure system over the Atlantic, north of the Caribbean, rotates clockwise producing higher than normal east to northeasterly trade winds. This phenomenon, called the Christmas Winds, sometimes lasts for weeks at a time. Conditions on the one-hundred-mile Anagada Passage (which we must cross twice more this month) are 20–25 knots of wind and 8–13-foot seas during the day. It is an overnight passage with winds of 30 knots or more and seas 15 feet or higher at night with scattered thundershowers. If this persists, our crossings will be most difficult.

January 14. Friday. Dancing with a Norwegian Princess. We finally caught a weather window to cross the Anagada Passage from the Virgin Islands to St. Martin. We planned to leave by 10:00 a.m. but didn't get away until almost noon. We motorsailed from St. Thomas to St. John. Just off Cruz Bay, the bell on the fishing line rang and we landed a nice sized kingfish. I filleted it and put it in the fridge. Soon we were short-tacking up Sir Frances Drake's channel in the British Virgin Islands. By late afternoon, we made it to a calm spot off Cooper Island where we stopped for dinner. Jennifer and Linda had made lasagna yesterday and we baked it this afternoon while underway.

We watched the sun set and raised the anchor and the sails. We planned to go out Round Rock Passage. Linda was at the helm and we tacked to put us on course for St. Martin. I just happened to notice a very large cruise ship, the *Norwegian Princess,* was off our starboard quarter, showing red and green and a couple of miles away. In other words, she was headed directly for us. It was nearly dark, and the cut was still a mile away. She flashed a spotlight on us and called us on the radio. We agreed to stay on the starboard side of the channel. The cut looks quite narrow on the chart and from the sea and I hadn't been through it before.

The large cruise ship steamed slowly by our port side and passed us just before we reached the narrowest part of the opening. There was more room than it looked like on the chart, but still it got our juices flowing.

I just came off the 2:00 to 4:00 a.m. watch. When I took over for Jennifer, there were literally a dozen ships and boats in sight. Most were 6–12 miles away. Several sailboats passed within a mile or two. Everyone who wanted to do this passage must have been waiting for this weather window too.

When I took over for the 8:00 to 10:00 a.m. watch, I was dismayed to see the windsurf board was nowhere in sight. I fretted for a while and finally saw that it was loose and sitting precariously on the side deck. I clipped my harness on the jack line, went forward with waves crashing on deck, and tied it on a little better.

One of the arms holding the wind generator broke from vibrations. I had forgotten to tie it off before we left. I tried during the night but was unsuccessful. It is not an easy job—in the dark with a bouncing boat hanging onto the radar arch and standing precariously high on the stern rail.

Not everyone agreed that this passage was benign. Linda and Jennifer especially said it was harder than our first trip.

January 16. Sunday. Yesterday was beautiful, sunny and clear, cool, with moderate winds, and a calm anchorage. Mark spent much of the afternoon windsurfing and was really getting the hang of it. Linda and Jennifer made the first half of bouillabaisse while Mark and I went ashore to watch the second NFL playoff game at a local casino. At half-time we went back to get them so we could all watch the second half. During a lull in the action, I put $3 worth of quarters in a slot machine and won $15 on the last pull. Later Jennifer and Linda took ten quarters each and played until Jennifer won $75. We decided to quit while we were ahead and cashed in the remaining $80.

It was only the beginning of our luck. We went back to the boat and reluctantly added the kingfish we caught in the Virgins to the stew. Large kingfish are known to harbor ciguatera, a neuro-toxin. Was this one small enough to not contain it? We found out by morning that it did not. It certainly was tasty.

The effects of a cold front arrived as forecasted in the middle of the night. The winds suddenly built to 25 knots, with higher gusts. The boat began to rock and roll, and the jury-rigged wind generator began to vibrate loudly. I was up checking things every hour or two. I was confident we wouldn't drag since we had survived several nights of 30 to 35 knot winds in the same place while here in December. I wasn't sleepy so about 4:30 a.m. I got up and began studying a dental journal on CD-ROM. I decided to take one more peek topside. I almost didn't notice the large ketch anchored directly in front of us, less than two boat lengths away. I didn't remember them there earlier and decided they must have come in after we went to bed.

How rude of them to anchor so close to us in such a large, roomy place, I thought. I almost went back to my studies when I decided to watch the boat for a while. Was it getting closer to us, or was it my imagination? Yes, it *was* getting closer—much closer. No one was aboard and its anchor was dragging, causing them to bear down on us.

I started our engine, which woke everyone up. I told Linda to motor out of the way of the offending boat and position us to set a second anchor. Our usual hand signals didn't work too well after dark, so Mark and Jennifer relayed my requests. The high winds made the maneuver tricky, but we finally got the other anchor down keeping us out of the path of the boat *Random Wind,* a large local ketch.

Now our dilemma was: should we try to save this boat from dragging on the rocks that were just a few hundred yards away? Mark and I donned life vests and took the dinghy in the windy, wavy, anchorage over to *Random Wind.* Only one anchor was visible, so I let out more scope, hoping to stop the movement. We got off the boat when it was about fifty feet from the rocks behind it.

We returned to *Halimeda* and called the coast guard. They sent a boat over to have a look. Since no one was aboard, they could do little. Soon the boat was turned sideways and heeling over, which indicated that it was aground. We could only hope that the bottom was sandy and that it didn't reach the rocks just yards away.

By daybreak, the owners had gotten the word and were aboard trying hard to save their vessel. Someone used a dinghy to set two more anchors. One was used to turn the bow into the wind, the other was tied to a halyard causing the boat to heel, reducing the draft (making the boat float in less water). This worked and they got the boat free. They cast off both anchors so the person in the dinghy could retrieve them. They nearly got the line of one entangled in the propeller in the process.

As they motored by me, I could see that the anchor that drug was a CRQ Plow that was much too small for this large a vessel. I had a similar anchor on our previous boat and found it didn't hold very well. They didn't have much chain, not enough scope, and might have not listened to the weather forecast. I guess we weren't the only lucky ones last night.

I saw the boat in a repair yard a week later. The captain said someone had taken their mooring, so he anchored the boat and went ashore without checking the weather forecast.

January 28. Friday. My how time flies. It has been an eventful two weeks. Hal and Linda Lee, good friends of ours from home, arrived Tuesday on the 11:00 p.m. flight after missing a connection for their scheduled 7:30 p.m. flight. Linda and I welcomed the opportunity to talk while we waited for them at the airport. My, how this trip has changed me; before we left, I could barely stand to wait three minutes, let alone three hours! I can only wonder if this newfound patience will continue after I return home.

On Wednesday, we cleared customs and sailed to Marigot on the French side. It was crowded and we had trouble finding a spot to anchor. After the third try, the anchor held and we went ashore. While I cleared in, the crew picked a waterfront restaurant for lunch. We had salads and panini, a tasty pizza folded in half and baked. We had the most wonderful chocolate soufflé for dessert.

After lunch, we walked four blocks to the grocery to restock. We walked back to the boat and sailed to Grand Case, an anchorage a few miles up the north coast. Anguilla, an island north of St. Martin, didn't block the large swell as I had hoped. This made landing a dinghy exciting, if not dangerous. Still Hal, Linda, and I managed to go ashore to make dinner reservations at L'Auberge Gourmande, a French restaurant recommended by a friend from home. He didn't steer us wrong. Everything was delicious.

We were anchored far enough out to avoid the worst of the swell, but the anchorage was rollier than I would have liked. We got up the next day and motored around to Orient Bay which is lined by a mile-long, crescent-shaped, broad, white sand beach. The entrance can be tricky, especially for the uninitiated. One or two boats are lost here every year mainly due to errors in navigation. We had been there several times in years past. With good conditions, electronic navigation, and an experienced crew, we felt confident. We made it in without a hitch.

But I was surprised and a little dismayed to see the amount of development that had taken place since our last visit. What was only a few years ago a long stretch of open beach is now covered with shops, bars, beach chairs, umbrellas, and tourists. The verdant mountains behind the beach were nearly covered with new condos and hotels now. Club Orient, a clothing optional resort, is still going strong. The last time we were there, it was at one end of the beach and a new hotel was at the other with very little in between. Such is progress, I guess. What hasn't changed much is that the nudist colony is still largely populated with corpulent old people you would rather not see in the buff.

Mark got the windsurf board and took advantage of the good conditions to practice. Hal and I took a long stroll on the nude beach for "exercise." Everyone else relaxed aboard. We had planned on leaving for St. Barts that afternoon but didn't seem to have the energy. Linda and Hal cooked a delicious linguini with clams, fresh asparagus, and garlic toast points for dinner. We watched a movie and turned in.

The next day there was once again not enough wind to sail so we motored to St. Barts. We anchored, went ashore to clear customs, and did a little shopping and exploring. Hal and Linda seemed impressed with the wide variety of quaint, upscale, duty-free shops.

For dinner, we returned to L'Escale, the upbeat restaurant we enjoyed on Christmas Eve. Unfortunately, the crowd was very sedate, and the "show" just wasn't the same.

On Saturday, the Lees, Linda, and I took a cab to Baie de St-Jean where we did a little shopping and beaching. The beach was nearly deserted. It was a beautiful day with good light for pictures. I filled the memory card on my digital camera and got several keepers.

That night, Linda and Hal made the most delicious chicken enchiladas. They even made a few just with spinach for Jennifer. We felt guilty having our guests slaving away in the galley.

Sunday evening found us at The Rock, the main restaurant atop Eden Rock, the unique seven-room, seven-suite upscale hotel scattered on a pile of huge boulders sticking out from the beach on Baie de St-Jean. A James Bond-prototype pilot built Eden Rock in the early 50s. It was patronized in its heyday by Greta Garbo, among other movie stars and celebrities. A couple recently spent a fortune renovating it and filling the rooms with antiques from their hometown, Nottingham, England. They did a superb job. The views of it, and from the place, are unmatched.

We had drinks at the tapas bar outside the two open-air kitchens. The smells wafting from them nearly drove us insane while we waited for our table. The cuisine was simple, French, and simply outstanding. We passed on the 5,200-franc ($1,000) caviar but sampled most other items. Great appetizers and desserts bracketed one of the best meals of our entire trip. I had veal, Linda lamb, the others had fish. The waiter was English with a great sense of humor.

Unfortunately, the rest of the evening wasn't as pleasant. The wind shifted and the swells increased, causing *Halimeda* to roll uncomfortably. I got up in the middle of the night and rigged a bridle to the anchor chain hoping to cause the boat to pitch fore and aft instead of from side to side. This is a more tolerable motion. Unfortunately, the wind was variable enough so that it only worked part of the time.

Linda awoke about 2:00 a.m. and hourly spent the next eight hours violently expelling the contents of her gastrointestinal tract from both ends at once. I finally called Marine Health Services, our medical service. They advised the drug Tigan, which mercifully stopped the siege.

Linda finally got some rest while we cleared out, did some final shopping, and motorsailed downwind to St. Martin. The seas were 6–8 ft and the winds 20–25 knots. It was a fast trip with the waves pushing us back and forth. We made it just in time to clear in and make the 5:30 p.m. bridge opening. We settled into the mercifully flat calm lagoon where we enjoyed Jennifer's seafood and vegetable pasta dinner and a quiet night's sleep.

The Lees easily made their 11:15 a.m. flight the next morning. We were sorry to see them go. We certainly enjoy their company and they were great boat guests. I think they had a good time too.

January 29. Saturday. We had planned to head to the Virgins soon after the Lees left, but didn't make it. There was some debate as to whether Linda's problem was food or the flu. I settled the argument when I made a series of three spectacular Technicolor yawns (pukes) starting after midnight. It took me a couple of days to recover. The weather was okay for a Thursday night passage, but when I tried to start the engine, I got nothing. I managed to get a mechanic to remove what was now the *second* broken starter motor of the trip. Fortunately, I found the last one on the island; unfortunately, I have been unable to get the mechanic to reinstall it yet. If the guy shows up today then maybe we'll go tonight, maybe Monday. Such is the nature of the islands. Cruising involves repairing your boat in a series of exotic places.

February

February 6. Sunday. We ended up doing the Anegada Passage for the last time on Monday night. It was rollier than Linda and Jennifer liked, but not too unpleasant. Wind was off our starboard aft quarter at 18–22 knots, but the seas were only 4–6 feet. I had a single reef in the main and the staysail. We only made 4 knots through the water, but with the current boost we made 6 knots over the ground. If it had been light, we would have had more sail up. We didn't want to arrive before dawn, so it worked out just fine. As usual it only rained on Jennifer's two watches. She has become our designated rain driver.

We cleared in at Spanish Town, Virgin Gorda, British Virgin Islands. We provisioned and headed to North Gorda Sound where we anchored off the Bitter End. Mark met a couple who were seriously into windsurfing. They loaned him a video and gave him some pointers.

On Thursday, we tried to send email, but the place wouldn't let us use a disk and it was $40 per hour. We had a very mediocre lunch at the Pusser's in Leverick Bay. About what we expect in the English Islands. We watched Forrest Gump

Thursday evening at The Bitter End. They have free movies nightly on a large TV in an outdoor theater.

On Saturday, we sailed fifteen miles to Anegada. It is seven miles long, two miles wide, and only twenty-eight feet high. A huge reef surrounds it that has claimed many boats over the years. Fortunately, we avoided it. Computer navigation makes it almost too easy.

Anegada is noted for lobster. There were cages filled with them floating beside the docks. We had great lobster for dinner, grilled on the beach.

This morning we went for a walk searching for wild orchids and flamingos. We were moderately successful. The orchids were tiny and the flamingos far away. Jennifer fixed quiche and biscuits for brunch. After noon we set sail for Cane Garden Bay, twenty-five miles away on Tortola.

We saw whales sounding in the distance. They are quite impressive animals. At first, I thought it was a large powerboat slamming into a wave two miles away. The second time we saw them they were much closer, maybe five-hundred yards. Close enough to see but not so close as to threaten the boat.

February 9. Wednesday. Back in the U.S.A.! We cleared out of BVI customs on the 7th at West End Tortola. I received a stern lecture by an agent since I had originally said we would leave the 5th. He mentioned stiff fines or worse. When we cleared in at Cruz Bay, St. John, USVI, the USDA lady grilled us to be sure we had no imported meat or fresh fruits and vegetables. She stressed that we could *not* bring our garbage ashore but had to store it onboard until we reached a port with an incinerator. She didn't know if Puerto Rico had such facilities. It will get pretty ripe if we have to wait until Miami. We should have dumped it in the BVI before leaving. We simply forgot. Traveling from country to country is such fun.

Yesterday Jen and I walked early then took the ferry to St. Thomas. We took a cab to Coral World, a huge modern aquarium with many great exhibits. We saw sharks, turtles, lizards, and myriad fish in very natural settings. Even though we are knowledgeable about marine life, we saw some new and interesting creatures. Spanish lobsters have no pinchers like Maine lobster or long tentacles like the spiny Caribbean lobster. We saw an industrious jawfish building and rebuilding a nest-like cave out of coral rubble.

We stopped at a pottery kiln and bought some neat souvenirs (adorned with lizards) and then went on to a windsurfing shop where Mark bought some upgrades for his board. We walked back to the dock and had lunch at the infamous Duffy's Love Shack. The music was loud, the service fast by island standards, and the food good for a non-French island. Then it was on to an internet café where we emailed and learned of the tragic death of Derrick Thomas.

Today we got up and hiked to town. We spent the better part of the morning trying to do email. Our standard place refused to let us use disks saying they feared a virus problem. A second place looked great, but their phone line was down.

Finally, we found a computer repair store with one machine. Of course it was busy, so we had to wait.

Tonight, we did our first night scuba dive and it was fascinating—not scary at all. A whole different group of creatures are active after dark. The normally shy squirrelfish with their huge eyes were no longer hidden in dark holes but instead swim about. The lights really bring out the color of the coral. It was such a cool experience.

February 17. Thursday. We spent a few more days enjoying St. John's water, hiking trails, sun, and beaches. Mark got to test out his new sail, mast extension, and harness. We trekked to the Annenberg Sugar Mill ruins. It is really an amazing bit of architecture. The view of the reef below and the islands in the distance was incredible. All the doors and archways are lined with brain coral stones. They are soft enough to cut when first taken from the sea but become hard when exposed to the air, just like native Kansas limestone.

We spent two more days at Crown Bay Marina in St. Thomas. I did some much-needed maintenance. The wiring on our bow running light had corroded and the light itself rusted so I replaced the fixture again. I went up the mast again to hang a new radar reflector and my heart rate hardly went up at all. I'm getting to enjoy the view.

We had a lumpy but short sail to Culebra, and island off Puerto Rico. We followed the cruising guide's suggestion to anchor off and clear customs in the morning. The official chastised us and warned that we could be fined $5,000 for failing to clear in immediately! He issued a warning that was placed in our computer record. At least he was friendly.

He also said we needed the original boat documentation papers. I just carry a copy and keep the original onboard. We met a couple on the way in who warned us of this problem and were sent back to get theirs. At least he didn't make us walk the half-mile to the dock and dinghy ten minutes to the boat twice more to get them. Maybe he took pity on us since we were from Kansas. Mark thinks it was because Jennifer was along. His theory is that a pretty, young blonde can get away with murder.

We then walked a couple of miles to Flamingo Beach. It is a long, wide, gorgeous white sand beach somewhat protected by a reef. Only a few other people were there.

Last night we anchored at Bahia de Almodovar on the east coast of Culebra. I spent the night with the Doyons here on the way down. It was a weekend then and the anchorage was filled with local powerboats. This time we are sharing it with just one other sailboat.

It is a fantastic place, protected by two large reefs that block the waves but not the wind. Less than half a dozen widely-spaced homes dot the surrounding hills. After Mark used the flat, open water to windsurf, he said it was nice not to have to dodge other boats. After dark we watched the light of St. Thomas twenty miles east. On his *Son of a Sailor* album in the song "Manana," Jimmy Buffett describes the opposite view from Cane Garden Bay on Tortola, BVI. It goes something like, "I hear it gets better, that's what they say as soon as you sail onto Cane Garden Bay ... While the lights of St. Thomas, twenty miles west, I see General Electric is still doing their best."

February 20. Sunday. We are anchored behind Ilsa Pineros, just north of Roosevelt Roads Naval Base on the east coast of Puerto Rico. The Navy owns the island, so we aren't allowed ashore. We shared this large and relatively quiet spot with just one other sailboat.

I got up early as usual, got the weather, read until just before dawn, and went up on deck to enjoy the spectacle. The full moon over our stern had not yet set. It was shining brightly on El Yunque, the cloud shrouded, rain forested mountain behind us. Pineros is a low, lush island with a good reef and a small sand beach. The sun rose brightly in a slight cloud. Jimmy Buffett describes the opposite astrological phenomenon of the sun setting while the full moon is rising in one of his songs. Both events give one a chance to reflect on the two heavenly bodies that most affect our lives at sea being responsible for the weather and tides.

Friday, we sailed from Bahia de Almodovar to Cayo de Luis Pena on the west side of Culebra. It is an uninhabited bird sanctuary that was supposed to have hiking trails. We dinghied to the beach and searched in vain for them. Instead we walked along the boulder-strewn coast. The edge of the island has rocky beaches punctuated with huge lava mounds. Purplish-pink coral fans and a few bleached-white brain corals had been driven onto them by some previous storm. We hiked and scrambled for almost a mile until we reached the southern point where we saw a vertical lava wall plunging into the sea, abruptly ending our trek.

On the way back, I stared lovingly at *Halimeda* anchored alone a few hundred yards offshore. She has only a few minor flaws and has been an outstanding home for this adventure of ours. I can think of no other craft so well-suited for this type of voyaging.

Since the anchorage was rolly, we decided to head for Culebera where we had spied a mooring on the way in. We tied up and settled in for the evening. Jennifer fixed black bean quesadillas with her wonderful homemade pico de gallo and Mark's homemade guacamole. We watched *The Big Chill* and turned in.

More extreme rolling than usual awakened me about 5:30 a.m. I got up on deck and finally realized we were off our mooring and drifting offshore. It was still quite dark, and I was a little disoriented. I started the motor and began motoring slowly into the wind. The electronic chart of this area was about 350 yards off, so I didn't trust it too close to the coast until it got lighter. We finally decided to head to our next stop instead. I don't know if the knot Mark tied to the mooring came undone or if someone untied it during the night.

We set off on a nice twelve-mile reach to Isabel Segunda on the north coast of Vieques. For years the U.S. Navy has used the western half if this eighteen-mile-long island as a practice bombing range. Last year a bomb went slightly astray and killed a civilian security guard. Ever since, there have been protests seeking a halt to the bombing.

Mark read in *Hot Licks,* a book about hot pepper sauce, that they make a very good one on Vieques. We took a mooring and went in search of it. We found a well-stocked grocery store that didn't carry it. If fact, they said they didn't know it existed. After getting a few items, we walked around. I walked into a shop selling t-shirts protesting the bombing hanging outside. The owner asked in a New York accent if she could help us. I asked about the hot sauce and she told us they had moved to St. Augustine, Florida, and that she carried it! We bought several bottles and a t-shirt.

We then ambled off to a huge picturesque cemetery on a hill on the coast. It was filled with large above-ground mausoleums adorned with crosses and statues. I took several pictures, as the view of the ocean and the islands beyond was delightful. If one could somehow enjoy the view from the grave, this would be an ideal spot to spend eternity.

On the way to Vieques we caught a large barracuda which we cut off and a small kingfish which got away. I was wearing the same white long-sleeved shirt that I wore when we caught the last fish. I remember because I got blood on it while Mark was cleaning the fish. I also wore it when we caught another fish once. I had joked that it was my lucky shirt and it certainly was. After lunch, as we sailed to Isla Palominos, we caught a very nice kingfish, which we landed successfully. Jennifer navigated and

Mark finished cleaning it as Linda and I furled the sails and picked up a mooring.

Isla Palominos is an idyllic little island off the east coast of Puerto Rico. It is owned by the upscale resort El Conquistador. The Doyons and I had stopped here on our way to St. Thomas last May. It is simply beautiful. We had a delightful dinner aboard as the nearly full moon rose over the island. It was quite a romantic setting.

The mooring held this time, so we spent a quiet night. In the morning we sailed to Isla Pineros. The wind was up, and it was a boisterous sail. There were 4–6-foot waves on the beam that rolled us 35 degrees and more each way. Fortunately, it took only a little over an hour. Once we rounded the point and motored up the narrow channel things settled down nicely. After setting anchor in ten feet of water, we gave the boat a good cleaning and spent the rest of the afternoon off reading. It is so nice to have the time to read and enjoy good books.

February 22. Tuesday. We just arrived in Ponce, Puerto Rico's second city—the Chicago of Puerto Rico. We are anchored off the Ponce Yacht Club. Last night we were in Salinas. It was somewhat disappointing since Van Sant called it his favorite anchorage. We ate lunch at the marina. The food was so-so, the fish soup inedible.

We anchored in the lee of Cayo Santiago, also called Monkey Island. It is a small island off the southeastern coast of Puerto Rico. It is home to about a thousand free-range rhesus macaque monkeys. Annoying jet skiers swarmed around us all afternoon until nearly dark. After they left, we were the only boat anchored there. We did watch the monkeys romping all over the island. After dark, a bright yellowish red moon came up through the trees. It looked like the monkeys had built a campfire.

The next day we got a free ride back from the grocery store. A nice guy took pity on us carrying groceries and gave us a ride the mile back to the marina. He said he had been in the army. Since it was President's Day, he had it off. He was halfway through a six-pack of Coors Light (one in his hand, two between the front seats, and three empties in the trunk) so he was in a good mood. He told Mark not to worry: he didn't have any guns. He had worked in the States, and just got back from Pittsburgh where it was *cold*.

Tomorrow we will head to the west coast of Puerto Rico. Then we will need to do the Mona Passage to the Dominican Republic, something that can be worse than the Anegada. The forecast is for light winds so we should have an easy time of it, but it will probably be an offshore trip of up to forty-eight hours.

February 28. Monday. From Ponce we sailed directly to Boqueron on the west coast of Puerto Rico. The anchorage was huge and well protected, but the town was disappointing. Once more we were told there was no internet access.

We had sailed not far from another sailboat for most of the trip and they called and offered us a fish as they had just caught two. We told them we'd meet them in Boqueron. They gave us what he thought was a kingfish. It turned out to be a small and tasty tuna, which we marinated it in Teriyaki sauce and grilled. It was delicious.

Thursday morning we got up and tidied up the boat. Jennifer prepared enchiladas and baked pumpkin bread. It was nearly noon before we got underway. The seas were flat and the winds light for the first few hours since we were protected by a long point of Puerto Rico to the north of us. Soon the wind and seas built up and we shut the motor off.

The Mona Passage has a worse reputation than the Anegada. There is a large hourglass shoal on the western third of the trip. The Puerto Rican Trench just north of it has some of the deepest waters of the ocean, over five miles deep! Wind and current can drive huge, confused waves over the edge of the shallow water of the shoal. One needs to either sail around the north end or quickly cross the narrowest part in the middle. Due to the wind direction, we chose the latter.

We could sail on a beam reach for several hours in 15–18 knots of wind. This is *Halimeda*'s favorite point of sail and we kept a steady 7.5 knot speed over ground. The seas were relatively flat, at 3–6 feet, and the boat didn't roll much. Mark baked the enchiladas and we enjoyed them as the sun set.

This great sail continued until the end of my 2:00 to 4:00 a.m. watch. It was now time to head north into the waves and across the shoal. We had to motor and slam into steep, confused macaque monkeys. Annoying jet skiers swarmed around us all afternoon until nearly dark. After they left, we were the only boat anchored there. We did watch the monkeys romping all over the island. After dark, a bright yellowish red moon came up through the trees. It looked like the monkeys had built a campfire.

The next day we got a free ride back from the grocery store. A nice guy took pity on us carrying groceries and gave us a ride the mile back to the marina. He said he had been in the army. Since it was President's Day, he had it off. He was halfway through a six-pack of Coors Light (one in his hand, two between the front seats, and three empties in the trunk) so he was in a good mood. He told Mark not to worry: he didn't have any guns. He had worked in the States, and just got back from Pittsburgh where it was *cold*.

Tomorrow we will head to the west coast of Puerto Rico. Then we will need to do the Mona Passage to the Dominican Republic, something that can be worse than the Anegada. The forecast is for light winds so we should have an easy time of it, but it will probably be an offshore trip of up to forty-eight hours.

February 28. Monday. From Ponce we sailed directly to Boqueron on the west coast of Puerto Rico. The anchorage was huge and well protected, but the town was disappointing. Once more we were told there was no internet access.

We had sailed not far from another sailboat for most of the trip and they called and offered us a fish as they had just caught two. We told them we'd meet them in Boqueron. They gave us what he thought was a kingfish. It turned out to be a small and tasty tuna, which we marinated it in Teriyaki sauce and grilled. It was delicious.

Thursday morning we got up and tidied up the boat. Jennifer prepared enchiladas and baked pumpkin bread. It was nearly noon before we got underway. The seas were flat and the winds light for the first few hours since we were protected by a long point of Puerto Rico to the north of us. Soon the wind and seas built up and we shut the motor off.

The Mona Passage has a worse reputation than the Anegada. There is a large hourglass shoal on the western third of the trip. The Puerto Rican Trench just north of it has some of the deepest waters of the ocean, over five miles deep! Wind and current can drive huge, confused waves over the edge of the shallow water of the shoal. One needs to either sail around the north end or quickly cross the narrowest part in the middle. Due to the wind direction, we chose the latter.

We could sail on a beam reach for several hours in 15–18 knots of wind. This is *Halimeda*'s favorite point of sail and we kept a steady 7.5 knot speed over ground. The seas were relatively flat, at 3–6 feet, and the boat didn't roll much. Mark baked the enchiladas and we enjoyed them as the sun set.

This great sail continued until the end of my 2:00 to 4:00 a.m. watch. It was now time to head north into the waves and across the shoal. We had to motor and slam into steep, confused waves 6–10 feet high. Fortunately, this only lasted two hours when we were able to fall off the wind and sail again.

We spent most of Friday on a pleasant reach with the coast of the Dominican Republic in sight, 10–20 miles off our port beam. The seas had built to 4–6 feet, with an occasional 8–10. *Halimeda* handled them better than we did. Due to sunspots, I couldn't receive a very good weather forecast on the SSB, but what I did get called for "light and variable winds." I told Linda she probably wouldn't need Meclizine, but, I was wrong, of course. She was miserable until she took one and was out of it afterwards. She simply cannot become accustomed to the motion. The rest of us did okay.

By early Saturday morning we had a beam sea that rolled the boat every couple of minutes. If we were able to sail, the pressure of the wind dampened the motion to an acceptable level. At the end of Mark's 4:00 to 6:00 a.m. watch, the wind had died. Leaving the mainsail up helped the motion of the boat, but the waves caused it to slam back and forth. This had already broken one sail slide, so I hesitated to allow it to continue. When we took it down, though, the boat really rolled miserably.

Since we only had a couple of hours to go, I decided to leave the mainsail down, much to the consternation of the crew. We had made such good time that we got to the entrance before dawn. I motored into the seas for a while and reversed to the entrance twice before the sun came up and we were able to enter the anchorage. The entrance was better marked than we had been led to believe and once we got behind the first two reefs, the waves subsided.

The guide says to wait aboard until the Commandante comes to the boat. After an hour, I decided to go ashore. Ronnie, a local, had come by the boat offering to sell me diesel and water. I told him to come back another day. He happened to be on the dock and offered to help me. I followed him along the long pier to the edge of town. He led me across a substantial footbridge and up a dirt path to a small building atop a hill. Two uniformed young men and several others were sitting around eating breakfast out of metal bowls. I was told to sit and wait until they finished. Finally, one a guy wearing a black Chicago Bulls Dennis Rodman jersey called me over to a small table. He was maybe 5' 4" and weighed at least 200 pounds. He turned on the TV and began to fill out the form for me. He spoke no English, I no Spanish. Fortunately, Ronnie translated for me. After several minutes, I signed the form and we were off.

We walked a few blocks down the street of the town. Ronnie got on the back of a small motorcycle and motioned for me to do the same. I had read that this is a form of taxi here. He drove me to what was evidently the local political headquarters. A small open room with political posters covering the room. A uniformed, jovial, roly-poly man with a small, black mustache was drinking coffee on the porch. We went inside where he opened his briefcase and began to stamp and sign our passports. All the while he talked loudly to several others seated around the room and outside on the porch. Ronnie gave me a small plastic cup of strong, sweet coffee. After the official was half through, Ronnie told him we were entering, not leaving, so he had to mark out what he had done and start again. The process was relatively painless and quite entertaining.

I went back to the boat and got Mark to go back into town to do email. The connection was fast and the computer quite up to date. We ran into Ronnie again on the way back to the boat. He insisted on buying us a beer at his family bar and restaurant. He introduced us to his sister, mother, and father and kept pouring beer for Mark and Coke for me. We left after a long and entertaining time.

Yesterday was Independence Day. They had a parade in town, but we didn't make it. We did go to the small marina around the corner and had a great barbeque. We met a few other cruisers including our friends, on *Sola Fide*, who we had met in Trinidad and again in St. John. It is indeed a small world.

After lunch we hiked to a large, modern resort on the coast. It is evidently an all-inclusive place since we were not allowed entrance to the facilities. The beach was public, so we could walk to it around the resort. We strolled up and down the beach, which was wide, large, and covered with sunbathers. I suspect they cater mainly to Europeans. The guests all wore plastic ID bracelets to differentiate them from the locals and us poor yachties.

Linda, Jennifer, and I walked to town and did email. It was quite reasonable at 35 DR peso's (about 2 USD) per hour. Back at the boat, Mark had baked some wonderful muffins made with chocolate chips, oat bran, and bananas. For dinner, Jennifer made great homemade pizza.

March

March 7. Tuesday. We are anchored at Sopadilla Bay on the south side of Providenciales, one of the Turks and Caicos. These are a group of a dozen islands that are a British Crown colony, one-hundred-and-forty miles north of the Dominican Republic. They are mainly low, limestone outcroppings with sparse vegetation and even sparser population. The water surrounding them is quite shallow compared to what we are used to. We are anchored in about seven feet of water, giving us only a foot and a half under our keel.

I really enjoyed our stay in the Dominican Republic. I got to know Ronnie a little better. He lined us up with his uncle who drove us an hour and a half to the Puerto Plata airport in an old Chevy. He was a fast but careful driver who knew when to pass, when to wait, and how to swerve to miss the large trucks, small cars, swarms of motor scooters, animals led, driven, or ridden, and pedestrians.

I bid my crew farewell as they headed back home to plan the wedding and find Mark and Jennifer a new home in Portland. These are exciting and fun-filled times for us all.

On the way back, we drove by an old fort dating from Christopher Columbus times. At least that is what I think he said as he spoke no English.

In Luperon, I renewed my friendship with Captain Karl, who helped me sail from Florida to Puerto Rico last May. He is moving from the hustle and bustle of Santa Domingo to Luperon. He said the number of cars in Santa Domingo has tripled in the last few years. Karl joked about how important family is in the Dominican Republic. They keep in constant touch and tell each other everything. His daughter is almost two and is growing rapidly.

I also enjoyed visiting with the many cruising sailors passing through. Most were heading south so we swapped local knowledge of the places we'd been. We met up with John and Leslie on *Sola Fide* once again. They are three-fourths through a two-year "pretirement."

On Friday, Ronnie's uncle again drove me to the airport to pick up Glen9 and Nancy Doyon, the dentists from Philadelphia, who helped me sail to St. Thomas from Puerto Rico last summer. It was great to see them again. They own an Island Packet 35, moored in the same marina in Rock Hall, Maryland, where we will take *Halimeda* in early May once this trip is over.

That evening, friends introduced me to a young Israeli who was seeking passage north. She said she could cook and was an artist. She had been traveling the world for several years and was trying to get to the Bahamas to work as a "Cosmic Dancer." Although she was quite attractive, I foresaw potential trouble and declined to give her a ride.

On Saturday morning we went into town and did a little shopping. On the way back from the airport, we had stopped in a *supermercado* (supermarket) in Puerto Plata that was very well stocked and reasonably priced. After clearing out, we raised and washed the muddy anchor and set sail for the Turks and Caicos.

As I was raising the anchor, small mouse-like droppings on the foredeck puzzled me. I was confident we didn't have a mouse aboard. Once we unfurled the genoa, a small bat dropped out into the water. We were unaware of this little stowaway. I hope he knew how to swim.

We had one of the most pleasant sails of the trip with winds 10–15 knots off starboard beam. We screamed along at 7.5 knots in very calm, flat seas. Glen commented he had been in much rougher anchorages. Who says Island Packets aren't good in light winds?

We were rewarded with one of the most spectacular sunsets of the trip. The sky was ablaze in colors ranging from dayglow orange to fire engine red streaked across the sky in broad brush strokes that would have shamed the best artist. It lasted unusually long for the tropics. Life is good!

The autopilot was uncharacteristically acting up—slowly heading 30 or more degrees off course. I finally realized that we were stowing a metal-framed pack near the fluxgate compass. I thought this was the cause, but moving it didn't fix the problem. Glen and I took turns steering every two hours all night with help from Nancy. Fortunately, the benign conditions continued. The wind eventually clocked to the stern and died after midnight, so I rolled in the genoa and staysail and dropped the main. Since the seas were still flat, we didn't roll like we did on the way into Luperon.

Dawn broke to clear skies and light winds. We heard on the radio that *Sola Fide* was anchored off French Cay, our destination. We spoke on the radio and bid them farewell as they headed north later in the morning.

French Cay is an uninhabited island barely a mile across and only a few feet high. A small burned-out wrecked tug is on one end and two abandoned Haitian sloops were beached nearby. Hundreds of seabirds flitted back and forth. There was some scrubby vegetation and a little beach which we shared with a few powerboats in the afternoon. A U.S. Coast Guard helicopter flew over, presumably looking for drugs or bad guys. Soon we had the place to ourselves out in the middle of the ocean with nothing else in sight.

We snorkeled in the gin-clear water over the reef and saw beautiful coral and fish, notably a queen triggerfish, a dinner-plate-sized French angelfish, and a four-foot barracuda.

For dinner we fixed pasta with red sauce, TVP (textured vegetable protein that tastes amazingly like beef), and fresh snow peas we had purchased for less than a dollar in Puerto Plata. Once more the sky was ablaze with incredible color and beauty, reminding me of the old saying, "Red sky at night, sailor's delight."

Yesterday morning we got up, had breakfast, listened to the weather, and set off for Sopadilla Bay, three hours north. I was amazed by the crystal-clear water and trusted the cruising guide that the clearly-visible coral heads were all at least ten feet from the surface. I was enthralled by the shadow of our sail on the sandy bottom just below. The colors of the water were a gorgeous robin's egg blue. French Cay soon sunk below the horizon. Shortly afterwards, Provo appeared in the distance ahead.

We anchored and got ready to go ashore. One neighbor came by to welcome us and give us local knowledge. He said hitchhiking was easy and safe here. It was important, though, to raise the hand with all fingers extended like a stop sign instead of putting the thumb out, like in the States. Evidently that gesture means "up yours" here and is frowned upon.

We were anchored next to *Cop Out,* an Island Packet 38 from Keizer, Oregon. I stopped by on my way to customs and exchanged life stories with the handsome couple aboard. They are both retired policemen who were married seven years ago. Soon afterwards, his son married her daughter and they have since given them three grandchildren. They sold their house to their kids and headed across the country, towing a trailer, in search of an Island Packet. They found one in Palmetto, Florida, just north of where we kept *Halimeda*. They have been cruising south for the last ten months. They haven't been in as big a hurry as we have been.

Clearing customs was relatively painless since the official was pleasant, polite, articulate, and friendly. I then went back to the boat and picked up the Doyons. We tied to a dock labeled "private." Since the house was deserted, we used it.

We then set out on a hike to town, reportedly two miles away. The first part was rocky and rough. Eventually we came to a wide, well-paved road. We had been going for what seemed like too long a time when we decided we must be headed the wrong way. We hiked for a few minutes back towards the boat when we finally got up the courage to catch a ride. We passed up several pickup trucks with people in the back that were screaming 60 mph down the smooth but curvy road.

We finally picked an SUV, figuring that at least we wouldn't fall out on the turns and bumps. The gentleman kindly told us we had been heading towards town the first time, so we hiked a little longer over ground we had already covered with our hand out. A handsome young man driving an SUV stopped. He had handcuffs on his belt. He had no uniform nor was the vehicle marked. He said he was a policeman from Dominica and had been recruited for a 3-year term, a common practice. His tour was nearly up, and he would be glad to get back home. I could see why he would miss the lush, green mountains of home on this arid, flat rock.

When queried, he said crime wasn't much of a problem and most of the bad guys were locked up. The population was only 25,000. He said petty thievery was the main problem and violence rare. He was very friendly and dropped us near a rental car store. We got a tiny car and drove over more of the island, making it to a dive shop where we made a reservation. We had tasty appetizers at an outdoor bar near the waterfront and dinner at an excellent restaurant nearby. The drive back and the short hike to the dinghy in the black, dark night weren't too bad. We turned in early and slept well.

Today, Glen and I did two great scuba dives off West Caicos, an island about ten miles away. The coral was in wonderful shape, the fish life abundant, the water crystal clear, and the weather delightful. We saw two large rays, a big grouper, garden eels, and myriad of fish. We were in sixty feet of water and swam over the edge and down a wall that drops to six thousand feet. Quite a thrill! A sensation almost like diving off a cliff. On the way back, the driver stopped the boat not far from ours to show us a ten-foot-long hammerhead shark.

On the way to the dive site I was tired, so I laid down on the deck of the boat in the shade of the scuba tanks. Glen and I had attached our regulators to two of them. After about fifteen minutes, I felt refreshed and got up to look around. Not five seconds after that, the boat rolled and the tank with my regulator on it fell onto the deck where my head had just been. I didn't realize you needed to reattach the shock cord to the top of the tank. I'd rather be lucky than good.

March 12. Sunday. We did a night dive on Wednesday that I did not enjoy. I was cold and there was one dive master to eleven divers, the visibility was terrible, and my mask kept fogging and filling with water. I was lost most of the time. The only thing I saw was a large lobster, which we couldn't take as it was a protected park.

We flew around the island in a small seaplane on Friday. The views were spectacular and the water landing neat. In one of his songs, Jimmy Buffett says that is just about his favorite thing to do. The takeoff got my heart rate up—it looked like we were going to hit a small island. Glen owns a Piper Cub on floats.

I see a flying boat
And I get a lump in my throat
And I say Someday I Will
"Someday I Will"—Jimmy Buffett

There is a twelve-mile-long, cream-colored, powdery sand beach in Grace Bay on the northern coast protected by a reef about a half-mile offshore. We ate lunch at a place called LeDeck in the middle of it. The view was spectacular—the prettiest beach I've seen. They are developing it at an alarming rate, but it hasn't gotten crowded yet. There are only a couple of large, all-inclusive resorts that have bunches of tourists. The rest is nearly deserted.

The boat is messy right now, though I finally found a place to do laundry, so at least that's done. I'll probably wait a few days to clean the boat so I won't have to do it twice. This island is mostly rock and sand, so the boat gets really dusty. The anchorage is shallow (7.4 ft at low tide!) but the boat seems to be holding okay. It is a little crowded but not too bad.

Mostly people come and go, but unless I get a really bad weather forecast, I'll stay put. There is a slightly more protected spot around the corner if things get nasty. I can probably find a neighbor to help. It is a long way from here to the airport and the last half-mile of road is terrible, but it is a long way to take the boat around to the north coast and there is a cut in the reef up there that can be dangerous-to-impossible if a large north swell comes up.

About 1:30 a.m. last night the boat was really hobby-horsing (pitching fore and aft). The wind was gusting to 25 knots and a chop was rolling in. I was afraid it might pull the anchor out, so I decided to set a second anchor. I did it in the dark, as flashlights adversely affect my night vision. I started the engine, motored to the spot I had decided was best, and moved smartly to the bow. The secondary anchor has thirty feet of chain and the rest rope. I thought I had it laid out and ready to go. As I wrapped the rope around the windlass, I pinched a couple of pea-sized chunks of skin off of my index finger. It made a bloody mess on the foredeck, but I should heal in time.

Internet access is pricey here. I pay $15/hour at the best place I've found. I paid 60 cents a minute yesterday! The grocery stores are well-stocked but more expensive than in the Dominican Republic. They are supposed to be cheaper than in the Bahamas though, so we should probably try to provision here for the rest of the trip, if possible. Mark will be happy to hear that they have over fifty types of hot sauce for sale at two area restaurants.

March 15. Wednesday. I had a little excitement today. There is a couple anchored next to me. He came by yesterday to ask if I knew of a mechanic. His engine was overheating. I told him about a guy I had heard of but knew nothing about. This morning

I stopped by on my way to do email to see if he had had any luck. They had found a mechanic, but he refused to ride in the dinghy to his boat. Instead he planned to sail to the commercial dock not far from here. I helped him raise his anchors. He was somewhat in front of our boat so I was a little worried he might drift down on us before he could set the sail. He unfurled the genoa and his wife managed to get by and behind *Halimeda* but sailed close to the front of the boat anchored on the other side of us. He got the sail trimmed just in time.

The dock was a concrete pier at least four feet higher than the boat's deck. The plan was for him to climb up on the dock; I would toss him the lines. Fortunately, there were some huge chains hanging off the side of the dock so I could attach the bow line to one of them. He then was able to climb up on the dock and I got the springs and the stern line to him.

Once he was secure, I left and went to town. I didn't walk today because after lunch the wind really picked up and I wanted to get back to the boat to be sure it was okay. Not long after I arrived, they returned all smiles and waving thumbs up. They called me on the radio. It turns out they just had a bad impeller. They invited me over to their boat for a Coke at 5:30.

They are a fascinating couple. Their boat is from Falmouth, Massachusetts, near Cape Cod, but they both had fairly thick accents. It turns out they were originally from Hungary but have lived in the States for some forty years and have been retired for about four. He is in his 70s, but they look amazingly fit. We had a great evening discussing sailing plans, history, places we'd been, politics, and astronomy. It turns out they were in St. Barts for New Year's too and are also Jimmy Buffett fans. They were fascinated by my tales of the concert we attended.

They had sailed in Venezuela and agreed that the political situation made them quite tense. They did really love the waters and the islands. They were also extremely pleased with Bonaire. It would have been nice to go there, but you can't do it all.

I got a haircut today. It is short, and they trimmed my beard differently. It was getting scraggly. I had shaved the moustache to keep water out of my mask, but it didn't seem to help much. I probably need a new mask, but with so little time left, I will get along without. The dive master thinks it is too wide for my face.

The wind really piped up after I got back on the boat. It was forecast to be 20–25 and I think that is what we have. It is fairly protected from the waves here, but it is so flat that the wind isn't blocked at all. I ran the watermaker for an hour today and haven't run the generator at all.

The finger is healing nicely and isn't festering. I probably can straighten things up tomorrow, Thursday, and clean on Friday. I don't think it is too dirty, but I'm sure our head needs a going-over as it is dusty here.

Things are a little different here. It took me several tries to find the laundry. I was told it was on the way to the airport. I stopped there and was told it was just down the road on the other side. I stopped there and was told it was next door. I stopped there and was told it was down the street. I finally found it in an unfinished cement building with no sign anywhere.

When I went to immigration, I suspected they had moved from where the '98 cruising guide said. A fellow sweeping the sidewalk pointed it out. He said it was in the white house across the road. The "house" was a two-story, large, cement commercial building with "SAMS" on the front. There were several doors, some of which led to shops. I finally found the immigration office, but there was no sign on the outside or inside the office. It's as bad as Trinidad is about signs.

The first time I went there was the morning after a holiday weekend and it was packed. I decided to come back later. The one thing I did notice about both customs and immigration is that they were extremely friendly and helpful, quite different from most places we've been. I was *supposed* to go to immigration within seven days of arriving to get an extension for the cruising permit. I was supposed to pay something for it too. Well, come late Saturday afternoon, I realized they would be closed on Sunday and Monday. Tuesday would make it eight days after I arrived. I stopped back by customs to ask what to do and, I couldn't believe it, the guy looked up my papers since I didn't have my copy with me. He then gave me a cruising permit for free (the cruising guide says you can only get it at immigration, three miles away in town). He didn't even hassle me! I'm sure he was getting ready to close. Seems like there is always something good about every place we go that makes up for the difficult things.

I better close and try to get a little sleep for a change. It is too cold for one blanket and too hot for two. The breeze is nice, though. There is a three-quarters moon tonight. There is supposed to be some weird glowworm phenomena about three days after the full moon here, which should be when the kids are back. Hopefully the wind will have calmed down enough for the water to clear up some so we can see it.

March 27. Monday. There really hasn't been much excitement here lately and I guess that is good. Mercifully, Jennifer and Mark returned last week. Mark's sister Emily, Jen's best friend, Amy, and her good friend, Whitney, spent their spring break with us. It was great to have company again.

We didn't get to do much sailing, as this area doesn't have multiple protected anchorages. The water is quite shallow in the routes between anchorages. I seem to be between weather stations, so I only get partial forecasts.

One day we sailed to the south end of West Caicos, about fifteen miles away. I was expecting a north swell. Unfortunately, it was from the south, making my planned anchorage untenable so we turned around and sailed back to Provo.

The next day we did a dive trip to French Cay, the tiny island I had visited with the Doyons. The water wasn't quite as clear as it was off West Caicos, but the coral was incredible. We saw a spotted eagle ray with a six-foot wingspan and an eight-foot-long tail. Quite impressive.

Since things were calm at French Cay, the next day we sailed there. It is about fourteen miles from Provo, and we had *great* winds. They were on our beam 16–18 knots out of the west. *Halimeda* really kicked up her heels and screamed along at 7.5–8.3 knots for much of the way. The theoretical maximum sustained speed for a boat her length is 8.2 so we were really flying. I had all three sails up and everything was cooking. The water was flat since we were on the banks. The water was only 12–15 feet deep much of the way and crystal clear.

Once again, I was expecting southerly winds and got northerlies. I simply must get better at this weather forecasting. It was a lot easier in the Caribbean. Initially we were doing okay, but after an hour or so, I could see a frontal line approaching. This time of year they are fairly benign. It rained hard and the wind swung around to the north. The highest gusts were only 35 knots. I had the engine on and sat at the helm in case our anchor drug, but it stayed put. I had snorkeled over it to be sure it was dug in. On the other side of the cay the sand is only a couple of inches thick over solid rock, not good for holding. Here it was about a foot thick and that must have been enough. I had checked the areas where we might have swung to be sure there were no shallow spots. It is so strange to be anchoring in nine feet of water, most places further south were much deeper. Deep water takes more chain and is a test, shallow takes less chain and is usually easier. However, the worry is that waves will cause you to hit bottom.

Unfortunately, the wind stayed out of the north making it exactly on the nose for the trip back to Provo the next day. Since the channel was so narrow, we couldn't raise the sails. By then the chop had built to the point that it made for slow going. The short, steep waves would almost stop the boat. Usually we can motor in flat water at well over 7 knots, this trip we were lucky to average 3.5 and the waves would often slow us to less than 2 knots. Still it was a nice day and the guests got some sun.

The next day we dropped our three guests off at the airport early in the morning and went back to the boat for a nap. We should have waited. The next day we heard that their flight had been cancelled due to mechanical problems and they'd spent most of the day at the Provo airport and had to overnight in Miami. There are only two flights a day here so you can't catch another one an hour later like at most hubs in the States.

Tomorrow Linda finally returns. I missed her more this time than any other time. We were apart almost four weeks, the longest we've ever been apart. At least I have been able to call her and get email. Absence does make the heart grow fonder.

April

April 1. Saturday. Today was not a good day. It started out on the wrong foot. It was uncharacteristically rainy and cold this morning. A very unusual cold front swung much further south than ever before. In fact, they reported snow and ice on some of the higher elevations here on Provo. It was the first time in living memory that this had occurred.

As a result of the rain, I slept in. Unfortunately, one of the port lights (side windows) on the boat had a leak I didn't know about. It soaked and ruined half our books, Linda's computer, and our spare GPS navigation instrument. Not a good start to the day. All our dried beans, some of our rice, and Mark's baseball card collection was soaked too. Fortunately, Jennifer's Barbie doll collection was stowed on the other side of the boat and escaped unharmed.

After the cleanup everyone was in a foul mood, so I decided to cook breakfast in hopes of cheering us up. I made my nearly famous goat meat, red beans, and okra omelets but for some reason they didn't taste right. Maybe the eggs were old. It didn't improve the mood much.

After breakfast, Linda and I got in a little spat. She insisted that I install an electric flush toilet since she was tired of pumping the handle fifty times every time she went. I maintained it cost too much—over $200!—and that it would make too much noise. We finally compromised on the propane-operated model, which is about half the price and a little quieter. The only other problem with it is the potential for explosion and fire, but we decided to take the risk.

Our arguing must have infected Jennifer and Mark; they started debating wedding issues. They were locked in their cabin so I couldn't hear all that was said. They haven't spoken to each other since, but at least they are both still on the boat.

We wanted to leave today so I went to clear out customs and immigration. As it turned out, I had failed to check one box on one of the many forms I filled out when I cleared in nearly a month ago. The official became very angry and threatened to arrest me and impound our boat. Finally, he calmed down and agreed to let me go if I paid a $5,000 fine. It seemed a little excessive to me, but I promptly wrote a check and left.

Today just isn't my day. We went to raise the anchor and found it had become stuck under a rock. No matter how hard we pulled, it wouldn't come loose. We had to take a hacksaw to cut the chain and leave it there. Fortunately, we have a spare—we will be able to anchor again.

Once we got the sails up and were underway, my mood improved. It was such a great sail that everyone started to cheer up a little. I knew it was too good to last. As we were leaving the island in a very narrow channel, a boatload of Haitian immigrants sailed in front of us and cut us off. They stopped and demanded something. Since none of us speaks Creole, we couldn't understand what it was they wanted. Finally, a little boy who spoke some English told us they were asking for Grey Poupon mustard. Fortunately, we had a case onboard. We gave them two bottles and they went away happy.

We were all snoozing in the cockpit, just sailing along slowly in light winds, when a huge blue whale surfaced right beside the boat. We were so shocked we didn't know what to do. The only bad thing was that we had left the windows open and our books got soaked again.

We must have been tired as we somehow all fell asleep while underway. As a result, we managed to sail right up on a beach. Since it is soft sand the boat wasn't hurt. Still it is kind of embarrassing to be sitting high and dry on the beach. There aren't any towboats here so I was afraid we would be stuck.

Fortunately, there is a tow truck available. We need to drive a big stake into the water and take a rope from the boat around the stake and back to the truck on land. I hope it works. If not, we may need to hire a helicopter and they are expensive …

… And the alarm just went off. It turns out that the above was just a vivid bad dream. How appropriate that it happened on April 1st.

April 3. Monday. We left Provo, Turks and Caicos, and motored for two hours to West Caicos. We picked up a dive mooring off the western shore and spent the night. Only three other boats were visible, about two miles away. We were hanging above the wall where I dove with Glen. The boat was in fifty feet of water; we could see the bottom clearly even in the fading afternoon light. Just a few yards off the stern, the wall drops straight down over 6,000 feet! On the next passage we will pass over water 15,000 feet deep. Let's hope we don't drop anything.

We got up at first light and sailed seven hours to Mayaguana, the first Bahamian island of the trip. (The remaining islands will all be in the Bahamas.) We anchored on the west coast with no other boats in sight. We got up at first light and sailed six hours to Samana. Good evidence points to this as the place where Columbus first landed and discovered America.[1] It was a magical feeling to think that this famous mariner probably saw this same spot over five hundred years ago. Since there are no permanent residents, and only a few tumbled down buildings

[1] See *National Geographic,* November 1986. vol. 170.

and a couple of fishing shacks ashore, it must look much like it did way back then.

We reached the anchorage by sight, navigating through a narrow, winding cut in a shallow reef. We were the only boat. We were behind a long, narrow island in a large, protected sand-bottomed spot surrounded by reefs. The water was crystal clear, and the snorkeling was some of the best of the trip. I saw a rare Spanish lobster that has neither pinchers like the Maine variety, nor feelers like the Caribbean kind. We saw several queen triggerfish, trunkfish, a small stingray, many blue tangs, and brightly-colored parrotfish. This island is somewhat out of the way and the anchorage difficult to find, making it more pristine than most places.

We decided to spend two nights there to rest. After sleeping in, we ate breakfast and dinghied to shore. We went for a long walk on the mostly deserted beach and saw two local fishermen that had come from Acklins Island, twenty miles away.

Next, we went snorkeling at several places around the anchorage. The coral was in great shape and the fish life abundant. I quit early and the others went to one more spot, about fifty yards off the stern of the boat. They saw a six-foot shark. They calmly swam back to the boat only to realize that the shark had followed them. He swam around the boat several times, as if looking for a hand out, or a hand! A large barracuda also swam by. Since we were eighty miles from the nearest hospital, it was good that we escaped injury.

Yesterday, we slept in and waited for good light to leave through the cut in the reef. The wind had piped up, making the exit exciting. I'm glad the conditions were milder when we entered. We then set off on a twenty-hour overnight passage to Georgetown, in the Exumas. As forecast, the winds were 15–20 knots and the waves 6–9 feet. This made for an exciting and challenging passage. Still, the boat and we handled it well. All but Mark felt a little queasy, as it had been a while since we had bounced that much.

The entrance to Georgetown is a five-mile tortuous passage through reef-strewn shallow waters. We had sloppy conditions and marginal light, but the GPS guided us flawlessly. We picked a spot to anchor well away from other boats, had a big breakfast, and I went ashore to clear customs. I returned with our mail containing a dozen sailing, computer, and news magazines. We took a long, well deserved nap, showered, and went ashore for a fish dinner and to watch the NCAA men's basketball championship game. Tomorrow we will be off in search of laundry and internet access.

April 11. Tuesday. We are anchored behind Highborne Cay, about thirty miles southeast of Nassau near the northern end of the Exumas. Georgetown is near the southern end of that Bahamian island chain. So far, I have been less than impressed with the Bahamas. It cost 100 USD to enter the country. I have become accustomed to waiting a while to clear in, but here it took nearly two days! After paying my entry fee at the unmarked customs office, I was told that the immigration officer wouldn't be in town until 10:30 a.m. the next day. Upon arriving at the immigration office, we waited until after noon with no officer in sight. We decided to go have lunch. Once back, he finally arrived and was slowly processing the long line of entrants. He only allowed one party in his office at a time. After taking thirty minutes with the party ahead of me, a friend of his cut in line and spent another twenty minutes talking with him about personal matters. When I finally got my turn, it took him all of one minute to stamp my papers.

The only internet access was three miles out of town. Taxies are few and expensive, so I walked most of the way. I hitchhiked the last half mile with a very friendly, one-armed local who told me he was starting a fly fishing business. Internet access was in a "resource center" for the College of the Bahamas. I entered a room containing thirty PCs, but each had two large signs proclaiming, "DO NOT USE THIS COMPUTER!" The only computer available was a Mac, which could not read my PC disk so I could not download my messages. I was not impressed.

I tried to register my cellular phone without success. I got a recorded message proclaiming my call was being forwarded to the "roaming center" after which I was either cut off or got a busy signal. It may be just as well as the cruising guides say that a $500 deposit is required to use the service.

There is room in the various Georgetown anchorages for thousands of boats. I estimate that over five hundred were visible from where we anchored. The water is relatively shallow, the holding fair to good, and the dinghy rides to town quite choppy and wet. The grocery store was well-stocked except for fresh produce. We must have been between mail boat arrivals.

We had a fairly good meal at the Two Turtles restaurant. After dinner, we watched the first half of the NCAA men's college basketball championship game at a TV mounted inside the cover of a small, square outdoor bar. Mark managed to insult two groups of fellow viewers. First, he complained that he didn't like one of the sportscasters. The fellow seated near us said that he was a childhood friend of this celebrity and grew up next door to him. Next Jen and Mark were debating which car to buy. She said they should consider the Volvo, he said they were too young to buy one. The two ladies next to them said they both owned Volvos. One had bought one just last week. Oops … at least everyone was good-natured about it!

The next day we pulled up to the only fuel dock in town and filled up with diesel and water. It turns out that the water was only partially desalinized—now our coffee, milk, juice, and water are all too salty to drink.

Even though a cold front had just passed, and winds and waves were fairly high, we decided to leave. The western route out of Georgetown is even more tortuous and reef-strewn than the eastern entrance. The exit was very rough, the clouds and waves made eyeball navigation difficult. Once again, the GPS and extremely accurate Explorer Charts saved the day.

The Exumas are a group of 365 small, low islands that form a long, curved chain. On the eastern side is the deep Exuma

Sound. On the western side, the shallow water is called the Exuma Banks. The passages between the islands, called "cuts," are narrow, rough, and contain strong currents. We had to exit the Banks through a cut and sail outside on the sound for about 25 miles. Since the sound is exposed to the winds for nearly a hundred miles, the waves were 8–12 feet. The winds were 20–25 knots. This makes for exhilarating and challenging sailing. Fortunately, the winds were abaft the beam, so we had a broad reach, one of the fastest, easiest points of sail. With a little boost from the current, we went screaming along at 8 knots, or more, over the ground.

The cut back onto the Banks was narrow, exceedingly rough, downwind, and had a strong current. These conditions make maneuvering difficult and potentially dangerous. Mark took the helm and I navigated. Jennifer watched for rocks ahead and breaking waves astern. Linda stayed below and prayed. The waves would take the boat and toss it from side to side. Mark constantly was rapidly turning the wheel one way and then the other trying to maintain some form of straight course. He did a great job in difficult conditions.

Once we'd finally made it through the cut, the water was as calm as a millpond, though the current was still strong and the route quite narrow between shallow sandbars. We quickly found a good but small anchorage behind Musha Island where an upscale mini-resort is being built. We had it all to ourselves. Everything was fine until about 6:30 a.m. the next day when someone lit a bonfire ashore directly upwind from us. They must have been burning construction waste as the smoke was extremely foul. Black soot and ash descended on the boat. It was hard to breath. We quickly raised anchor and left this otherwise beautiful spot. Turns out magician David Copperfield was building an exquisite resort that sleeps twenty-four. (Now, in 2019, it costs $42,000–$60,000 *per night*!)

Sailing inside on the Banks to our next anchorage was calm and relaxing compared to our trip up the Sound the day before. The wind was still good, but the islands blocked the waves. Once again, the wind was on the beam and we made great time.

We anchored behind an island called Big Major's Spot. It has two interesting features. Some scenes from the James Bond movie *Thunderball* and the movie *Splash* were filmed in an underwater cave near there. It was cold, rough, and a long way from where we anchored so we didn't explore the cave. The second feature is a swimming wild pig that lives on the beach by the anchorage. When you dinghy up to the beach, he swims out to meet you. We gave him some leftover salad, took videos and pictures, and went back to the boat. He was quite large but less than handsome.

The next day we sailed to Wardwick Wells, an anchorage with moorings inside a national park. All the moorings were full, so we had to anchor over a mile outside in shallow, rough water. We dinghied over and snorkeled. The coral was nice and the fish life abundant in the small area we visited.

In the afternoon Linda and I went to "happy hour" at the park ranger's headquarters. Several cruisers brought snacks and drinks and swapped stories. The ranger was gone but his wife and their two small children (one a baby and the other in the terrible twos) were holding down the fort. The older one, a boy, was running all over the place and screaming at the top of his lungs. He was also running around on the high dock. I hoped he knew how to swim!

We waited a second day in hopes of getting a mooring, but a cold front with high winds was forecast so no one left. We all went ashore and took a long hike. The terrain was rugged and the flora and fauna interesting. The paths were marked after a fashion and we had a rudimentary trail map. There were several holes in the rock, some trapping fresh water.

On Monday we got up and sailed thirty miles to Highborne Cay. The winds were 20–25 knots and the seas quite choppy even though we were inside on the Banks. This made for a fast but wet and wild ride. The last six miles were hard on the wind, so I furled the genoa and motorsailed with a single reef in the main. With two miles to go to the anchorage, I tacked—and the engine promptly died.

The wind was still blowing, three-foot steep waves were slamming us around, and the boat wouldn't tack with just the staysail and reefed main. I rolled out about a third of the genoa. It was slapping loudly since it doesn't have the right shape when roller reefed this way. Still, it did allow us to sail to within about 60 degrees of the wind at about 4–5 knots. More importantly, if I fell off the wind just a bit, we could tack. I had to wait until the genoa was backwinded before releasing the sheet. Fortunately, the anchorage was relatively wide open and only a few other boats were anchored there. Since I thought we would be protected on the Banks, I had failed to fully secure the anchor. It was hanging off the roller. Did I mention that our windlass began slipping badly a couple of days ago and was nearly useless? I was at the helm and Mark went forward to drop the anchor. With some difficulty, he got it down.

Since I had limited maneuverability, we stopped quite a way out and it was still quite choppy there. I tried the engine again and it promptly started. Mark and I raised the heavy anchor by hand, motored closer to shore in somewhat calmer and more protected water, and dropped the secondary anchor. The primary 55 lb Delta Anchor is on all chain and quite a handful to raise without the windless. The secondary anchor is a 60 lb Bruce, but only has thirty feet of chain and the rest rope. This makes raising it manually easier—rope is considerably lighter than chain. At least we know we can get by without the motor if we have room to maneuver.

April 12. Wednesday. Yesterday, we got up early and sailed thirty-five miles across the Yellow Banks to Nassau. The winds were still blowing 20–25 knots. Since we would be more on a beam reach for most of the trip, I had the genoa all the way out and the full main up. It was slightly too much sail for these conditions, but *Halimeda* does fine with too much canvas up. It makes for a faster, though rougher, passage.

Our main concern on this trip is that there are large, shallow coral heads along the way. If you have calm conditions and full sunlight overhead, they are quite visible. We had extremely rough water and a cloudy sky. Fortunately, just as we got to the area with the keel-busting coral, the sun broke through and we had enough light to spot them. I stayed on the foredeck getting soaked and pointed the way around and between them. Mark took the helm and Jen and Linda maintained a lookout from either side of the cockpit. We threaded our way through them without hitting one.

Nassau was choppy, crowded with boat traffic, and windy. We got the last available slip in the third marina we tried. The entrance to the marina was quite narrow, but we had several line-handlers ashore and I greased the landing without hitting anything. I've mentioned that Island Packets don't handle well under power, but I've finally learned a few tricks. Either that or I got lucky.

April 15. Saturday. Our short visit to Nassau was pleasant enough. After we got the boat settled in, we ate lunch at the Chinese restaurant that was part of the marina. The food was quite good, though not as good as Bo Ling's back home. We found a very complete grocery store with reasonable prices. I spent some time trading mechanical advice for dental advice with a marine mechanic. I decided to wait until we get to Miami to fix our windlass and he decided not to get his silver fillings replaced with composite.

Wednesday morning, Linda and Jennifer cleaned the boat while Mark and I changed the fuel filters on the main engine. Hopefully that will prevent another shut down at a critical moment. Mark and I walked over a mile to the nearest internet access. The place was modern, and the machines seemed fine, but they didn't have enough memory, so it took nearly five minutes to retrieve each message. Since I had eighteen in my inbox, I had to pick which ones to read. Internet access in the Bahamas has been abysmal.

We spent the rest of the day wandering around the Atlantis Resort on Paradise Island. It is an amazing place that just opened last year. It has a huge casino, over thirty-five restaurants, thousands of rooms, a gargantuan saltwater aquarium, an enormous beach/water sports complex, and a fantastic marina full of mega yachts. The décor was fascinating: huge fountains, immense columns, huge complex moldings and gargoyles, gigantic Chihuly blown glass sculptures, and intricate astrological mosaics on the ceilings. Towering bronze sculptures of dolphins, sea horses, and other marine creatures adorned the exterior roofs.

We ate a delicious, if pricey, lunch in a large, open restaurant while watching sharks, tuna, jacks, rays, scuba divers, and schools of smaller fish swim in the three-hundred-foot-long floor-to-ceiling aquarium that made up two walls of the restaurant. The other side opened into one of the main lobbies of the hotel with large double staircases and tall columns topped with giant seahorse sculptures and water cascading down them into pools. We were impressed.

We tromped from one end of the complex to the other, browsing the upscale shops, dropping coins in the slots, watching sports and the stock market tumble in the multi-TV sports bar, checking out the grand ballroom, and people watching. After two hours we finished off with ice cream overlooking the marina. It was a memorable visit and we all vowed to return.

The weather was marginal, but we decided to press on. The trip from the marina to the open ocean was action-packed. The waterway is narrow and congested. We had to maneuver under two bridges, dodge many boats, watch the depth, and gawk at cruise ships, mega yachts, navy vessels, and assorted other craft moored and anchored along our route. Oh, we also had to get out of the way of seaplanes landing and taking off. Jennifer steered while I navigated, stared, filmed, and photographed the sights.

Once we reached open water, things got a little lumpy. There were 20–25 knot winds and 6–8 feet seas. Friday the 13th came on Thursday this month. As I was moving a preventer line, I got whacked in the nose by a genoa sheet. I didn't even notice that it also flicked my glasses off and into the drink. I needed a new pair anyway and I'm just glad it didn't knock off my Le Select/Jimmy Buffett hat. Then, out of the corner of my eye, I saw the boom gybing just in time to duck. It most certainly would have knocked me unconscious into the sea. Not a pleasant thought. Finally, the boat rolled just as I was stepping from the cockpit into the companionway. I slipped and hit my temple on the opening. It wasn't hard enough to make me see stars, but it could have been much worse. I must be getting cocky. At least my luck is holding up.

Once we got the sails rigged, things settled down. We had a pleasant, if rolly, trip to Chubb Cay where we anchored, exposed to a quartering swell. I rigged a bridle so that we'd pitch more than rolled, which is a less distressing motion, but we spent a rocky night.

Yesterday we got up at dawn and headed to the Great Brahma Banks. Wind and seas were high for the two hours it took us to reach them. Once there, the seas settled down nicely. We had enough wind to sail most of the way. We passed through one rapidly-moving squall with 35-knot winds and lots of rain. Things settled down until about 4:00 p.m. when we got a call from a nearby boat asking us to call the marina ahead for a reservation for them. I hadn't noticed that the forecast had just changed, now calling for high winds that evening. We decided to join them. Soon we were enveloped in a large rainstorm. There was little wind, so we had to motor. Instead of passing as most squalls do, this one seemed to hang over us. It followed us for the next two hours all the way to the marina. We could only see fifty feet ahead of us at most. Lightning danced all around us threatening to wipe out all our navigation instruments, computers, radar, and autopilot. Fortunately, just as we reached the marina, it lifted enough that we could see the way in.

Navigation would have been very tough without instruments. Jennifer drove the boat and Mark and I handled the lines. Another smooth landing. We are getting better at this.

But the rain continued unabated. We elected to eat ashore and almost crashed a private party by accident. Cat Cay is a private, very upscale island south of Bimini and just fifty miles from Miami. The marina, and a restaurant, shop, and grocery are open to the public, the rest is private—off limits. I thought the private club was the public restaurant. We asked the lady who greeted us if this was a private affair. She said yes, the restaurant is the next building down.

Dinner was good. We ate in a small bar next to the restaurant where the dress code allows shorts. A group of fishermen led by a large, loud, inebriated man entertained us by bantering back and forth with us. Even though this is an upscale place, fishermen are similar the world over. "Give a man a fish and he will eat for a day, teach a man to fish and he will spend all day in a boat drinking beer."

April 17. Yesterday we arrived in Miami. The trip was uneventful. The bad weather had passed. Unfortunately, the wind went too so we had to motor the forty miles and our autopilot gave up the ghost, so we had to hand steer. Still, it was a pleasant, calm trip. As we approached Miami, we could see a huge, violent thunderstorm just south of our destination. We even saw a small funnel-shaped cloud drop from the base of the system. It didn't turn into a tornado, but it looked like it might. We asked, "Are we back in Kansas?"

This closes my outbound track. *Halimeda* is in Miami Beach Marina again, what had been the first stop on my trip down from Florida's west coast. My family hadn't joined me until St. Thomas, and they are leaving me here. I had help bringing the boat here from the west coast of Florida and will have students aboard for the trip to the Chesapeake. Still, this represents a closure of sorts.

I have many emotions. I remember writing about my ambivalence as I was preparing for this adventure. I feel that way again. Although I am sorry it is nearly over, in a way I am relieved too. We had a wonderful time, met fascinating people, saw incredible sites, had unforgettable experiences, ate fabulous food, got to know each other and ourselves better, grew in strength and confidence, and learned a great deal about this part of the world.

I am relieved that no one became ill or was injured and that the boat survived without major damage or breakdown. I haven't spoken about the sense of responsibility a captain feels to his or her crew and ship. It was doubly so on this trip since I had with me three of the four people I care about most in this world. Was it luck, preparation, planning, skill, or divine intervention? Who knows! I am just glad we pulled it off.

I will miss the great times and adventures we had; the spectacular sunsets, the warm weather, the beautiful water, swimming with a kaleidoscope of fishes and corals, the physical and mental challenge of sailing, planning, navigating, and exploring, the delicious food, the long talks, the time to read books, think, relax, and rest. I won't miss the hard work, the heat and humidity of some places, the insects chewing my flesh, the bumps, bruises, cuts and scrapes, the occasional anxiety, fear, and boredom, or the exhaustion after several sleepless nights in a row. On balance, though, it was a *great* trip.

I couldn't have pulled this off alone. I have many people to thank. I am so grateful to Linda for putting up with me and sharing my dream. She is much less enthralled with sailing than I am. She suffers from motion sickness, doesn't swim, and misses her friends and home. She has been a real trooper to endure the unpleasant parts of this trip. I have come to love and respect her even more.

Jennifer provided the inspiration years ago when she said, "Dad, when I graduate from high school, let's take a year off and sail around the world." Her intelligence and strength inspire us all. She can calmly steer the boat into the narrowest spot, direct us when we are steering, see and point out the best solution to the problem at hand, and whip up a mean pizza.

Mark has been wonderful to be with. He is so fun, so motivating, and has become a great sailor. His family and friends must have thought he had lost his mind for going along with his future in-laws in such close quarters for a whole year. Not everyone would delay starting his career, be away from loved ones, and take a leap of faith like he did. He has been a great help fixing things, taking late night and early morning watches, cooking, cleaning, washing dishes (one of his least favorite things), and helping with the web page. Besides, it has been great to have someone to talk with about computers.

Thanks to Libby for allowing us to be so far away for so long and for motivating us to go see Jimmy Buffett. Thanks for keeping in touch and coming to visit us. She is the one I missed the most on this trip.

I am so grateful for my business partners who worked so hard while I was away playing. Also, for my staff for pulling together and keeping the practice running smoothly while I was gone, to my brother-in-law and sister-in-law, Steve and Sandy, for keeping the house from falling apart while we were away, and to our office manager, Carol, for running both the practice and my personal life when I was out of touch. I owe them all— big time. Thanks also to all my friends and family who read my ramblings, wrote kind words of encouragement. That kept us going through the bad times and motivated us in the good. Thank heaven for the internet.

Linda and I went for a walk last night. The sky was ablaze with a spectacular red and grey sunset. It seemed a fitting metaphor for the trip to end with the calm and beauty of nature after a storm. I feel at peace.

May and the Trip's End

May 2. Tuesday. Miami Beach is a marvelous place. On South Beach, everyone seems to be young, buff, on roller skates, and speaking a beautiful foreign language. Walking up and down

Ocean Avenue, one feels a carnival atmosphere. Quaint sidewalk cafes, crowded open-air bars, and renovated small hotels make strolling entertaining. An old man with a Taco Bell dog dressed in a colorful cape in his bicycle's basket competes with a young man with one yellow and one brown boa constrictor on his neck for the attention of the passers-by. The dancing couples on stages are shown live on a street-side color TV monitor. A tattoo parlor has a short line of waiting patrons. The artist is visibly busy plying his trade just inside the large doorway. The sidewalk is filled with some tourists but more locals. Everyone is laughing, talking, skating, dining, dancing, and generally having a great time.

The cars of South Beach are exotic too. Ferraris, Rolls Royce's, Jags, and limousines are ubiquitous. Only a Ford Expedition and a Mercury Navigator both stretched as long as our boat into nearly-identical twin limos caught people's attention. I heard, and saw out of the corner of my eye, a canary yellow Ferrari screamingly accelerate. A loud bang happened just after I lost sight of it. I walked over to find it had crashed head-on into a tree. Evidently the driver was uninjured, because when I walked over to see if anyone was hurt, he had already left the scene. What a town! Even hundred-thousand-dollar cars are disposable.

Decommissioning a cruising sailboat is nearly as taxing as equipping one. We spent a day and a half packing up most of our personal items and loading them into a ten-foot U-Haul. Mark, Jennifer, and Linda "volunteered" to drive it back to Kansas City while I stayed onboard arranging for the servicing of some of the boat's systems.

May 5. Friday. The final leg of my journey on *Halimeda* called for me to act as mate while a captain from the Maryland School of Sailing guided four students from Miami to Norfolk, Virginia. The first couple of days of this offshore trip were uneventful and pleasant enough. We rode the Gulf Stream northerly for much of the passage. It amazed me to see *Halimeda*'s 7-plus knots through the water boosted to 11–12 knots over the ground. I'm just glad we weren't going south against the Stream.

My only disappointment on this leg was that they failed to launch the space shuttle across our path as planned. Someday I hope to sail these waters again and watch a night launch.

This trip turned into a bird-watching expedition. Numerous colorful small finches landed onboard to take a rest. They must have been tired—we were seventy-five miles offshore. A large white egret landed aboard for a while. A large sea eagle tried but couldn't find a perch to his liking. The small birds would sit quite close to us. I took a picture of one perched on my head.

According to our captain, Cape Hatteras is one of the five most dangerous places in the world to sail, right up there with Cape Horn. So, when the weather fax foretold of a developing gale on a collision course with us as we were about to round the Cape, visions of the Perfect Storm danced in my head. And then it arrived, true to form.

Chapter 20
A Gale Off Hatteras

I am sometimes asked, "What is the worst weather you've sailed in?"

Our year-long voyage in the Caribbean was nearly over, my family had left, and I was moving the boat from Miami, Florida, to Norfolk, Virginia, with a captain and four students from the Maryland School of Sailing for their offshore sailing classes. The captain was a sixty-something, ex-IBM executive with a lot of single handed ocean sailing aboard a 24-foot boat. We were set to sail up the coast.

After a year aboard, I was confident and comfortable. The students were excited and eager to set off. The first couple of days and nights were picture perfect. We had wind on the beam and a boost from the Gulf Stream. When the wind wasn't against them, the waves were benign, and we got an extra 2–4 knots boost of speed by the current. When your maximum speed *without* the current is only 7–8 knots, that's a lot of help.

We had settled into a routine of two people on watch for four hours and then eight hours off. There was little boat traffic, so we had plenty of time to tell stories and learn from the Captain. When sailing alone, sleep deprivation is always a problem, he said. Eventually one starts to hallucinate. He said that he sometimes clearly saw a little man with a thick Scottish accent sitting beside him in the cockpit. They were discussing sail trim one dark night when the Scot said he could better see the sail shape from the water—so the captain jumped overboard, alone and a hundred miles from shore. He immediately realized his mistake and was able to grab a line he was trailing behind the boat and, with great difficulty, pull himself back aboard.

As I said, the captain mentioned in passing that Cape Hatteras is one of the five most dangerous places in the world to sail, every bit as bad as the infamous Cape Horn. Local magnetic variations can mess with compass headings and cause you to sail off course. Diamond Shoals extends much farther off the cape than one would expect and shifting sands cause shallow water to cause grounding many miles from shore where there used to be deep water. The area is known as the Graveyard of the Atlantic. Over the centuries, thousands of ships have sunk in storms or from hitting the shoal.

Did I mention we had decided to sail around Cape Hatteras rather than take the easy way behind the barrier islands in the Intracoastal Waterway?

The next day I was checking the weather and an ominous forecast came across the Navtex weather report: "Developing gale off Hatteras." The unique geography of the region causes weather systems to be much worse than in other areas. I had sailed in thirty mph winds and 8–10 feet seas, but gales, by definition, are up to 50 mph. High winds cause high waves. High waves cause more damage to a sailboat than high winds do. Sailors deal with increasing winds by reefing or reducing the area of sails they have up. Increased winds have a geometric, rather than an arithmetic, increased force. In other words: doubling the speed of the wind *quadruples* the force on the sails rather than doubling it.

We were reefed down when the gale hit. One advantage of the cutter-rigged boat is that it is easy to decrease sail area and get what sail you have up lower and closer to the center of the boat. Still, as the wind reached 50 mph, the sound also quadrupled. It was screaming through the rigging. We steered to keep the wind on the side of the boat and make the chances of broaching less. The waves rolled the boat back and forth, pitching fore and aft, and yawing. One must experience the motion of a boat in a storm to fully appreciate the ferocity and violence.

Fortunately, the waves weren't coming from the stern, something that can "poop," or fill, the cockpit with water. We were doing everything right and the boat was handling the conditions better than we were. One student, a strapping 6' 4" rugby player, was steering the boat when he started to hyperventilate. Walls of green water crashed over the bow and rolled up to the dodger window. We were wearing our foul weather gear, but on deck the wind blew the water up our sleeves and down our necks. It wasn't bitterly cold, but we still needed to be aware of hyperthermia. Below deck in the cabin wasn't much better.

Then, while the rugby player was walking through the salon, the boat rolled. The table was down, and he was thrown against it. His weight tore the piano hinge holding the table from the bulkhead. We "hove to" to make repairs. This maneuver essentially puts the sails in neutral. You make very little progress, but the motion of the boat is much easier compared to the effect of pounding to weather in a gale. To achieve this, we simply tacked but didn't release the head sail. This caused the sails to work against each other, slowing the boat and causing a slick in the water to lessen the effects of the waves—very useful if you need to rest or repair the boat.

Another thing I noticed was an increase in the noise in the rigging or metal wires holding the mast up. At 50-plus knots of wind, it went from a loud whistle to a horrific scream, making conversation nearly impossible. We were all clipped to the boat with harnesses and tethers because falling overboard in these conditions would mean almost certain death.

Sea berths are important in a blue water offshore boat. On *Halimeda,* we had lee cloths tied beside narrow bunks to keep one from falling out of bed as the boat rocked, rolled, tipped, and dipped. It is the only place one can relax all one's muscles and rest. Anywhere else, even sitting down, you are hanging on for dear life. Moving about is even more strenuous. "One hand for yourself and one for the boat" is a saying among sailors. Always have a firm grip on something solid with one hand to avoid slipping, falling, or being tossed across the cabin or off the deck of the boat. Because falling off boat, scores of miles from land especially in rough weather or at night, is a near death sentence.

I remember reading a story about a guy who was sailing alone a couple of miles off the coast of Mexico when his lifeline gave way and he fell overboard. He was trailing a fishing line, but he slowly slid back until the hook was impaled in his palm. The boat continued to drag him though the water until he eventually was able to get the hook out and watch his craft sail away without him. Through super-human effort, he made it to shore only to find steep, razor sharp, jagged rock cliffs further lacerating his hands, feet and body. He kept swimming along the coast until he eventually found a beach. The area was deserted so he staggered until he finally found an uninhabited cabin with food and water. He decided to stay put until his wounds healed. Eventually a Mexican park ranger found him naked and disheveled. Unable to speak Spanish, he was arrested and thrown into a Mexican prison, not an ideal place for a gringo. Eventually, his friends found his boat and started searching for him. After several days of incarceration, they found him, and he was released. This story makes you want to be *sure* you stay aboard the boat, alone or with crew.

The gale lasted for twelve hours, with 12–16 feet seas, but we were screaming along in the Gulf Stream at 12 knots, so we made great progress the whole time.

By dawn the next day, wind and waves were back to normal. Later than afternoon, we pulled into Norfolk, Virginia, and let the students off, hopefully the wiser for their experience.

Later, I decided to sell *Halimeda* to Tom Tursi of the Maryland School of Sailing, but when Tom decided to replace her a decade later, I bought her back! The surveyor said, "I've done thousands of purchase surveys in my twenty-year career and can't ever remember doing one for someone buying a boat back!"

Chapter 21
Home Again

The students left at Norfolk and Captain Bill and I took two days to sail *Halimeda* up the Chesapeake to Rock Hall, Maryland, her home for the upcoming season. We did a drive-by of carrier row, spent a night on an island in the middle of the Bay, had our GPS go out as we passed an abandoned ship used by the Navy for target practice, and feasted on blue point crabs near Annapolis. I then spent a day and a half removing the rest of my personal gear from the boat and placing it in storage. It was not quite as big a job as loading it up a year ago had been.

Glen Doyon and his wife Nancy had helped me sail *Halimeda* from Puerto Rico to St. Thomas, and from the Dominican Republic to the Turks and Caicos. Glen volunteered to fly me to Ohio to meet Libby. He had a Piper Cub that was built in 1946, two years before I was born. He and his brother restored it when they were in college. The plane has floats, so Glen flew it to the marina and landed just fifty yards from *Halimeda.* The wings were covered with a treated fabric that gave when you touch it. It was a delightful evening, so we flew with a window and door open. The view was amazing. The cars, trains, houses, and animals looked like toys. The countryside was quite green. We saw a herd of deer grazing near a pond full of ducks and geese. Horses, cattle, and people were all clearly visible, a few hundred feet below us.

I had to sit in the front seat, with my bag stuffed between my feet as there was very little space. To add to the excitement, Glen told me we might be out of fuel when we still had twenty minutes to go. He said I shouldn't worry if the engine quit, as he would just land on the water. We were over a river for most of the last half of the trip, so I wasn't really concerned.

We made it to the seaplane base in Philadelphia, where he keeps his plane, without incident. When he filled up the plane, it took 11.7 gallons of gas. The plane holds 12. At four gallons an hour, that meant we'd had just over four minutes of flight time left. A few years later, Glen had engine failure on another plane and landed on a Phoenix freeway during rush hour. Any landing you walk away from is a good one.

The next day, Glen flew me in a friend's twin-engine plane to Oxford, Ohio. I made sure it had plenty of gas. When I arrived in Ohio, Libby and I drove the ten hours to Kansas City. It was great to catch up on her life and to finally be home again. All good things must come to an end. I was on my way home at last. I kept asking myself *Am I really going home, or did I leave my home on the boat?* What a journey it had been.

I saw my first patients in over a year and didn't know who was dreading it more, them or me. I was amazed that I hadn't lost my touch. It's like riding a bicycle, I guess. It was great to see my staff again; they had kept things running so smoothly in my absence.

Soon after I was back in the swing of things, it was thundering and lightning one night. Jennifer came in and asked if it felt good not to worry about getting struck like we always did on the boat. Lightning at sea is one thing I wouldn't miss. As the days went on, I knew I would miss all the good times we had. But I had memories to savor.

To this day, I can't believe we pulled it off. It really was a dream come true.

Chapter 22
Running Aground Mid-Life

Be good and you will be lonesome
Be lonesome and you will be free
Live a lie and you will live to regret it
That's what livin' is to me
—Jimmy Buffett quoting Mark Twain, in "That's What Living Is to Me"

I met Linda on a blind date when she was seventeen and I was eighteen. My dorm roommate had a date with her friend, but he liked Linda better, so he suggested we double date and try to switch during the evening. I liked Linda better too; the switch didn't happen. When we got back to the dorm, I told CJ, "I'm probably going to marry her."

We dated through college and got married after my fourth year. I sometimes wonder if I married her because she could work and help put me through school, or did I *really* love her? Now I ask myself: why didn't I try communicating with her? Why didn't we work harder on the marriage?

The late 60s and early 70s were difficult times. Vietnam and Watergate consumed the news. I guess I was more worried about staying in school to avoid dying in a rice paddy in southeast Asia than working on my marriage. I knew she would get a well-paying job after she graduated. She made $8,000 the first year and we thought, "How could we even *spend* that much money?" Gas was 36 cents a gallon, beer was a quarter. We were paying $135 a month to rent a nice two-bedroom apartment. I would write a check for $5 and it would last most of the week. I later realized that although you can marry more money in an hour than you can make in a lifetime, if you only marry for money, you will earn every penny. We were both so focused on school when we were first married that we didn't take time to work on our marriage.

* * *

Chicago is a major dental town. Its dental society holds an annual meeting every February. Some years it is better attended than the national American Dental Association's meeting. When I was a junior in dental school, a local dental supply house sponsored a trip to the Chicago midwinter dental meeting. Being a farm boy from Kansas, I guess I just assumed that Chicago was about like Kansas City. We rode the train, leaving Kansas City's Union Station at midnight. There was plenty of beer on the train and a crap game in the men's restroom. Nobody got any sleep on the way, but when you are twenty-two you don't really need much sleep. I was amazed when I got to Chicago to see that it was much larger than Kansas City. We would joke, saying, "Golly, look at all them tall buildings." We secretly really felt that way.

As a budding dentist it was great to see all the types of equipment and supplies. Companies often introduce new products at this meeting. There were lots of parties sponsored by the companies and I tried to attend everyone I could. This was my first time hailing and riding in a cab. It was also my first time staying in a hotel.

Over the years I attended the same meeting nearly every year and was amazed at its growth. For the first few years it was held at the historic old Chicago Hilton on Michigan Avenue, but when the meeting outgrew the space it was moved to the huge McCormick Convention Hall.

* * *

My parents neither drank or smoked and discouraged me from doing so. We didn't know about drugs back then. Mother was a member of the temperance union and a devout Methodist. Her father and mine used Copenhagen chewing tobacco surreptitiously in the barn. I do not remember any member of my immediate family drinking alcohol. It wasn't served at family gatherings or holiday celebrations. My mother's family emigrated from Sweden, and Scandinavians do have a reputation for having problems with alcohol, so I'm sure there were abusers on her side of the family. My dad's mother's father was reported to have had a serious drinking problem that led him to abandon his family and disappear in Kansas City to a life of sin and degradation.

Because I didn't grow up around alcohol, I didn't know how to handle my first exposure. When I was about fifteen, we were riding around town in a friend's car when someone of age, which was eighteen for 3.2% beer in Kansas at the time, procured a quart of beer for each of us. We ended up in the drive-in theater on the edge of town. I was feeling okay after drinking the beer but wanted more. Someone said our classmate worked the projector and that he cleaned the lens with grain alcohol. He added a few ounces to our empty beer bottles, and we drank it straight. I didn't realize it was stronger than the beer I had just had. By the time I got home, I was violently ill. I told my mom I had the flu. I paid for it dearly the next morning in church.

Unfortunately, that didn't dissuade me from obtaining more beer. We found a gas station out in the country that would sell beer to minors on Sunday, both illegal. We enjoyed driving around in the country and drinking beer. I remember one Christmas break driving with some of the basketball team and passing around a pint of gin. When I had to get up and go to work the next day there was an awful smell in my car. The point guard had vomited on the floorboard on the passenger side. On another occasion, I was driving to an away football game when I managed to lock a case of beer *and* the keys to my car in the trunk. We somehow figured out how to take the back seat apart and retrieve them both. How we avoided getting caught, killed, or injuring ourselves or others, I'll never know.

By the time I finished dental school, alcohol had become a real problem. I asked a psychiatrist patient to help me cut back. He said, "Just quit drinking." So, I did for a year. I found if I had a Coke or glass of water in my hand, it calmed me down in social situations. I went to an ex-nun for counseling during that time and was bragging that I had quit on my own. She said, "That's great, but if you ever start again, you'll have to go to A.A."

I didn't know much about A.A., so I didn't think about it again. I had made it a year, so I figured I didn't really have a problem. I decided to try to drink and before long I was drinking every day after work. I could never drink and work, but I drank almost every day. I could not drink in moderation—one or two drinks were not enough. When we went sailing with another couple at the lake, and each brought a case of beer, I drank most of mine.

Linda finally put her foot down and said I either needed to quit or she would leave me. I found an A.A. meeting above a storefront in a neighboring suburb. It was a smoke-filled room with about twenty-five people of all ages and both genders. When they found out it was my first meeting, four members took me into a smaller room and gave me what they called a first step meeting. They each told me their story of how they drank and how they quit with A.A. The only thing I remember is that one of them said, "You don't look too bad." I had quit a couple of days before. He continued, "I have lost jobs, cars, businesses, a wife, and my family. I've been in prison. Think of it this way: alcoholism is like an elevator ride down. You can get off at any floor, you don't have to ride it all the way to the bottom."

In some A.A. literature I read about a guy who said, "I had a blackout. I just flew from N.Y. to L.A. and have absolutely no memory of the trip."

"So what's the problem?" someone asked.

"I was the airline pilot," he replied.

I read about another guy who got up in the morning and walked out to his car and fell to the ground at what he saw: a young child and his bike impaled on the front bumper.

These stories scared me straight. I admitted I was powerless over alcohol and my life was unmanageable. It all made sense to me. I started reading the *Big Book,* following the 12 Steps, and got a sponsor. I didn't make ninety meetings in ninety days—the advice they give you when you first begin—but probably did at least thirty. I liked the fellowship, the group wisdom, and felt I was on my way to recovery. I came out of my fog. I experienced emotions, like anger, that alcohol had been suppressing. I lost weight, got along better with Linda, and was more present with Jen and Libby. But after a couple of years, I rarely went to meetings. I thought I had it licked.

Over New Year's, we went sailing in the British Virgin Islands on our Moorings charter boat *Lady Jayhawk.* I ordered a fruit punch at a restaurant, but they brought me a rum punch instead. I realized the mistake immediately. I drank it anyway. I had another and got a light buzz.

I gradually got back into my old habit of drinking after work until I had forgotten the stress of the day and dozed off in a chair. Eventually Linda found out but didn't confront me.

Then I went alone to a dental meeting in Chicago over Labor Day weekend. I had a couple of glasses of wine with dinner and an after-dinner drink or two. The next morning, I left the meeting after an hour and went back to my room. In less than an hour I drank everything in the mini bar. I caught an early flight home and had a couple of beers on the way. I drove to the lake and drank until I passed out while sailing. I woke up to find I had gone aground. I got unstuck. While driving home I crossed the center line and was stopped by a cop. He asked if I had been drinking and I said I had a couple beers earlier at the lake. He let me go.

That night and the next day I was deathly sick. I had never felt worse in my life. It was the old cliché: at first you fear you will die and then you feel so badly you hope you will. The next day, I drove three hours to my hometown to celebrate my aunt and uncle's 50th wedding anniversary. I was still suffering all afternoon and evening. The next day I tried to give blood, but they rejected me due to messed up liver enzymes. They thought I had hepatitis.

The episode convinced me I would never be able to drink again so I went back to A.A. and became a regular, completing the 12 Steps. Most say you never fully recover and that you can never drink in moderation, so I have never tested it. That was Labor Day in 1991. I haven't had a drink since. I still have friends who drink, but it doesn't bother me to be around them.

In retrospect, one of the reasons I drank was escape. Just like sailing, it allowed me to not face my problems with Linda or the stress of work. It prevented me from tackling issues I didn't have the courage or wisdom to deal with. Like the Serenity Prayer says: "God, grant me the serenity to accept the things I cannot change; the courage to change the things I can; and the wisdom to know the difference." I am proud of being sober and glad I found sobriety when I did. I don't want to chance riding the elevator to the bottom.

But even sober, I felt that I couldn't love fully. I had been eleven when my father died. I was an only child growing up on a farm. I knew very little about the opposite sex. At age twelve, I was heartbroken for the first time by my first girlfriend when she dumped me for a classmate. I often felt this experience prevented me from fully loving anyone; I didn't ever want to feel pain like the loss of my dad and my first true love again.

The End of Our Marriage

After the year-long break from reality, Linda and I were empty nesters. I think the trip changed us both. We still didn't communicate very well and had a midlife crisis of sorts. We decided to remodel our kitchen and the stress of that drove us apart. Linda became enamored with one of the painters, a tall thin guy with a ponytail who was also an artist.

I have always believed in omens or signs. Twenty-five years ago, while walking through a lumber yard parking lot, I found a carpenter's pencil on the ground and took it as a sign to start building a small wooden boat. I had purchased the plans for it a year before and had never started on it. When Linda replaced the photos of our family on our fireplace mantle with art work of the painter, I took it as a sign that our marriage was over.

I moved out when Linda disappeared for a long weekend without telling anyone where she was going. We tried counseling but neither of us was committed to the marriage any longer. In a way, I was relieved. I may have pushed her away.

Chapter 23
To the Star

Less than a year after selling *Halimeda,* I bought another Island Packet, downsizing to a thirty-seven-footer. I renamed her from *Rum Runner* to *Ad Astra*. If you took Latin, you may know it translates as "To the Star." The first half of the Kansas state motto: "Ad Astra Per Aspera," means "To the Stars Through Difficulty." The difficulties refer to the hardships "bloody Kansas" endured while becoming a state before the Civil War. Since I was born, raised, and lived in Kansas, and the star is part of the Island Packet logo, I thought it was the perfect name.

Linda and I had just told the girls we were divorcing, a sad and painful conversation we had with them just before Christmas. A sailing trip was just the escape I needed.

I found a woman online, a widow, who owned an Island Packet and wanted to sail with her two adult children, a daughter and son. It was not a romantic thing in any way; she was a good woman who needed someone with a boat and the experience it takes to do an off-shore trip.

The four of us sailed 300 miles of open ocean from St. Petersburg on Tampa Bay, to Panama City, Florida. It took us about fifty-two hours. It was the second week of March and a series of three cold fronts had moved through, one right after the other, making it a cold, rough trip.

What a long, strange trip it was. It was just before 6:00 a.m. and I was sitting at a concrete table on the pier at the marina in Panama City. It was a little chilly, but cold was a relative term after the last two nights I had just spent sailing across the top of the Gulf of Mexico.

The night before, I was hanging on for dear life strapped in the cockpit. My hands were freezing in a pair of half-rubberized, salt-water-soaked gloves. The wind was blowing steady 25 gusting to 30 plus. We were getting slammed by 6–8 feet seas that were very confused. Every couple of minutes we would fall off the face of a wave with teeth-jarring crash at the bottom. The off-watch crew below became temporarily airborne before falling back into their bunks. The boat would shudder, almost come to a stop, creak, and shake the water off the deck before slowly resuming her tortured, bucking course. Every few minutes a wave would break over the bow and explode atop the dodger, soaking us in the process. The water temperature was 58 and the wind chill half of that. I was wet, cold, tired, sore, sleep deprived and asking myself why I did this for fun. At least I was the only one not seasick.

But it was over now. I slept four hours straight through that afternoon and got another six hours of sleep that night, so I was catching up and thinking a little more clearly. Early the next morning I drove around until I found an open Waffle House. It was packed with drunk kids with club stamps on their hands looking like they had just stepped out of an MTV video. I took an empty seat at the counter between a guy with more chains than a prison gang and a pretty girl with dreadlocks. We all silently watched the chaos in the food preparation area for about fifteen minutes. It was becoming clear that it was going to take way too long to get a cup of coffee and some eggs, so I left and hit the gas station down the road. A similar crowd was lined up at the counter, vying for the few remaining pieces of deep-fried chicken. I finally wormed my way to the cash register and paid for my cup of decaf and a large bag of Cracker Jacks. Three very large, wildly made-up ladies caught my eye. I wished I had the nerve to snap a picture of them, but I decided not to. They looked like drag queens, but I'm pretty sure they weren't. Young black kids with John Deere farm caps and t-shirts were trading slang with the club kids. It was nice to see everyone getting along.

I was starting to feel like myself again and thought about why I did trips like these. The first night, before the wind picked up, we were motorsailing in calm seas and warm weather. The sun was slowly descending through a large group of small clouds so that its rays fanned out through them, shining lines that touched 120 degrees of the horizon. About twenty minutes before it set, a pod of at least twenty dolphins saw our boat and came charging up from half a mile away. They swam and played beneath the front of our boat as we stood on the bow sprit and watched them frolicking and swimming below. They occasionally looked back up at us as though they were trying to form a bond or communicate with us. Some calves swam upside-down beside their mothers, exposing their white underbelly. A handful of them swam on either side of the boat below us while the remaining swam up ahead, jumping out of the water and playing. All the while the sun sank lower and lower, getting redder and redder. It finally sunk and the sky glowed pinkish-red. The dolphins took off, doing a few more jumps as they swam away. I wondered later if they were wishing us a safe and pleasant voyage—or warning us of the impending maelstrom to come.

Having rested and recovered, we were back at it the next night. Away from land and lights, with a clear sky, the stars were incredible. I picked out my favorite three constellations lined up as though to guide us: Sirius, the brightest star, Orion's three-jeweled belt, and Pleiades, the Seven Sisters. I liked to think about the ancient mariners who use these same stars to navigate. We were spoiled with GPS and chart plotters. In a way, we are using man-made stars to navigate, but it does take some of the magic out of the process.

This must have been the road less traveled because we saw almost no other boats once we got out of sight of land. As we approached the coast, we had to round a cape with shallow water extending several miles from shore. As we passed over it, a couple of hours after it got dark, we suddenly came upon a fleet of nearly two-dozen shrimp boats grouped closely together dragging their nets.

Shrimp boats are so brightly illuminated that their navigation lights are nearly invisible. This makes trying to tell which direction they are going challenging. To make matters worse, they often change direction. Since they are short-handed, they are usually on autopilot and concentrating on their work, thus not looking out for poorly-illuminated sailboats like ours. Since they are fishing, they have the right of way. We needed to keep out of their way.

To make it even more difficult, they drag nets yards behind, so you must pass in front of them, which is hard to do if you can't tell which way they are moving. If you can't go fast enough, they could run over you without ever seeing you. Radar in these conditions can only track them to within a mile because the waves make the image useless once they get any closer. I once had misjudged one and passed too close in front of it. He did finally see me, shone his spotlight on me, and called me on the radio. He was quite cordial, though. He said something like, "What are you doing out here on a rough night like this if you don't have to be here?" I was asking myself the same thing.

I had been meaning to replace the engine room insulation for several months; large panels had been falling off. When I bought the boat, the surveyor recommended fixing the panel in front of the engine since the water pump pulley rubbed against it. I had noticed a piece was loose just before we left but had inexplicably neglected to take it out. At about 8:00 p.m. the first night we heard a loud *clunk.* The wind and waves had started so I figured something had slid around in the galley, probably just the cutting board.

Maggie's son Scott was off watch and trying to sleep in the main salon. He heard a clapping noise and started to smell something burning. He took the cover off the front of the engine and saw the insulation had become entangled in the fan belt causing it to come off the pulley, which was now stuck around the shaft but not turning the water pump or charging alternator. It was quickly getting eaten up by the friction of the shaft and the pulley.

We immediately stopped the boat and tried to remedy the situation. This belt charged our batteries and ran the pump to cool the engine, so we wouldn't be able to motor and would eventually lose our navigation lights without it.

With some difficulty, Scott was able to get the belt off. This boat had a high-output alternator, replacing the standard one, but since it was larger than the one that had come with the boat, we couldn't move the alternator far enough to loosen the belt.

The old belt was missing several teeth. The limited movement of the alternator made getting the new belt back on a challenge. We didn't want to run the engine at full speed because we were afraid the belt would break. We also worried that we might run out of fuel since if we had to sail without the motor—it would have doubled or tripled the time it would take us to get there.

But the belt held, we didn't run out of gas, and we made it.

Just like my life at the time, a lot seemed to be going wrong. But it was the sight of a green flash sunrise that reassured me that I was ultimately headed in the right direction. Green flashes just before the sun rises require just the right conditions, no clouds and a clear view of the horizon. In our year in the

Caribbean, we probably saw less than half a dozen. Although I eagerly awaited the sunrise at sea after a long hard night of sailing scores of times, I never had seen a green flash at sunrise. I hadn't even thought to look for it on this trip, but then there it was: the sky flashed bright green the instant before the sun emerged from the ocean and quickly turned red as the sun began to rise.

Chapter 24
Dating, Again, For the First Time

If one does not know to which port one is sailing, no wind is favorable.
—Lucius Annaeus Seneca

I had been married so young that my dating experience was very limited and was forty years in the past. Now I found myself single at age fifty-five and puzzled as to how to begin.

When my office manager told me a friend of hers might be interested in going out with me, I jumped at the chance. We hit it off right away and began dating exclusively. I took her sailing, which she seemed to enjoy. We dined out, talked, walked, and traveled some. After a few months, although we liked each other, it became clear to both of us, I think, that we were not a good enough match for the long haul. We decided to remain friends and date others.

My therapist strongly urged me not to marry for a while. "Paul, just have fun and *don't* get married!"

But places for me to meet dates were limited. I didn't go to bars anymore, or to church. Dating patients or staff is unethical. I was used to meeting people online to go sailing, but never romance. Then an ad for Match.com popped up. *I'm comfortable communicating via email and I like to write,* I thought. I dove in with both feet.

I would connect with someone whose picture I found attractive and with a profile that seemed to match my interests. I had coffee with several women, but none seemed to click. Then I met a wonderful woman, a master gardener. We had a three-month long relationship and she taught me a lot about life and love. But we finally agreed that it, too, wasn't meant for the long haul.

Throughout those first forays into dating again, Linda and I were still trying to wrap up the details of our life together—we had been married for thirty-three years.

I then dated a cardiologist who said she once had to decide whether to become a ballerina or go to medical school. She loved to dance and had dated professional athletes. *NY Times* columnist Maureen Dowd says in her book *Are Men Necessary?* that men have a hard time dating "up." I didn't believe it back then, but I realize now that dating that doctor had indeed intimidated me.

Dating showed me how much I had to learn about women and about myself.

When Hugh Hefner died, I thought a lot about the many ways he brought out openness to sex and made sex seem less "sinful." Was that a good thing? Did he help women enjoy sex and not feel guilty? Or did it push them to try to live up to impossible beauty standards? Are we meant to be monogamous? Is that an impossible standard too? What effect does ubiquitous pornography have on relationships? How about Tinder ... or birth control? I realize the argument can be made that these are both positive and negative. Maureen Dowd wrote a scathing criticism of Hefner, but a high school classmate of Judy's posted a glowing tribute to Hefner, espousing that Hef had shaped his life for the better.

Despite all the hard-won gains women have made in this country, untold numbers of American women go under the knife to look like Playmates. Are we okay with the reality that our girls are being raised in a world that Mr. Hefner made? I am not.

Having no sisters probably impaired my ability to relate to women. Having no brothers kept me from learning to fight for what I wanted. As an only child, I was pampered and spoiled. I have always thought I supported women and feminism. Having two daughters, I somehow understood the importance of honoring women and not holding them back. I know they are different than men, but not *less.* I was always drawn to strong women, maybe because I never felt strong myself and wanted someone I didn't have to protect. Linda was strong. I relied on her in many ways. My mother was strong—she had to be, she was widowed twice.

Then I met Judy online. We dated for a couple months, and then I broke it off. I just wasn't ready, I guess. I then began dating someone else exclusively for several months and then broke that off as well.

One day, Judy came back into my mind, I called her, and we started dating again. Six months later, we moved in together.

I am in a loving, trusting relationship with Judy. Oh, there are things I would change about Judy, of course, and I am sure there are things she would change about me if she could. She still suffers from chronic pain and doesn't like to go out much. I must push her to go out and do things. I like to travel; she is more of a homebody. But those things aside, it feels wonderful to love and be loved by someone I trust.

Chapter 25
Watery Emergencies

May Day

Linda, her nephew Charles, and I were anchored out in one of our favorite anchorages between Useppa Island and Cabbage Cay on the west coast of Florida. So far, it had been a good trip. It was a quiet, calm, moonless evening and the boat was open. It was as dark out as the inside of a cow. We were relaxing after dinner when I heard an outboard motor start and rev up immediately. It kept getting louder and closer when *boom*—a dinghy struck the side of our boat.

I grabbed a flashlight and ran up into the cockpit from which I spied an unoccupied rubber boat speeding in circles. No one was aboard. My heart was racing in panic. Had the driver fallen out when he hit our boat and was he now unconscious in the water beside us? I called out, searching with the light for someone in vain. I saw and heard nothing.

There are three types of radio calls: Sécurité, Pan-Pan, and May Day. The first announces something to be on the lookout for, say, a large boat leaving a dock with little room for other boats to maneuver around it. The second is made when you have a problem but don't need immediate help. For example, when a boat is leaking but the bilge pump is keeping up with the leak. You make the last—May Day—when you need immediate help. It is supposed to be used only when the boat is on fire, in danger of sinking, or someone is dying. I got on the radio and called a May Day.

The Useppa fire search and rescue responded, arriving on the scene in a few minutes in their boat. They were able to corral the little boat and stop it. They also performed a thorough search of the waters around my boat but to no avail. Eventually someone sheepishly called on the radio from a nearby motor yacht admitting that the dinghy was his. He'd had a little too much to drink, fallen out of the dinghy right after he started it in gear, and had climbed safely back onto his big boat.

We had done the right thing, though; someone could have been in the water. It got our adrenaline pumping to think a person could be badly injured or drowning and in need of our help. It was good to know that help was just a radio call away. The lessons learned were:

1. Do not disable the feature that prevents starting an outboard motor while in gear.
2. Attach the kill switch lanyard to your clothing so that if you do fall overboard the engine will stop.
3. Don't drink and drive a boat, especially at night.

Going Aground

There are two types of boaters in Florida: those who have gone aground and those who will. I began my sailing career in small boats on Kansas lakes where going aground wasn't a problem. If you hit bottom you could step out and push the boat into deeper water. As I started ocean sailing on larger boats in the Caribbean, the water was deep and crystal clear. Shallow water was easy to spot; "brown, brown, go aground" is a saying to remind you what to watch for. It was when we began sailing along the coast of Florida and Georgia that grounding became more of a concern. I now have plenty of experience hitting bottom. I always keep my towing insurance up to date and have used it so many times that I can't believe they haven't rated or cancelled me.

Now, I am not a careless boater, I just spend a lot of time exploring the coast shorthanded. Sometimes it isn't even my fault. I've run aground in a channel in what should have had plenty of water; it had shoaled in. Fortunately, our boat was a long-keeled Island Packet and the bottom is usually soft, so I've never damaged the boat when I touched bottom.

Navigation errors are a common cause of grounding. Ideally someone other than the helmsperson should be assigned as navigator to closely monitor the position and keep up any changes to the charts with notices to mariners. That isn't always possible with recreational boaters out for a day of fun on the water. Modern electronic charts can be updated more easily than the old paper charts.

* * *

It was a beautiful, sunny day off the Florida coast. One crewmember was at the helm as we took a side channel going into a marina, another was steering as we were going out. I wasn't watching the chart plotter either time. The area is wide and the marks far apart. Two green markers, one on the ICW and the other on the side channel, are easily confused and if you do

that, you hit sand, which is what we did. If the tide is low, you can wait, if it is high, you need to call for a tow. I called and waited until the tide came back in and they pulled us off without damage.

We did have a real problem the next year just downstream from downtown Jacksonville, Florida, on the St. John's River. Again, it was a beautiful sunny day; we were the only boat in the middle of a two-mile-wide, calm, flat river. We were motorsailing, doing seven knots, and looking for the entrance to a marina when I hit sand. The boat came to a sudden stop. It wasn't damaged, but Judy was.

Judy was at the top of the companionway steps. She turned to go down and was thrown eight feet down the stairs to the cabin floor, breaking three vertebrae in her back. There is a charted mile-long shoal marked only on either end but not in the middle where we hit it. I momentarily wasn't paying attention to the chart plotter and hadn't looked at the chart ahead of time. Judy's injury was the result. If she had been anywhere else on the boat, she would not have been injured. No other crewmembers were hurt.

I called 911 and Mayday at the same time; a fire and rescue boat came alongside us in minutes. They strapped her on a backboard while I motored to a nearby dock. As the EMTs lifted her off the boat, Judy sternly said to them "Whatever you do, DON'T drop me in the water!"

I rode with Judy in the ambulance to Baptist Medical Center, just across the river, where she was admitted, evaluated, and x-rayed. She had compression fractures of her thoracic vertebrae. T9 was displaced about three millimeters, endangering her spinal cord. Fortunately, one of the best neurosurgeons in the area happened to be on call that weekend.

He recommended surgery first thing in the morning. He placed two 20 cm (8 inch) titanium rods screwed to seven of her vertebrae on each side of her spine with two 3-inch-long, quarter-inch inch screws. Judy was amazingly strong and tolerant.

I should have been paying more attention. Thankfully this happened within sight of the hospital, minutes away from help. I had nothing but praise for the entire team who assisted in her evacuation. They were there immediately, very professional, did the right thing, and were compassionate and caring. Two of them even visited her in the ER that evening to see how she was doing, and one gave me his card and said to call him if we needed anything. Amazing!

Always review the chart ahead of time, as I do now without fail, so you understand what the intended course looks like. Know where the deep and shallow waters are. Look for places where navigational marks can be confusing. If possible, in tricky situations assign a navigator *and* a helmsperson to keep the boat on course. Oh, and be sure to pay your towing insurance premium.

Chapter 26
Sailing Away with Judy

Ode to Judith Ann
I was attracted by your beauty
I was captured by your charm
I was attracted by your smile
I was captured by you mind
I was attracted by your shape
I was captured by your soul
I was attracted by your strength
I was captured by your heart
I was attracted by your grace
I was captured by your spirit
I was attracted by your style
I was captured by your poise
I was attracted by your talent
I am eternally captured by your love

We had *Gratitude* in Brunswick, Georgia, for the hurricane season and took Judy's daughter, Lindsey, and her family sailing. Judy and I had been engaged since the previous October but had not had time to plan the wedding. While Lindsey was visiting, she helped us search for locations around Brunswick. We took a very nice slip in Golden Iles Marina on Lanier Island, just across a stream from St. Simons Island. I asked the dock hand for a recommendation. She suggested Epworth By The Sea, which was within sight of the fuel dock just across the river.

We had been to the annual Golden Isles Kingfish Classic tournament near there the day before, so we drove over. The site was beautiful, there was a tiny prayer chapel right on the water, and a dock for *Gratitude*. Huge oaks with yard-long moss beards draped on the branches populated the site. John Wesley, a founder of the Methodist Church (which I attended as a child), had built a church there that still stands. Next, we explored in town. King and Prince, a beachside resort, was a possibility, but it was dated.

Finally, we found the perfect place: St. Simon's Lighthouse. They had a gazebo, a shaded lawn, an old keeper's house, now a museum, and a matching visitor's center with a dining room, catering kitchen, and museum store.

This was the place. Now we needed to pick a date. March or April would be a good time. Then Jennifer called to tell us she was pregnant and due in March. Okay, how about the end of May? The weekend of the 20th was Judy's granddaughter Maggie's graduation. The next weekend was Memorial Day, so June 5th might work, but the facility was only available for a midday wedding. We decided to just have our kids and our grandkids present. Finally, we picked July 2nd, 2009. We found some new condos for everyone to stay in.

It was good to have had Lindsey there to support us in planning. As we drove her and her kids to the airport, it was raining so hard we could barely see. Small tree limbs were in the road and the water was over the road in several places. I couldn't get a cell signal, making finding the airport a challenge. When I dropped them off and parked the car, I heard there was a tornado warning. I'd lived in Kansas all but three years of my life and had never seen a tornado; now I was about to get hit by one in Georgia! Fortunately, it passed with little damage and the sun was out by the time we got back to the boat.

* * *

The wedding was great. All five of our kids, their spouses, and our eleven grandkids, as well as Judy's brother and his wife, attended. The family assembled by the ancient lighthouse while my son-in-law Mark and I sailed *Gratitude* from the marina, anchored in front of the lighthouse, and dinghied ashore. We had a simple, outdoor ceremony with a female minister officiating. The weather was perfect. Afterwards we had dinner in the building next door.

We took everyone out to dinner on July 4th by sailing to the historic Jekyll Island Club for dinner and then back to St. Simon's to watch the fireworks from the boat. In 1858, a 106-foot racing schooner called the *Wanderer* was used to smuggle four hundred slaves here from Africa. Early in the 20th century, members of this exclusive club built palatial winter homes here and some still stand. The members were so rich they owned one sixth of the wealth in the country. The Federal Reserve was secretly planned here in 1910.

Judy and I spent our honeymoon on the boat, of course.

Gratitude

Chapter 27
A Hard Rain's Gonna Fall

You don't need a weather man to know which way the wind blows.
—Bob Dylan

In 2012, Libby, Jennifer, and I were all free to go on a sailing trip together. Just my girls and me. We planned to move my sailboat *Gratitude* from Jacksonville, Florida, up to Brunswick, Georgia.

We caught the tide right so the twenty-five-mile trip to the mouth of the St. Johns River only took three hours. We motorsailed offshore in light winds and calm seas for another six hours to St. Mary's River. A wildfire's thin clouds made the partly sunny day very pleasant. We spent the night at Fernandina Beach, Florida. I used to be obsessive about checking the weather but had become much more relaxed. I did note there was a 40 percent chance of thunderstorms, but that was common for the time of year.

We left Fernandina Beach about noon. As we approached Kings Bay Naval Submarine Base, a strong thunderstorm enveloped us. It had been a warm trip so far, so we were lightly dressed. The cold rain felt good, initially. It intensified and visibility dropped to a boat-length or less. Lightning was flashing with an instantaneous explosion of thunder, indicating it was right next to us. A line from my good friend Captain Oliver Holmes flashed through my mind, "It's like fishin' with a hammer; if you hit 'em, you get 'em." I just hoped it wouldn't hit us.

Our main worry with being hit by lightning was losing all our electronics, including the chart plotter I was using to navigate between the shallow water on one side of the narrow channel and the huge submarine dock on the other side. Without the plotter, we would be flying blind. Offshore you can run with the wind without worrying about going aground; the confined space of the ICW makes visual navigation imperative, but the waves are almost non-existent, so it is a tradeoff. Winds were forecast up to 60 mph; the highest we saw were 40. Thankfully, the golf-ball-sized hail didn't appear either.

The river was about two hundred yards wide there, but we needed to make a turn into a narrow and poorly-marked channel in order to continue our journey so we elected to retrace our track, feeling our way in the blinding rain between the dock and the shore. It seemed like an hour, though it was probably only twenty minutes, before the constant flashing and claps of thunder subsided and the rain changed to a steady downpour. The wind eased to 20 mph and visibility lifted enough we could see a nuclear submarine docked on our left and the yellow poles across the channel marking the shallow water.

In Bob Dylan's song "A Hard Rain's Gonna Fall" he speaks of the horrors of nuclear war. I couldn't help but think of the irony of being next to a submarine, full of nukes, in a very hard rain.

And what did you hear, my blue-eyed son?
And what did you hear, my darling young one?
I heard the sound of a thunder, it roared out a warnin'
Heard the roar of a wave that could drown the whole world
     ...
And it's a hard, and it's a hard, it's a hard, it's a hard
And it's a hard rain's a-gonna fall

Chapter 28
Transitioning to RV Life

I heard someone say the natural progression of a sailor's life is from a sailboat, to a motorboat, to a motorhome, to a rest home, and then to a funeral home. Although I've owned and operated several motorboats throughout my life, Judy and I decided it was time to skip directly from a sailboat to a motorhome.

The similarities between the two are numerous. One usually needs to make reservations at an RV park, just like at a marina. Once there, you must hook up "shore power," water, cable, and deal with sewage. The provisioning and cooking are similar, if not a little easier, since land-based facilities are usually closer. One can spend a few days "anchored out" without hookups or stay in a park. And there is a built-in RV community which one is immediately part of—just like the boating community. The main advantage of both lifestyles is the ability to freely travel and explore new parts of the world.

Navigation, weather, and route planning are all somewhat easier on land, however you are required to stay on roads and traffic is often more intense on land.

Electronics have made it much simpler and more precise to travel on both land and sea. The integration of GPS and chart/map plotters specifically have made it a lot easier, but one must still know basic navigation and not rely on instruments entirely. Paper charts and maps both have limitations; navigating while piloting has its own perils. I began sailing the islands before GPS, so I learned compass and chart navigation, which helped me transition to the electronic version.

I installed a radio with Apple Car Play. When I decide on a destination, I just copy the address into my iPhone calendar and touch the address. The map comes up on the display and reads me turn-by-turn directions. Siri is available when I have a question, want to make a call, or find a restaurant or gas station—all at the touch of a button and a voice request.

Although the RV has speed control, technology hasn't progressed to the point of universal self-driving cars. I loved setting the autopilot on in the sailboat when we are in open water away from much boat traffic and relaxing, going below to get a beverage, reading a book, checking email and Facebook. All I needed to do was check the horizon periodically for other boats. Driving the RV demands much more attention.

Both a sailboat and an RV require a dinghy or car to more easily access shore-side facilities. Towing or stowing both present their own unique set of problems. Backing up in either case is perilous. I only caught my dinghy painter once, when backing down on the anchor late one night off the coast of Florida and, so far, I have only run over curbs while towing the car.

Air

Is it better to be blissfully ignorant or anxiously informed? I learned that monitoring RV tire pressure and temperature can improve tire life and might avoid a disastrous blowout at highway speeds. I found a set of wireless monitors on Amazon and installed them. They come with a safety nut to keep them from vibrating loose from the valve stem. I lost one on the initial installation. I purchased an air hose that should allow me to add air from the coach's air brake system. That didn't seem to work; not sure if it was inadequate pressure or improper insertion. Next, I found that although they have a valve stem for adding air, with my hub caps, I couldn't fully insert the air hose fitting on two of the rear wheels without removing the sensors.

We stopped at three places on the way from New Orleans to Florida trying to add air. The hose was too short at the first, the pressure inadequate at the second. At the third place I realized I couldn't add air without removing a hub cap. I didn't have the right tool or knowledge to do that, so I only succeeded in letting some air out of the one with the lowest pressure. Time for a professional.

We camped in Navarre, Florida, overlooking Santa Rosa Sound, a beautiful wide body of water protected from the Gulf by a narrow spit of land, a half a dozen high-rise condos, and a couple of miles of sparsely populated low-rise condos and homes on the beach. Eventually it becomes part of the Gulf Islands National Seashore. I rode my bike on the bridge across the sound to Navarre Beach. The path beside the bridge was protected by a fence on one side and a low concrete barrier on the other and was only a couple of feet wide, not wide enough to easily pass a walker. I bumped into the chain with my handlebar and then ricocheted into the concrete with my front tire on the way across the bridge, but no damage was done. I decided to take my chances on the roadway on the way back. The smooth, new, two-lane asphalt road didn't have a designated bike path, but it was wide and drivers heeded the sign to share the road with bicycles.

As the sun set over the sound that night, the clear blue sky above the water gradually turned yellow, then orange, then pink before turning inky black. The weather was delightful and there was a breeze off the sound. The song "Six Days on the Road" came on the radio.

> *Well I pulled outta Pittsburgh a rollin' down that Eastern seaboard*
> *I got my diesel wound up and she's a runnin' like a never before*
> *There's a speed zone ahead alright well I don't see a cop in sight*
> *Six days on the road and I'm a gonna make it home tonight*

Chapter 29
My Religion

There's a song that they sing when they take to the highway
A song that they sing when they take to the sea
A song that they sing of their home in the sky
Maybe you can believe it if it helps you to sleep
But singing works just fine for me
—James Taylor

Religion, and the small Methodist church in Beattie, were integral parts of my parent's lives when I was growing up. We always attended church on Sunday. I went to Sunday School and Vacation Bible School where I memorized Bible verses. I can still quote a fair number. As I got a little older, I attended the adult services and sometimes even listened to the sermons.

Mom and Dad would sing in the choir. Eventually, so did I. I loved the music. A few of my favorites were "The Old Rugged Cross," "What a Friend We Have in Jesus," "Jesus Loves Me," and "Blessed Assurance." "How Great Thou Art" still brings tears to my eyes. "Abide With Me," "Nearer My God to Thee," "Bringing In the Sheaves," "Sweet Hour of Prayer," "Peace in the Valley," "In the Sweet Bye and Bye," and "The Church in the Wildwood" are also old standbys I love.

The church, the music, the Bible, and the sermons all had a comforting effect on me as a young boy. They assured me that there was a heaven, a life after death, and they taught me how to live my life and how to treat other people.

The church provided isolated farmers, most of whom toiled alone all week, a place and time to rest for the Sabbath and to socialize after the services. Church suppers, quilting bees, weddings, baptisms, and funerals bound the members into a community and gave us a way to celebrate by sharing life's joys and weep in its sorrows.

Once we moved into town, after my father's death, I still attended church and youth groups. I began to question, however, the overriding premise of an omniscient and omnipotent God who watched over me and every other human and who cared about us all. Furthermore, I began to doubt the existence of heaven and hell. I still agreed with the church's teachings of right and wrong, good and evil, and treating others like I'd like to be treated. I became far from sure that if I sinned, I would be sent to eternal, fiery damnation, or that if I was somehow perfect, I would reside in a blissful paradise without pain or woe forever.

Over the years, I came to believe that science could explain how the universe was formed. Behavioral studies could better guide me how to interact and help others than a prophet from two millennia ago in a book written and rewritten many times by fallible humans. Social studies were a good way to show how to live and get along with others in this complex, diverse, rapidly-changing society. Well-designed research was better at teaching me proper diet and exercise habits than those made up by ancient peoples. Science and modern medicine were always evolving and improving. That was my religion.

I felt that man had created God in his own image, not the other way around. God was just an imaginary friend for adults; a figure for believers to tell their thoughts and hopes to and to ask for help in times of trouble. Give me the journals *Nature* or *The New England Journal of Medicine* over Luke, Peter, Isaiah, and Daniel.

Furthermore, growing up on the farm, living outside in nature's beauty and bounty, I came to worship the environment as my church. Camping, hiking, boating, fishing, hunting, and sailing became my preferred forms of worship. Sharing the great outdoors with my family and friends became my devotion. I longed to study and explore the forests, prairies, rivers, seas, and oceans of the world.

I also wanted to learn about cultures different from my own. I began to study history, something missing from my science-based pharmacy and dental school curriculum. I learned from writings and teachings written before, during, and after Biblical times. I viewed the "Good Book" as just that—a book to study and learn from along with the multitude of other good books about history, science, and social studies.

I love expanding my knowledge and experiences, talking to strangers from faraway lands and different cultures, in person and online. One of my favorite things is sailing across the sea, using wind to propel me just like the ancients did, but using our modern materials and designs to get there faster, safer, and more comfortably than they did. I am equally as thrilled to see a pod of dolphins frolicking in my wake as I am by singing along to "Amazing Grace." I relish reading about a new scientific discovery, using the latest technology to read, write, photograph, navigate, and communicate with others who know more than I do, or to share my knowledge with those who don't have my experience. These things are my church, my religion.

Aside from what it teaches you,
there is simply the indescribable degree of peace
that can be achieved on a sailing vessel at sea.
I guess a combination of hard work and
the seemingly infinite expanse of the sea—the profound
        solitude—
that does it for me.
—Billy Campbell

Chapter 30
Dreams

We are tied to the ocean. And when we go back to the sea, whether it is to sail or to watch, we are going back from whence we came.
—John F. Kennedy

My father's dream may have been to leave the farm and work on the railroad. Of all his siblings, he was the only one to stay home, taking care of his widowed mother and keeping the family farm going through the Depression. His brother Aaron left to work construction as a steelworker in Kansas City and later in Chicago. His brother Alvin moved to Topeka and worked in government. His sister Lilly married and moved to Oakland, California. And his sister Pearl ended up in the Board of Trade in Kansas City. But I do not remember my father bemoaning his choice to stay on the farm or express any jealousy of his siblings. He knew he was needed, so he stayed put.

I, on the other hand, have always been in a hurry to go someplace else. Men on my dad's side of the family died relatively young. My dad's father died at age fifty-one, my dad at fifty-eight; I assumed I would die young too. That made me want to cram as many experiences into my life as possible.

My mother was anxious when she was late and always rushed to arrive early to work, church, or social gatherings. I learned from her that it takes real work to be on time! Some say I have ADHD. I work very hard to be on time, especially when I was in practice. I become very uptight when I am late. When I was little, I wanted to go to school before I was old enough to go. I recall trying to learn math and reading on my own. And when I finally graduated from high school, I wanted to get away from our small town and go to college so badly that I went to summer school at Kansas University the summer before my freshman year. In dental school, I went to summer school when others didn't so I could graduate in three and a half years instead of four. After two years in general practice, I wanted to move on. Then, after grad school, I was in such a hurry to start practice, I didn't even stay to attend my graduation.

It is no surprise, then, that I always wanted to retire early. Although divorce kept me working longer, I finally quit work at age sixty-five.

But it was hard for me to slow down. It sounds counterintuitive, but in retirement I have had to work hard at relaxing. I don't have the patience to meditate, but I try to use the principles when I am rushing to remind me to slow down. I started, but didn't finish, an online eating program where you try to get in touch with your feelings. You practice eating when you are hungry, stopping when nearly full, eating slowly, paying attention to the taste and texture of the food, chewing slowly, and enjoying it. Don't multitask during meals: no phone, TV, internet, email. This is very difficult for me, but I have lost a little weight and am making progress.

What's the old joke? I want patience and I want it *right now!*

It may seem ironic, then, that my passion is sailing. You would think I would have wanted to get a speed boat or an airplane to get there faster, but no, I love sailing. Sailing *forces* me to relax, slow down, enjoy the time on the water with friends and nature. I can't sit still long, though, I am always tweaking the shape of the sails, adjusting things, fixing things, trying to perfect the course and trim to maximize the speed and efficiency of the rig.

While exploring the Florida Keys with Judy, we stopped at a sporting goods superstore. I was amazed to find the sister ship of Hemingway's *Pilar* displayed in the middle of the store, fully restored to look like his boat. I took it as a sign that I should resume writing this memoir. Although I've spent the last thirty years exploring most of the islands of the Caribbean, a few of the Greek Isles, the East Coast from Maine to Texas, all three coasts of Florida and the Keys by sailboat, and *Pilar* is a powerboat, that boat represents the history of these islands and especially of their most famous writer, Earnest Hemingway.

Hemingway lived a full life boating, traveling, fishing, fighting, loving, drinking, and writing all over the world, but much of his time was spent in the Keys and Key West. His life and writings inspired me to tell the story of my life; to recall all the good times and preserve them in case my descendants are interested in reading them one day. I also hope in some small way to inspire others to live out their dreams as I have been so fortunate to be able to live out mine in paradise.

Don't it always seem to go
That you don't know what you've got 'til it's gone
They paved paradise
And put up a parking lot
— Joni Mitchell

After coming of age in the 60s, this popular 70s song became an anthem for me, just as it did for other tree huggers and early environmentalists. At the time, I didn't fully appreciate the meaning of the song. We may have won some battles but are still a long way from winning the war that this song alludes to.

In the late Anthony Bourdain's *Parts Unknown* episode on Jamaica, he extolled, as only he could, the natural beauty, simplicity, rich culture, delicious indigenous cuisine, and most of all the locals who populate the remote northeastern coast of this lush island. All these features combine to make it a true paradise. A recurring theme of the show was who "owns" paradise—who has the right to enjoy it, and who can afford the time and money it takes to experience it? I was saddened when Anthony told of the planned development of the last public beach on the island that might prevent the locals from continuing to enjoy their birthright: swimming, sunning, fishing, and gathering with friends and family on that beach. By gating and fencing off these beautiful spots, visitors may be protected from perceived harm, but the price paid is to remain isolated from the real culture, natural beauty, purity, and peacefulness these places have to offer. I only hope that my grandchildren get a chance to experience some part of this region as I have before it becomes an enclave solely for wealthy owners and cautious tourists, walled off from the locals who make this part of the world such a unique and vibrant place.

Yet, this currently seems to be the trend promoted by Trump: to fear "the other." To block those with "other" skin color, religion, or customs from contaminating the white, Christian America. This attitude takes advantage of our natural fear of the unknown and goes against the melting pot diversity on which America was founded. Monoculture doesn't work in agriculture or in human society. "Pure" blood lines lead to genetic defects and prevents the growth of ideas and industry. It is not natural. The Caribbean is a mixture of islands that are each microcosms of the many nations that "settled" them. The Europeans robbed the indigenous people of these islands, people who had lived there more or less in harmony with nature and each other. Europeans brought their diseases and guns, using God as an excuse to steal land, enslave, rape, and kill. They devastated the land by cutting down the native forest to plant sugar cane for rum and money.

Through travel, I have learned to love these other cultures and different people, despite the right wing's push to make them "other." I am grateful to have had these experiences.

Now, thinking back on my pattern of eagerness to *get away*, I wonder if I sometimes missed "smelling the roses" and enjoy the present moment. I do have a vivid memory of stopping and feeling present at the halfway turn around point of our year-long trip. I was sitting on a beach in Trinidad on a beautiful sunny day thinking how my dream had really come true and that I had sailed all the way there with my family. I was savoring the moment, taking in the scene. Local families were playing and swimming. I had sailed nearly two thousand miles to get there. It was a feeling of satisfaction. A goal achieved. I had learned a lot about myself and gained confidence in my ability to handle the boat and to handle the time off from work.

All these efforts and missteps took me where I am today ... I didn't leave Linda when I could or should have, but I don't regret it because I am sure our daughters might not have turned out as great as they have. I then got to date, something I had missed by marrying so young. Now I know I am a one-woman man. I am truly happy with Judy and am so lucky and blessed to have found her. She is such a warm, kind, beautiful, and loving person.

There is only one happiness in this life, to love and be loved.
—George Sand

* * *

We spent the night in a hotel on the beach in Florida. I got up before dawn, drove to McDonalds, and bought coffee and the freshest egg McMuffin I can recall. I drove back to the beach and ate on a park bench. The warm, moist, soft trade wind caressed my skin as I watched Orion's Belt point down to Sirius, the brightest star in the sky, low above the Atlantic. Gentle waves were whooshing on the sand, fifty yards away, and a menagerie of small dark clouds were peeking above the horizon. A brilliant full moon setting over my shoulder was illuminating the clouds. The dawn slowly turned the sky light blue, then pink, then orange. Fishing boats dotted the sea, zooming up and down the coast with their red and green navigation lights twinkling on the water.

When it was light enough, I could just see the outline of a huge ship creeping south. It looked like a long, low building floating on the junction between sea and sky. I could barely make out its lights blinking a dozen miles away. Walkers and joggers softly plodded their way along the sidewalk beside me.

Siri told me the sun would rise in twenty-one minutes. Fishermen and women already lined the pier, looking over the rail and anticipating their catch. The sky was now a lighter blue, with large, faint pink, God rays streaming up from the still point from which, at any moment, I expected the sun would burst from the ocean.

Epilogue

We have since sold the motor home, bought and sold two power boats, then returned to a Leopard 40 catamaran sailboat and are once more plying the ocean by sail. We moved to a condo in Stuart, Florida, where we keep *Sailfish* at a dock in front of the condo.

I hope you have enjoyed reading the story of my relationship with the ocean and my travels sailing to many beautiful and diverse islands.

I was able to live out my dream. I hope that you, too, can discover your dream and then fulfill it.

See www.stuartsailing.com.

THE END

Made in the USA
Columbia, SC
21 February 2020